THE AMERICAN DREAM

AND

THE NATIONAL GAME

THE AMERICAN DREAM

AND

THE NATIONAL GAME

by

Leverett T. Smith, Jr.

Bowling Green University Popular Press
Bowling Green, Ohio 43403

Copyright © 1970 by Leverett T. Smith, Jr.

Copyright © 1975 by The Popular Press, Ray B. Browne, Editor.

The Popular Press is the publishing division of the Center for the Study of Popular Culture, Bowling Green University, Bowling Green, Ohio, Ray B. Browne, Director.

Library of Congress Catalog Number: 75-15290

ISBN: 0-87972-112-X Cloth

Source Acknowledgments

The sources below have graciously allowed me to reprint excerpts from material still under copyright:

A truncated version of Chapter 4, Section 3, appeared last fall in *Heroes of Popular Culture,* pp. 73-85 (Bowling Green University Popular Press), as "Ty Cobb, Babe Ruth and the Changing Image of the Athletic Hero."

From *Man on Spikes* by Eliot Asinof. Copyright © 1955 by Eliot Asinof. Used with permission of the author.

From *Seven Days To Sunday: Crisis Week with the New York Football Giants* by Eliot Asinof. Copyright ©1968 by Eliot Asinof. Reprinted by permission of Simon and Schuster.

From *The Hundred Yard War* by Gary Cartwright. Copyright © 1968. Used with the permission of Doubleday and Company.

From *Only A Game* by Robert Daley. Copyright © 1967. Reprinted with the permission of The New American Library.

F. Scott Fitzgerald. *The Crack-Up*. Copyright © 1934 by Esquire, Inc., copyright © 1945 by New Directions Publishing Corporation. Reprinted by permission of New Directions Publishing Corporation.

From *The Southpaw* by Mark Harris. Copyright © 1953 by Mark Harris. Reprinted with permission of the author.

From *The Short Stories of Ernest Hemingway* by Ernest Hemingway. Copyright © 1954. Used with the permission of Charles Scribner's Sons.

From *Green Hills of Africa* by Ernest Hemingway. Copyright © 1962. Used with the permission of Charles Scribner's Sons.

From *By-Line: Ernest Hemingway* edited by William White. Copyright © 1967. Used with the permission of Charles Scribner's Sons.

From *A Moveable Feast* by Ernest Hemingway. Copyright © 1964. Used with the permission of Charles Scribner's Sons.

From *The Sun Also Rises* by Ernest Hemingway. Copyright © 1953. Used with the permission of Charles Scribner's Sons.

From *Death in the Afternoon* by Ernest Hemingway. Copyright © 1961. Used with the permission of Charles Scribner's Sons.

From *The Old Man and the Sea* by Ernest Hemingway. Copyright © 1950. Used with the permission of Charles Scribner's Sons.

From *Violence Every Sunday* by Mike Holovak and Bill McSweeny. Copyright © 1967. Used with the permission of Coward, McCann and Geoghegan, Inc.

From *In the Shadow of Tomorrow: A Diagnosis of the Spiritual Ills of Our Time* by Johan Huizinga. Copyright © 1936. Reprinted with the permission of the author.

From *Instant Replay* by Jerry Kramer. Copyright © 1968 by Jerry Kramer and Dick Schapp. Reprinted by arrangement with The New American Library, Inc., New York, N. Y.

From "Two Tramps in Mud Time" from *The Poetry of Robert Frost* edited by Edward Connery Lathem. Copyright © 1936 by Robert Frost. Copyright © 1964 by Lesley Frost Ballantine. Copyright © 1969 by Holt, Rinehart and Winston, Inc. Reprinted by permission of Holt, Rinehart and Winston, Inc.

From the book *Run to Daylight!* by Vincent Lombardi. Copyright © 1963 by Vincent Lombardi, W. C. Heinz and Robert Riger. Published by Prentice-Hall, Inc., Englewood Cliffs, New Jersey.

From *You Know Me Al* by Ring W. Lardner. Copyright © 1925. Used with the permission of Charles Scribner's Sons.

From *The Old Glory* by Robert Lowell. Copyright © 1964, 1965 by Robert Lowell. Reprinted with the permission of Farrar, Straus & Giroux, Inc.

From *Understanding Media* by Marshall McLuhan. Copyright © 1964 by Marshall McLuhan. Used with permission of McGraw Hill Book Company.

FOR

Leverett Tyrrell Smith

1907 – 1963

A parent gives life, but as parent, gives no more. A murderer takes life, but his deed stops there. A teacher affects eternity; he can never tell where his influence stops.

–Henry Adams

ACKNOWLEDGMENTS

This book was written and revised in a variety of communities and I wish to pay my respects to all of them here.

My own family is the most important of these, particularly my wife, Jan. Without her presence, I could not have held a balance sufficient to write this book. Her attitude toward the project itself, which varied from aloof detachment to outright disdain, was particularly helpful in keeping my thoughts about it in proper perspective. My children, Rab, Jessica and Harry, and my mother, Eleanor Hoyt Smith have also contributed in their own ways to the book. They all helped me by being themselves.

The book is a revision of my doctoral dissertation written in the American Studies Program at the University of Minnesota, and I am pleased to have been a part of the community there. Of the many faculty members there, I wish to remember here those who served on my committees; Don Gillmor, David Noble, Mulford Sibley, Donald Torbert and Mary Turpie. I have a special debt to Bernard Bowron, who directed the original dissertation. Not only has his direction given the book what focus it has, but also his teaching has helped me understand the kind of teacher I wish to be.

During our three dreadful years in Pennsylvania while the book was being revised, we were particularly glad to have the friendship of Fred, Lucianna and Catherine Bohne. We are grateful to all our friends in the community of Rocky Mount and at North Carolina Wesleyan College. For all these people, I wish I had written a worthier book.

Rocky Mount, North Carolina
1975

TABLE OF CONTENTS

INTRODUCTION

WRITING FROM PARIS IN MAY OF 1910, HENRY ADAMS GLOOMILY PREdicted the end of the usefulness of human intellectual activity. He sought to explain to Barrett Wendell the purpose of his *A Letter to American Teachers of History,* a volume he had recently sent to fellow members of the American Historical Association. He seemed to feel that the end of an era was at hand; "we have arrived. Nothing remains but to simmer out and to stop the appearance of boiling—of motion. There *is* no more motion, and can be none, except to recognise the fact." The *Letter to Teachers* was, for Adams, simply that; "a letter to Teachers . . . to teach teachers how to teach. . . . It is a scientific demonstration that Socialism, Collectivism, Humanitarianism, Universalism, Philanthropism, and every other ism, has come, and is the End, and there is nothing possible beyond, and they [American teachers of history] can all go play, and, on the whole, baseball is best."[1]

Adams, according to this image, saw baseball as a symbol of a world irrevelant to that in which he was used to living. He does not seem to have been alone in doing this. Originally a gentleman's sport, played by the upper and middle classes during their leisure time, between 1870 and 1910 baseball had evolved into a professional sport, providing entertainment for a large urban audience and a possible ladder to success for athletic young men who were inclined to use it as such. This evolution resulted in a public image which has been characterized by David Quentin Voigt as "schizoid, for while it was being idolized by some, it was being villainized by others."[2] Baseball's sins were seen to result from the conditions of urban life, and the chief habits of ball players as presented in the daily newspapers were drinking and gambling.[3] According to Chief Meyers, onetime catcher for the New York Giants, baseball "was not well thought of. . . . Ball players were considered a rowdy bunch. We weren't admitted to hotels, that is first-class hotels. Like the sailors in Boston, on the Commons—'No Sailors Allowed.' We were in that class. We were just second-class citizens, even worse."[4] The wife of a Methodist clergyman, discouraging her son's ambition to become a baseball player, characterized baseball as "not a serious occupation." And her husband, the Reverend Jonathan Townley Crane, in his book *Popular Amusements,* "prophesied that baseball was in decline because so many vices cluster around the ballground that 'everyone connected with it seems to be regarded with a degree of suspicion.' "[5]

The point of view that baseball is irrelevant if not immoral conflicted with another which was also forcefully presented during these years. Many players were able to build respectable middle class careers on the side and the sport as a whole could be seen rather differently than Adams saw it. Appropriately enough Mark Twain expressed this point of view when he described baseball as "the very symbol, the outward and visible expression of the drive and push and rush and struggle of the raging, tearing, booming nineteenth century."[6] Baseball here becomes a symbol of the dynamic element in American life. In *A Connecticut Yankee in King Arthur's Court* too, baseball appears as one of the modern blessings Hank Morgan confers on the middle ages. He speaks of "a project of mine to replace the tournament with something which might furnish an escape from the extra steam of the chivalry, keep those bucks entertained and out of mischief, and at the same time preserve the best thing in them, which was their hardy spirit of emulation. . . . This experiment was baseball."[7]

Neither of these images, that of baseball as immoral and irrelevant or as the very symbol of the new forces changing

American life, dominates at present though. A new image of baseball and of professional sports in general has appeared since then.[8] During the 1966 World Series, James Reston of the New York *Times* found time in one of his columns to meditate on the relation of sports to modern American life. "Sports in America," he suggests, "are an antidote to many of the trends of our time." The complexities of life in twentieth century America, he finds, "make it impossible to identify the point of decision in our national life." Life, in other words, is chaotic; it appears to have no meaningful shape. However, says Reston, "we know who won Sunday's game, and there was a sense of pageantry and beauty, on an Indian summer day, and the whole nation was watching." He concludes,

> Sports in America are something more than a diversion. They are a unifying social force, and a counter to the confusion about the vagueness and complexity of our cities, and in this long-haired age, even the confusion between our sexes.[9]

A good deal of fiction and social criticism reflect this same point of view. For example, the central character of Frederick Exley's *A Fan's Notes* engages in the following meditation as he tries to understand what draws him to professional football.

> Why did football bring me so to life? I can't say precisely. Part of it was my feeling that football was an island of directness in a world of circumspection. In football a man was asked to do a difficult and brutal job, and he either did it or got out. There was nothing rhetorical or vague about it; I chose to believe that it was not unlike the jobs which all men, in some sunnier past, had been called upon to do. It smacked of something old, something traditional, something unclouded by legerdemain and subterfuge. It had that kind of power over me, drawing me back with the force of something known, scarcely remembered, elusive as integrity–perhaps it was no more than the force of a forgotten childhood.[10]

This interest in sports as something which gives form to an otherwise chaotic world, which simplifies the complexities of human experience, is also manifest in the academic community. Though historians have not responded to Adams' suggestion that they "go play," many social scientists have gone *to* play, or to the idea of the game as a coherent notion of human action, in order to explain human behavior. Gregory Stone, for instance, addresses himself both to the world of sports as an area of study and to the notion of the game as a concept which will make human activity comprehensible. "Indeed," he says, "we can conceive of life as a series of games—contests and engagements—that mark the progress of careers, culminating in losses and victories for the participants."[11]

What emerges from this talk about sports and games is clear. In the late nineteenth century they were considered either irrelevant if not immoral or a manifestation of the dominant spirit of the nation. By the second half of the twentieth century they are being considered as a kind of repository for values thought to have been lost in the confusion of the modern world and also as a useful metaphor or concept for interpreting human behavior.

In order to describe how this change occurred I will need to use materials from both "high" culture and popular culture. What I hope to accomplish by this is indicated in the following quotation from the writings of Johan Huizinga:

> . . . knowing in the historical sense rarely if ever means indicating a strictly closed causality. It is always an understanding of contexts . . . this context is always an open one, which is to say that it may never be represented in the metaphor of links forming a chain, but only in that of a loosely bound bundle of sticks to which new twigs can be added as long as the band around them allows it. Perhaps more suitable than a bundle of sticks might be a bunch of wild flowers. In their variety and their difference in value new notions added to the conception of a historical context are like newly found flowers in the nosegay: each one changes the appearance of the whole bouquet.[12]

The notion of "context" seems adequate for what I will attempt in this book. Literary works will be placed in the context of popular culture; popular culture will be placed in the context of literature. Each, hopefully, will tell us something about the other.

"High" culture will be represented by works of literature and social criticism. These two kinds of "high" culture can be viewed uniformly if we remember that one of the functions of literature is the criticism of society. Since my general subject matter involves the changing relation of sport and society, I will try to discover in each work what values are attributed to games, sports, or other kinds of leisure activity. Naturally, I have to restrict myself to works which consider leisure activity in some way, but this has not proved a problem since most of the major figures of the nineteenth and twentieth centuries at one time or another find it necessary to deal with some aspect of the problem. Thomas Carlyle, Charles Dickens, Nathaniel Hawthorne, Henry David Thoreau, Thomas Hughes, Mark Twain, Thorstein Veblen, Robert Frost and Robert Lowell all have considered the value of leisure activity at one time or another and I will devote a chapter to analyzing a selection of their writings. Ernest Hemingway and Ring Lardner, two writers for the understanding of whose works the notion of leisure is essential, I will deal with more extensively in separate chapters. A consideration of this literature should reveal a dialogue taking place concerning the nature and value of leisure activity over the past one hundred thirty years.

It is important to recognize the formal relation literature has to an entire culture. Gertrude Jaeger and Philip Selznick have commented on this relation in an essay in which they develop a theory of culture. They argue that, even for the social scientist,

> symbolic expression, including artistic expression, is central to the study of culture . . . and not peripheral to it. It means that studies of high culture are not a thing apart, a peculiar and embarrassing intrusion on the world of sociology and anthropology. High culture has no monopoly on symbolic expression, but it is there that the vehicle of consummatory meaning—the representative object, the stylized form of action, the distinctive outlook on world and self—is given its most sophisticated and sensitive development.[13]

"High" culture here has two functions. It has first the traditional one to which Lionel Trilling and R. W. B. Lewis assign it: symbolic expression provides us with representative objects, the culture in "its most sophisticated and sensitive development."[14] In addition, Jaeger and Selznick, unlike Trilling and Lewis, are asserting the greater importance of a subject matter thought peripheral to their field. The fact that representative objects are getting systematic and sensitive development in works of "high" culture, holds interesting possibilities for the historian interested in the relation of "high" to popular culture.[15] Not only may works of "high" culture involve themselves consciously with all the contradictions present in the culture as a whole and present them in coherent form, but once analyzed, they may yield patterns which can be used as models in studying more popular forms of the culture. This is the second function suggested by Jaeger and Selznick. This book will attempt to test this idea and this is why I have chosen to consider works of "high" culture first, before moving to popular culture.[16]

What materials from popular culture have I chosen? Since I want to examine the changing public image of professional baseball, I have chosen an event to study that I suspect has contributed to a change in the shape of the image of the sport in the public mind. In 1919, eight Chicago White Sox players were bribed to throw the World Series. The events precipitated by this act created the structure of the baseball community as we know it today: a community that defines itself as distinct from the world of gambling and sin, as a special community outside the ordinary legal structure of American business. The complex event which brought about this situation actually involves three events: the uncovering of the scandal and the prosecution of the players, the appointment of Judge Kenesaw Mountain Landis as Commissioner of baseball with dictatorial powers, and finally the development of a new style of play in baseball, triggered by the emergence of Babe Ruth as a power hitter.

These events in themselves are not so important to my book as the public response to them and what I can find out about the effect they were calculated to produce. I expect that both will bear in some crucial respects a resemblance to the pattern of ideas found in the works of "high" culture.

The emergence of professional football as a competitor with professional baseball both for the sports dollar and for the title of "the National game" will be the subject matter of the concluding chapter and will provide a kind of synthesis of materials. The overwhelming popularity of professional football in the nineteen sixties has produced a considerable literature which is concerned to explain the basis of that popularity. George Plimpton's *Paper Lion* is probably the most famous. This kind of popular literature will fall midway between the kinds of evidence obtainable from highly formal literature and that found in the newspapers, and an analysis of it should pull together any loose ends that exist in the first two sections of the book. I will focus on the public image of Vince Lombardi, former coach of the Green Bay Packers and Washington Redskins, both through articles about him in newspapers and magazines and through his own book *Run to Daylight!* In these Lombardi emerges as both a critic of contemporary, business-oriented society and a good businessman and a shrewd manager of men. His popular image presents the same kind of dialogue between the values of a majority culture and those formulated in opposition to the majority culture that we find in literary works.

On what basis can we place literature and social criticism in the same context with events and writings from the world of professional sports? Artists and social critics are admittedly interested in the values of the society around them and it has become increasingly important to understand the phenomenon of leisure as the industrial revolution progresses.

In this context, that the image of professional sports has changed in the course of the twentieth century is an important event in the collective psychology of Americans. What do this image and social criticism have in common? The following quotation, a professional baseball player's attempt to come to terms with what it was that gave him satisfaction during his career, contains the suggestion of an answer to this question.

> I certainly enjoyed those years, though. I did get a little discouraged at times, but I guess you do at any job. Of course, when you play every day it gets to be sort of like work. But, somehow, way down deep, it's still play. Just like the umpire says: "Play Ball!" It *is*. It's *play*.[17]

Tension exists in this statement between an idea of work and an idea of play. It is unclear whether the speaker thinks of himself as having worked at play or played at work. The source he finally settles on as the source of his enjoyment is the element of play in what he is doing. Americans have generally considered hard work as the way to wealth and the way to personal salvation. Those who must give up this dream generally regard their life's work as a job: they work to live, rather than living to work. The course of their satisfaction is now play, but what is play?

I

JOHAN HUIZINGA'S WORLD OF WORK AND PLAY

LIKE ANY OTHER CONCEPT, PLAY CAN BE UNDERSTOOD IN MANY WAYS. The concept that serves to unite the diverse subject matters of my essay is set forth in Johan Huizinga's *Homo Ludens: A Study of the Play Element in Culture. Homo Ludens* was published near the end of Huizinga's life, in 1938, and before we consider his theory of the nature of play, it seems best to consider some of the contexts in which the theory appears. Huizinga was trained as a philologist and followed the profession of history, but *Homo Ludens* falls within neither of these academic disciplines. R. W. Colie offers the best description of the kind of book it is.

> From 1935 on, Huizinga's principal work was not historical, though it was cultural. In that year, only two years after Hitler's coup, he published *In the Shadow of Tomorrow: A Diagnosis of the Spiritual Ills of Our Time*, a highly polemical, pessimistic analysis of contemporary mass culture. Ten years later, the book he had been working on during his isolation in De Steeg was posthumously published, *The World in Ruins: A Consideration of the Chances for Restoring Our Civilization*, a sequel and a corrective to *In The Shadow of Tomorrow.*[1]

Homo Ludens is only partially an "analysis of contemporary mass culture" and perhaps not even principally that, but we should be aware that it forms part of a body of work in which Huizinga offered a systematic criticism of modern society. Another scholar has described the role Huizinga played during these years as that of "the scholar as warning prophet and guide towards salvation,"[2] a description which a brief examination of *In the Shadow of Tomorrow* will reveal as being just.

In the Shadow of Tomorrow was a relatively popular book. Its first edition in 1935 was sold out at once and by 1938, the year *Homo Ludens* appeared, it had been through seven more and had been translated into nine foreign languages.[3] It was also a controversial book. Huizinga was taken to task for what others regarded as his "faulty reading of modern culture" and some argued that he did not actually offer a reading of modern culture at all but simply recorded his revulsion from it.[4]

Huizinga presented his vision of the present and future as follows.

> The gods of our time, mechanization and organization, have brought life and death. They have wired up the whole world, established contact throughout, created everywhere the possibility of cooperation, concentration of strength and mutual understanding. At the same time they have trapped the spirit, fettered it, stifled it. They have led man from individualism to collectivism, the negation of the deepest personal values, the slavery of the spirit. Will the future be one of ever greater mechanisation of society solely governed by the demands of utility and power?[5]

The concluding question seems rhetorical: Huizinga's fears are evidently greater than his hopes. The chief manifestation of "the slavery of the spirit" he calls "puerilism." He devotes a whole chapter to it, defining it as "the attitude of a community whose behavior . . . instead of making the boy into the man adapts its conduct to that of the adolescent age."[6] The country where this phenomenon could be studied "most thoroughly in all of its aspects" was, according to Huizinga, America. Huizinga had visited America and in 1918 had published a book called *Man and Mass in America*, a book which both Colie and Pieter Geyl think of as a precursor of *In the Shadow of Tomorrow.* In speaking of the latter book, Colie remarks that it "points out at length the grimmer aspects of mass culture that Huizinga had first sketched in *Man and Mass in America*, a book partially a continuation of Alexis de Tocqueville's *Democracy in America*."[7] Geyl suggests that "what drove him [Huizinga] to that study *Man and Mass in America* . . . was undoubtedly that he was already beginning to watch the development of western civilization with misgivings, and in America he discerned some of its, to his thinking, most ominous tendencies in alarming force."[8]

"The modern puerilism," Huizinga felt, presented itself in two ways. These amounted to a confusion of the roles of work and play in the world. "On the one hand," said Huizinga, "activities of a professedly serious nature and universally regarded as serious . . . come to be permeated with the spirit of play and to bear all the characteristics of play; on the other, activities admittedly of a play character come to lose the true quality of play because of the manner in which they are carried on."[9] Modern puerilism has, of course, "found its way into sport. It is present wherever athletic rivalry assumes proportions tending to push intellectual interests into the background, as in the case in some American universities. It threatens to creep in with over-organization of sport and with the disproportionate place which the sporting page and the sporting magazines have come to occupy in the mental diet of untold numbers."[10]

Homo Ludens has all the limitations of this point of view. Pieter Geyl has said of the book that Huizinga's "obsession with decline and ruin and the rancor against his own time had taken complete control over his mind" and that therefore *Homo Ludens* must be considered a "brilliant, but wrong-headed improvization."[11] Geyl argues that "the entire argument seems to have served no other purpose . . . than to pronounce once more the verdict of guilty over present day civilization, which has allowed play to degenerate into puerilism,"[12] and seems to miss the whole point of the book, which is, as Colie states, to develop "a theory of the functions of play, always seen against the ostensibly more serious 'normal' modes of life."[13]

How does Huizinga define play? He protests that the English translation of the title of his book *Homo Ludens: A Study of the Play Element in Culture* is a mistranslation. He wants to consider the element of play as an aspect of all human activity, rather than as a distinct element within human culture. This results in some confusion as to the nature of play. If play is an element *in* culture, we should be able to isolate several cultural activities we could designate as play activities. If it is an element *of* culture, we should be able to see it as a dimension of all human activity. Huizinga himself seems to feel both possibilities are true, for he offers a set of formal characteristics which constitute a definition of play.

He begins his characterization of play by saying that it is "a voluntary activity. . . . By this quality of freedom alone, play marks itself off from the course of the natural process. It is something added thereto and spread out over it like a flowering, an ornament, a garment."[14] Huizinga continues:

> freedom must be understood here in the wider sense that leaves untouched the philosophical problem of determinism. It may be objected that this freedom does not exist for the animal and the child; they *must* play because their instinct drives them to it and because it serves to develop their bodily functions and their powers of selection. The term "instinct," however, introduces an unknown quality, and to presuppose the utility of play from the start is to be guilty of a *petito principii.* Children and animals play because they enjoy playing, and therein precisely lies their freedom. (pp. 7-8)

A second characteristic of play follows. "Play is not 'ordinary' life or 'real' life. It is rather a stepping out of 'real' life into a temporary sphere of activity with a disposition all of its own." (p. 8) The two social manifestations of this characteristic of play deserve mention. Play functions "in the higher forms . . . as a contest *for* something or a representation *of* something." (p. 13) It "always belongs to the sphere of festival and ritual–the sacred sphere." (p. 9) We catch a hint of this characteristic in James Reston's mention of the "pageantry and beauty" involved in baseball's World Series. The festival involves the same kind of ritual action. Huizinga asserts that "feast and play have their main characteristics in common." As above, he seems to feel the festival a social manifestation of play. He describes their common characteristics.

> Both proclaim a standstill to ordinary life. In both mirth and joy dominate, though not necessarily–for the feast too can be serious; both are limited as to time and place; both combine strict rules with genuine freedom. (p. 22)

These last anticipate further characteristics of play.

"Play is distinct from 'ordinary' life both as to locality and duration. This is the third main characteristic of play: its secludedness, its limitedness. It is 'played out' within certain limits of time and place. It contains its own course and meaning." (p. 9) Here, play working itself out in time, necessarily creates its own meaning in the course of its action, regardless of the world's condition, between the start and finish of the play time. This idea is more easily understood in terms of space.

> Inside the playground an absolute and peculiar order reigns. Here we come across another, very positive feature of play: it creates order, *is* order. Into an imperfect world and into the confusion of life it brings a temporary, a limited perfection. Play demands order absolute and supreme. (p. 20)

This order becomes institutionalized as rules which "are absolutely binding and admit of no doubt." (p. 11)

Huizinga's critique of the modern world in *In the Shadow of Tomorrow* involved the idea of the degeneration of play into puerilism. This involved a loss of the sense of the temporal and spacial limitations of the play world, which Huizinga considered essential to true play. "The most fundamental characteristic of true play," he says

> whether it be a cult, a performance, a contest, or a festivity, is that at a certain moment it is *over*. The spectators go home, the players take off their masks, the performance has ended. And here the evil of our time shows itself. For nowadays play in many cases never ends and hence is not true play. A far-reaching contamination of play and serious activity has taken place. The two spheres are getting mixed. In the activities of an outwardly serious nature hides an element of play. Recognized play, on the other hand, is no longer able to maintain its true play-character as a result of being taken too seriously and being technically over-organized. The indispensable qualities of detachment, artlessness and gladness are thus lost.
>
> To a certain extent something like this contamination has been present in all cultures as far back as we can see. But it is the dubious privilege of modern western civilization to have given this diffusion of the two spheres of life its greatest intensity. With great numbers of both the educated and the ignorant, the play attitude towards life of the adolescent has become permanent. At an earlier stage we have already alluded to the prevalence of a state of mind which might be called one of permanent adolescence. It is characterized by a lack of a sense of decorum, a lack of personal dignity and of respect for others and the opinions of others, and an excessive concentration on self. The general weakening of judgment and of the critical impulse has prepared the soil for the spread of this attitude.[15]

Though he describes it as a degeneration, Huizinga correctly sees that a change of attitude toward play has taken place in the modern world; a change which, my essay shall argue, reaches throughout the total culture in America only after the first world war. Throughout the nineteenth century play seems to have gradually gained the status of an ideology. This process is what Huizinga has described; an appropriation of the characteristics of play as a set of values with reference to which man could live in the workaday world. A review of the quotations from Reston, Exley and Stone will reinforce the idea that the characteristics of play, as Huizinga describes them, are susceptible of elevation into a kind of value system. Tracing now the development of a literary tradition from which a tendency to regard sports as a source of values developed will be useful.

I

Ralph Barton Perry's designation of the Puritan as a "moral athlete" sums up his attitude toward the Puritan sense of morality. It also seems to describe the nature of the Puritan's stance toward the rest of the world. According to Perry, "in order to perfect and prove his spiritual strength the Puritan engaged in exercises and went into training, much as a youth sets out to excel in sport."[16] He notes a curious consequence of this, both for the American athlete and the Puritan, "that by his intense effort to surpass records or defeat opponents he makes work out of what should be play."[17]

Michael Walzer's *The Revolution of the Saints* analyzes this aspect of Puritanism. Walzer suggests that Puritanism's importance to the modern world is best seen in terms of political ideology rather than theology. He describes the relation of Puritanism to the liberal world as "perhaps one of historical preparation, but not at all of theological contribution."[18] Walzer sees Puritanism as an important element in the process of change from medieval society to modern society. "In the history of Western Europe," he says,

> and especially of England, the sixteenth and seventeenth centuries mark a crucial phase of the modernizing process, a "crisis" manifest finally in the mid-seventeenth century English revolution in which the Puritan saint is the central protagonist.[19]

He concludes by saying that "Calvinism in its sixteenth- and seventeenth-century forms was not so much the cause of this or that modern economic, political or administrative system as it was an agent of modernization, an ideology of the transition period."[20]

What form did this ideology take? What kind of man did it produce? Walzer describes the change.

> In the old political order, the saint was a stranger . . . he had moved outside the world of political limitation and into the new world of self-control. His new freedom made radical aspiration and exploration possible; it also made fanaticism possible—and even necessary. . . . By calling himself elect, the saint specified his exclusive allegiance to God's Word and (presumably) to the community of the future, where men would live in fellowship on the 'Lord's hill.'[21]

This movement from the world of political limitation to a new world of self-control is the subject of a whole chapter in Walzer's book, "The New World of Discipline and Work," in which the shape of the Puritan's behavior is very much that of Perry's "moral athlete." The world the Puritan rejected could be easily described as one of "idleness and confusion." Walzer suggests that "the Puritan demand for continuous, organized, methodical activity—to banish idleness—was a reaction to the breakdown of country stability and . . . to the sudden appearance of the mobile urban man." These men were to the Puritans signs of the disorder of the times and their commitment to method gave them a vantage point from which to view the "men without work in the cities; noisy, jostling crowds, vagabonds on country roads; great houses filled with idle, merry men."[22] Thus work, as opposed to idleness and play, became not only "the primary and elemental form of social discipline," but also "the key to order and the foundation of all further morality."[23] Walzer concludes that the Puritans "sought in work itself what mere work can never give: a sense of vocation and discipline that would free them from sinfullness and the fear of disorder." All these things can be exemplified from the two accounts of what Harvey Wish calls "Plymouth's war on Merry Mount and the Maypole,"[24] those of Thomas Morton and William Bradford.

The title of Morton's defense of his action in the new world, *New English Canaan*, suggests that he shared with the Pilgrims the vision of the new world as a promised land, though for different motives. His book is in part a propaganda piece to lure new settlers: it emphasizes beauties of the New England climate and geography and stresses the area's commercial possibilities. The book is also a justification of his actions in the new world, for which he was twice forcibly removed to England by the Pilgrims. The incident of the Maypole he describes simply as a festival to commemorate the changing of the name of the settlement "from the ancient salvage name 'Pasonagessit' to 'Ma-re Mount.' The settlers," he says, "wished

to have it performed in a solemne manner, with Revels and merriment after the old English custome; they prepared to sett up a Maypole upon the festivall day of Philip and Iacob, and therefore brewed a barrell of excellent beare and provided a case of bottles, to be spent, with other good cheare, for all commers of that day, and because they would have it in a compleat forme, they had prepared a song fitting to the time and present occasion."[25]

All of this sounds reasonably orderly. It is to be done "after the old English custome": there is a desire to have things done "in a compleat form." "The precise separatists," however, according to Morton, were unhappy about it, "threatening to make it a woeful mount and not a merry mount. . . ." In this, he considers that they are "troubling their brains more than reason would require about things that are indifferent. . . ."[26] Morton implies here that the festival is a needed rest for his men from the trials of everyday existence, it is outside the sphere of everyday activity and not worth the pilgrims' bothering about. He regards the festival as play.

But Governor Bradford is a different kind of man, and lives, in spirit as well as in body, in a new world. In *Of Plymouth Plantation*, Morton is, for him, one of the "mobile, urban men" in relation to whom, according to Walzer, the Puritans formulated their morality. Bradford presents Morton as a rather scurrilous character, one who "had little respect amongst" his fellow colonists at Mount Wollaston and who was "sleghted [slighted] by the meanest servants."[27] Morton, he reports, with the aid of other miscreants, seized control of the colony when its leader was away, and set up a colony devoted to earthly pleasure. He describes this colony thusly.

And Morton became lord of misrule, and maintained (as it were) a school of Athisme. And after they had gott some gold into their hands, and gott much by trading with the Indeans, they spent it as vainly, in quaffing and drinking both wine & strong waters in great exsess, &, as some reported, 10. pounds

> worth in a morning. They allso set up a May-pole, drinking and dancing aboute it many days togeather, inviting the Indean women, for their consorts, dancing and frisking togither, (like so many fairies, or furies rather,) and worse practises. As if they had anew revived & celebrated the feasts of the Roman Goddes Flora, or the beastly practises of the madd Bacchinalians. Morton likewise (to show his poetrie) composed sundry rimes & verses, some tending to lasciviousness, and others to the detraction & scandall of some persons, which he affixed to this idle or idoll May-polle. They chainged allso the name of their place, and in stead of calling it Mounte Wollaston, they call it Merry-mounte, as if this joylity would have lasted ever.[28]

From this description, we imagine the festivities at Merry Mount to have been more unruly than Thomas Morton described them to be. More than that, the festival is inconceivable to Bradford's Puritan imagination. He objects to it first because of its licentiousness. Secondly the festival is a manifestation of idleness. To Bradford's mind anything outside the realm of hard work and prayer is idleness, and idleness breeds disorder and chaos. Finally, and perhaps most importantly, Bradford says that "they call it Merie-Mounte, as if this joylity would have lasted ever." In saying this, he accuses Morton and his men of extending their festival beyond its proper boundaries in time, making it the sole meaningful occupation of their life. In effect he accuses them of celebrating their leisure activities over their work activities. That Morton has no intention of doing this (he includes the festival among "things that are indifferent") underlines the fact that Bradford's objection has its formal source in his own way of looking at the world, for he, as well as the Puritans who were to settle in Massachusetts Bay, was engaged in making a Biblical commonwealth outside the daily corrupt practices of medieval Europe and this commonwealth, like Morton's festival, was to "have lasted ever."

II

Walzer's presentation of the Puritan's understanding of work as a moral orientation makes it seem akin to the Victorian's enthusiasm for work. Indeed, the nineteenth century proves to have been even more fanatical about the redemptive value of work than the seventeenth. Foster Rhea Dulles's history of recreation in America underlines this. In the first part of the nineteenth century, he finds "new forms of recreation found all the moral forces of the age arrayed against them." One of these was "a renewed emphasis upon the importance of work." This attitude he finds "strengthened and intensified by a revived Puritanism which again provided a moral sanction for the disapproval of recreation."[29] No single man represents these attitudes better than Thomas Carlyle, one of whose favorite sayings was "Laborare est Orare, Work is Worship!"[30]

In Carlyle's writings, as Walter Houghton says of the Victorian age in general, "Puritanism, business and doubt met together to write the gospel of work." Houghton styles Carlyle a "major prophet" of a "religion of work" which "could resolve both intellectual perplexity and psychological depression." Carlyle, says Houghton, tells us to "work and you will end your misery and forward the progress of civilization."[31] "In idleness alone there is perpetual despair." (p. 189) We need to investigate Carlyle's understanding of the nature and function of work, as it appears in *Past and Present*. It may be that what Carlyle understands as work, Johan Huizinga understands as play.

Work, like most anything Carlyle speaks of, must be taken doubly. In *Past and Present* he takes two chapters to discuss it, "Labour" and "Reward." In the second of these he considers the nature of work in the actual urban industrial world he sees around him.

> Industrial work, still under bondage to Mammon, the rational soul of it not yet awakened, is a tragic spectacle. Men in the rapidest motion and self-motion; restless, with convulsive energy, as if driven by Galvanism, as if possessed by a devil; tearing asunder mountains,–to no purpose, for Mammonism is always Midas-eared! . . . Labour is not a devil, even while encased in Mammonism; Labour is ever an imprisoned god, writhing unconsciously or consciously to escape out of Mammonism! (p. 199)

Thus for Carlyle we have only to remove the industrial context, both physical and moral, to be able to understand the genuine nature of work. "Genuine work alone, what thou workest faithfully, that is eternal, as the Almighty Founder and World-Builder himself." (p. 130) Work is part of the unchanging eternal world, not of the changing and sometimes chaotic actual world. Work being part of this unchanging world, it is really the same in both past and present, in both the medieval and the modern worlds. The question is how to release "industrial work" from the Mammonism in which it is encased.

To do this one must understand the primary qualities of genuine work. At least four can be seen in Carlyle's discussion of labor and reward. In the first place, work is a better way to self-knowledge than introspection. "The latest Gospel in this world is, Know thy work and do it. 'Know thyself': long enough has that poor 'self' of thine tormented thee; thou wilt never get to 'know' it, I believe!" (p. 189) Work here stands for a life of action rather than one of contemplation. It is in itself a non-intellectual activity, but at the same time has spiritual qualities; it is the true road to self knowledge. ". . . from the Worker's inmost heart awakens to him all nobleness—to all knowledge, 'self-knowledge' and much else, so soon as work fitly begins." (p. 190) Secondly, work is apparently instinctual rather than learned behavior. Man's real place in the universe is "Working as great Nature bade him. . . ." (pp. 152-153) "Labour is Life": Carlyle tells us, "from the inmost heart of the Worker rises his god-given Force, the sacred celestial Life-essence breathed into him by Almighty God: . . ." (p. 190)

If work is the manifestation of God in the individual, then, in the confused, disorganized world of industrial England, work can be an organizing principle in one's life, can be a "making of Madness sane." (p. 199) "Consider how," says Carlyle,

> even in the meanest sorts of labour, the whole soul of a man is composed into a kind of real harmony, the instant he sets himself to work! Doubt, Desire, Sorrow, Remorse, Indignation, Despair itself, all these like hell-dogs lie beleaguering the soul of the poor day-worker, as of every man, but he bends himself with free valour against his task, and all these are stifled, all these shrink murmuring far off into their caves. The man is now a man, the Blessed glow of Labour in him, is it not as purifying fire, wherein all poison is burnt up, and of sour smoke itself there is made bright blessed flame! (p. 189)

This passage has a triumphant sound, but its imagery suggests that the making of madness sane is only temporary: the reader may find himself listening for the murmuring of the hell-dogs in their caves. As a means of orienting one's life, work is, to Carlyle, a sacred activity. Work always gives order to a chaotic world. Carlyle uses two images to underline the sacredness of work. The first is that of the contest.

> Work is of a religious nature: work is of a *brave* nature; which it is the aim of all religion to be. All work of man is as the swimmer's; a waste ocean

threatens to devour him; if he front it not bravely, it will keep its word. By incessant wise defiance of it, lusty rebuke and buffet of it, behold how it loyally supports him, bears him as its conqueror along. (p. 192)

This image of the swimmer is followed by an image of man as a wrestler. "Thou, in thy strong soul, as with wrestler's arms, shalt embrace the World, harness it down; and make it bear thee on. . . ." (p. 193) Both swimmer and wrestler are contestants with the world. A second image suggests the ritual quality of work. Carlyle achieves this in general by setting his ideal society in a medieval monastery, where all action is plotted out for each individual monk. Everything he does becomes an outward and visible sign of inward and spiritual grace.

On the whole we do entirely agree with those old Monks, *Laborare est Orare.* In a thousand senses, from one end of it to the other, true Work *is* Worship. He that works, whatsoever be his work, he bodies forth the form of Things Unseen; a small Poet every Worker is. (p. 197)

One other quality of work emerges from this, but not until later in the book. As a result of work's being regarded as a contest or a ritual act, a set of rules may develop, differing according to the condition under which they emerge, but within which man must operate, in order that his actions be meaningful. Carlyle recognizes this when he says in his chapter "Captains of Industry" that "No Working World, any more than a Fighting World, can be led on without a noble chivalry of Work, and laws and fixed rules which follow out of that—far nobler than any Chivalry of Fighting was." (p. 263)

These qualities correspond in many important ways to the characteristics of play. Though he is not so theological as Carlyle, Huizinga is trying to describe an activity which, like Carlyle's work, is both non-material and non-intellectual; one, which, even if he doesn't like the word instinct, is instinctual in the sense that the fundamental impulse for it is unlearned. As a stepping out of "real" life, play corresponds to Carlyle's notion of genuine work. For Carlyle, work must transcend its industrial context to be genuine work. Play, as Huizinga describes it, is always removed from the context of the real world. To play, one must transcend the cares of the workaday world. The two social manifestations of this characteristic of play correspond exactly to the two images Carlyle uses in describing genuine work: contest and ritual.

As Carlyle sees work revealing the real order of the world, Huizinga describes play as bringing a temporary, limited perfection into the confusion of life. Although Carlyle would insist on the ultimate reality of his world of genuine work, while Huizinga stresses the temporary and limited nature of the world of play, we should remember that play can become a very serious thing and also that Carlyle's workman has not rid himself forever of his hell-dogs, who still murmur in their caves, awaiting their next opportunity to torment. They represent the actual world for Carlyle, if not the real one. Carlyle insists on the power of work as a power by which man can transcend, at least temporarily, the very conditions of existence (Doubt, Desire, Sorrow, etc.). In this important respect, Carlyle's world is a world of play, although he sees it as a world of work.

III

Huizinga himself becomes something of a Carlylian in his criticism of the play element of modern society. Later in *Homo Ludens* he offers this judgment:

> The 19th century seems to leave little room for play. . . . Work and production became the ideal, and then the idol, of the age. All Europe donned the boiler suit. Henceforth the dominants of civilization were to be social consciousness, educational aspirations, and scientific judgment.[32]

This is precisely the world Charles Dickens attacks in *Hard Times*, and he sees himself as a promulgator of Carlyle's ideas in so doing. In a letter to Charles Knight, Dickens discusses the problem of "industrial work."

> I earnestly entreat your attention to the point (I have been working upon it, weeks past, in Hard Times) *** The English are, so far as I know, the hardest worked people on whom the sun shines. Be content if, in their wretched intervals of pleasure, they read for amusement and do no worse. They are born at the oar, and they live and die at it. Good God, what would we have of them.[33]

Dickens included a passage very much like this in *Hard Times*, but with an important change. "I entertain a weak idea," he says, "that the English people are as hard worked as any people upon whom the sun shines. I acknowledge to this ridiculous idiosyncrasy, as a reason why I would give them a little more play." (p. 48) Can industrial work become genuine work through the addition of play? What Dickens did was to embody Carlyle's notion of genuine work in a symbol of play.

Sleary's horse riding establishment is Dickens' symbol of the alternative to the value system of the urban, industrial world of the nineteenth century in England. Though one might assume that this circus is as much a product of the forces making industrial England as the school of Mr. M'Choakumchild, Dickens does not present it as such. Its physical location is "the neutral ground upon the outskirts of town, which was neither town nor country, and yet was either spoiled . . ." (p. 8) Dickens emphasizes the separateness of the horse riding establishment in every way he can. The other characters in the book must go to it, it does not come to them. The two trips to the horse riding establishment serve to frame the action of the book. In the opening scenes, when we first see the entertainers, even their language is incomprehensible to the ordinary inhabitants of Coketown. (pp. 23-24) To Bounderby's way of thinking, they are outcasts. The word "idle" sums them up for him. (p. 20) But rather than being idle, they are hard and earnest workers in a world of play. The fact that Dickens sets them apart from the "real" world suggests this.

In contrast to the "hands" of Coketown, whose jobs are incomprehensible mechanical drudgery, the world of the horse riders is full of accomplishments which suggest a life of excitement and fulfillment.

> . . . all the fathers could dance on rolling casks, stand upon bottles, catch knives and balls, twirl hand-basins, ride upon anything, jump over everything, and stick at nothing. All the mothers could (and did) dance, upon the slack wire and the tight rope, and perform rapid acts on bare backed steeds. . . . (p. 27)

Like Carlyle's images of the genuine worker (the swimmer and wrestler), these are athletes. Their very work contains something of the nature of play. It is a continual contest with the conditions of existence.

Sleary's final statement of principle is given as a statement of the moral bases of his community and represents the basis of

Dickens' objections to industrial society.

> . . . there ith a love in the world, not all Thelf-interetht after all, but thomething very different . . . it hath a way of ith own of calculating or not calculating, whith thomehow or another ith at leatht ath hard to give a name to, ath the wayth of the dogth ith!
>
> . . . Don't be croth with uth poor vagabondth. People mutht be amuthed. They can't alwayth be a learning, not yet they can't be alwayth a working, they an't made for it. You *mutht* have uth, Thquire. Do the withe thing and the kind thing too make the betht of uth; not the wortht!" (p. 222)

How to reach the kind of love of which Sleary speaks is the problem of the book. Dickens has already indicated, in his depiction of Slackbridge the labor agitator, that he considers the reformation of industrial society an impossibility. Thus the reader is left with the possibility of self-reformation, or transcendence. The outline of Louisa Gradgrind's progress through the novel suggests the means of transcending the world of Coketown. The child of Gradgrind, the wife of Bounderby, the object of the intentions of Harthouse (the idler of the book), finally the companion of Sissy and her children; in all these roles Louisa moves toward the ideals Sleary announces. Her life begins to attain a sort of focus when she flees Harthouse, leaves Bounderby, rejects her father as an educator, and begins to recognize Sissy's good qualities. Sissy is the representative of the circus people to the world of Coketown and Louisa's success in transcending Coketown values can be measured by her relation to Sissy through the course of the book. Louisa's marriage to Bounderby, who epitomizes the values of the industrialist, alienates her from Sissy. This marriage does not last, because in great part of the Satanic machinations of the idle Harthouse, and Louisa flees Bounderby and all he stands for. At home, she collapses, then awakens to find Sissy's hand lying on her neck. "It lay there, warming into life a crowd of gentle thoughts." (p. 171) Converted by Sissy's touch, Louisa grows from that point through the rest of the book and, though she never remarries and has children, becomes a part of that family community symbolized by the circus performers and by Sissy. Dickens speculates on her future.

> happy Sissy's happy children loving her; all children loving her; she . . . trying hard to know her humbler fellow creatures, and to beautify their lives of machinery and reality with those imaginative graces and delights, without

which the heart of infancy will wither up, the sturdiest physical manhood will be morally stark death . . . she holding this course as part of no fantastic vow, no bond, or brotherhood . . . but simply as a duty to be done. . . . (pp. 226-227)

Here she becomes the spiritual counterpart of the actual family of the circus people.

IV

The same pairs Dickens opposed in *Hard Times*, mechanical civilization versus natural, imagination versus reality, work versus play, are present in Nathaniel Hawthorne's "The Maypole of Merry Mount," included in his 1836 *Twice Told Tales.* The colonists of Merry Mount are presented as "that giddy tribe whose whole life is like the festal days of soberer man," an echo of Bradford's vision of them.

In their train were minstrels, not unknown in London streets; wandering players, whose theatres had been the halls of nobleman; mummers, rope-dancers, and mountebacks, who would long be missed at wakes, church ales, and fairs; in a word, mirth makers of every sort, such as abounded in that age, but now began to be discountenanced by the rapid growth of Puritanism.[34]

To these are opposed that "grim" "stern band" of "toiling" "men of iron" the Puritans. Hawthorne, like Dickens, constructs "a sort of allegory" or moral fable out of this contrast. Both basically describe the journey of a soul through the world, but the goals of the two journeys are different.

Hawthorne first describes Merry Mount and its inhabitants:

But what was the wild throng that stood hand in hand about the Maypole? It could not be that the fauns and nymphs, when driven from their classic groves and homes of ancient fable, had sought refuge, as all the persecuted did, in the fresh woods of the West.

He discovers in the circle "a real bear of the dark forest." The bear's "inferior nature rose half way, to meet his companions as they stooped." (p. 883) With this, Hawthorne suggests that the revelers are, by choice, less than human. They engage in a "continual carnival." On this occasion the revelers are gathered together for a wedding. The Lord and Lady of the May are "to be partners for the dance of life." Their conversation as they await the blessing of "an English priest, canonically dressed, yet decked with flowers, in heathen fashion" further defines the limitations of the community at Merry Mount. The May Lord, "wonder struck at the almost pensive glance that met his own" as he looked into his Lady's eyes, exclaims "this is our golden time! Tarnish it not by any pensive shadow of the mind; for it may be that nothing of futurity will be brighter than the mere remembrance of what is now passing." (p. 884) This is precisely the problem.

> No sooner had their hearts glowed with real passion than they were sensible of something vague and insubstantial in their former pleasures, and felt a dreary presentment of inevitable change. From the moment that they truly loved, they had subjected themselves to earth's doom of care and sorrow, and troubled joy, and had no more a home at Merry Mount. (p. 885)

Hawthorne returns at this point in the story to a consideration of the two communities, that of Merry Mount and that of the Puritans. The leaders of Merry Mount were men "who had sported so long with life, that when Thought and Wisdom came, even these unwelcome guests were led astray by the crowd of vanities which they should have put to flight. Sworn triflers of a lifetime, they would not venture among the sober truths of life not even to be truly blest." Thus underlining the vanity of the colony, Hawthorne turns to its chief symbol, the Maypole itself. "It has made their true history a poet's tale." (p. 885) He describes its appearance during all four seasons of the year and concludes "Its votaries danced around it, once, at least, in every month; sometimes they called it their religion, their altar . . ." (p. 886) It seems clear from these quotations that this community is intent on following its animal, natural nature, to the exclusion of all else. Having rid themselves of care and sorrow (and troubled joy), the members of the community are children forever at play.

Hawthorne then turns to those "most dismal wretches" the Puritans, men "of sterner faith than those Maypole worshippers." (p. 886) He suggests points of comparison between the two groups, saying of the Puritans "their festivals were fast days." The whipping post "might be termed the Puritan maypole." These formal similarities serve to underline for Hawthorne the total opposition of the two groups. Their quarrel involves "the future complexion of New England."

> Should the grizzly saints establish their jurisdiction over the gay sinners, then would their spirits darken all the clime, and make it a land of clouded visages, of hard toil, of sermon and psalm forever. But should the banner staff of Merry Mount be fortunate, sunshine would break upon the hills, and flowers would beautify the forest, and late posterity do homage to the Maypole.

But Hawthorne's story shies away from this speculation, and returns to the wedding at Merry Mount. Those inhabitants, who in the opening passages of the story had been standing in the "broad smile of sunset," (p. 887) were now engulfed in the "evening gloom, which has rushed so instantaneously from the black surrounding woods."

"But some of these black shadows have rushed forth in human shape." The Puritans have arrived to put a stop to the revelries of Merry Mount. Here Hawthorne suggests an allegorical interpretation of the situation.

> The Puritans had played a characteristic part in the Maypole mummeries. Their darksome figures were intermixed with the wild shapes of their foes, and made the scene a picture of the moment, when waking thoughts start up amid the scattered fantasies of a dream. (p. 887)

Edicott, leader of the Puritans, signifying that "the Lord hath sanctified this wilderness for *his* peculiar people" (my emphasis), cuts down the Maypole and announces various punishments for the merrymakers "as earnest of our future justice." (p. 888) The Lord and Lady of the May are pointed out to him.

> There they stood, pale, downcast, and apprehensive. Yet there was an air of mutual support and of pure affection, seeking aid and giving it, that showed them to be man and wife, with the sanction of a priest on their love. . . . There they stood, in the first hour of wedlock, while the idle pleasures, of which their companions were the emblems, had given place to the sternest cares of life, personified by the dark Puritans. (pp. 888-889)

The allegorical significance of their situation is emphasized. The young couple, in marriage, have passed from the playground of youth (Merry Mount) to the cares and responsibilities of adulthood (the Puritan colony). Both conditions are vitally important to their developing understanding of their condition.

As the moral gloom of the world overpowers all systematic gayety, even so was their home of wild mirth made desolate amid the sad forest. They returned to it no more. But as their flowery garland was wreathed of the brightest roses that had grown there, so, in the tie that united them, were entwined the purest and the best of their early joys. (pp. 889-890)

For Hawthorne, unlike Dickens, there is no ideal condition of existence which can serve as an alternative to the social order, be it Puritan or industrial. Time and gloom make up, for Hawthorne, a major part of existence. Childhood dreams of play make them bearable, but cannot replace or transcend them. The end of Louisa's pilgrimage, we remember, was a life among Sissy's happy children. The new world of the Lord and Lady of the May is one of care and sorrow, and troubled joy.

V

In the year before the appearance of *Hard Times*, another book appeared that took as its setting "the neutral ground upon the outskirts of town, which was neither town nor country. . . ." At Walden pond, and in the book that presented his experience there, Henry David Thoreau sought, as Dickens did in *Hard Times*, to imagine an alternative way of life to that of the urban industrial society around him. The two books have different perspectives: Thoreau in *Walden* speaks from a point of view comparable to that of Sleary in *Hard Times*. We see the world through the eyes of a man whom honest, hardworking citizens like Bounderby could not fail to call an idler and who, much to his readers' horror, seemed disposed to brag about that fact.

Thoreau opens the book with an unequivocal rejection of the values of the actual workaday world. He announces that the ordinary working men are not free men at all but "serfs of the soil."[35] "I have traveled a good deal in Concord," he says,

and everywhere, in shops, and offices, and fields, the inhabitants have appeared to me to be doing penance in a thousand remarkable ways. . . . The twelve labors of Hercules were trifling in comparison with those which my neighbors have undertaken; for they were only twelve, and had an end; but I could never see that these men slew or captured any monster or finished any labor. (p. 2)

Human labor in the workaday world is, for Thoreau, never-ending and absurd. Consequently, the laborer is less than a man: "the laboring man has not leisure for a true dignity day by day; he cannot afford to sustain the manliest relations to men; his labor would be depreciated in the market. He has no time to be anything but a machine." (pp. 3-4) Laboring as they do, "the mass of men lead lives of quiet desperation." This despair, Thoreau insists, permeates all of contemporary life. He suggests that "a stereotyped but unconscious despair is concealed even under what are called the games and amusements of mankind. There is no play in them, for this comes after work." (p. 5) Because he characterizes human activity as despairing, the designations "work" and "play" are meaningless. One of Thoreau's tasks in *Walden* was to make them meaningful again.

Like Carlyle, he had first to establish that there was a real world, with reference to which one could live in the actual world around him. In the second chapter of *Walden*, "Where I Lived, What I Lived For," Thoreau does this. In the actual world

> shams and delusions are esteemed for soundest truths, while reality is fabulous. If men would steadily observe realities only, and not allow themselves to be deluded, life, to compare it with such things as we know, would be like a fairy tale and the Arabian Nights' Entertainments. (p. 78)

Thoreau then makes a distinction between appearance and reality. "I perceive that we inhabitants of New England live this mean life that we do because our vision does not penetrate the surface of things. We think that that *is* which *appears* to be." (p. 79) He appeals to humanity to "settle ourselves, and work and wedge our feet downward through the mud and slush of opinion, and prejudice, and tradition, and delusion, and appearance, that alluvion which covers the globe . . . till we come to a hard bottom and rocks in place, which we call *reality*, and say, This is, and no mistake; and then begin. . . ." (p. 80)

Thoreau went to Walden because he "wished to live deliberately, to front only the essential facts of life." (p. 74) The way he describes what he accomplished is significant.

> I learned this, at least, by my experiment: that if one advances confidently in the direction of his dreams, and endeavors to live the life which he has imagined, he will meet with a success unexpected in common hours. He will put

> some things behind, will pass an invisible boundary; new, universal, and more liberal laws will begin to establish themselves around and within him; or the old laws be expanded, and interpreted in his favor in a more liberal sense, and he will live with the license of a higher order of beings. In proportion as he simplifies his life, the laws of the universe will appear less complex, and solitude will not be solitude, nor poverty poverty, nor weakness weakness. If you have built castles in the air, your work need not be lost; that is where they should be. Now put the foundations under them. (p. 270)

Attainment of the real world is to a certain extent possible: this is what Thoreau learned at Walden. What is important for us to notice here is that the real world has many of the qualities Huizinga attributed to the world of play.

The world Thoreau describes is removed from the ordinary world. In moving into the real world, one "will pass an invisible boundary." What he finds in that world could be described as rules, which "are absolutely binding and admit of no doubt." "Universal" laws are established "around and within" him. This leads to the discovery that life is simple in reality; chaos and complexity are illusory. This simplicity actually operates as work does in Carlyle; to banish certain of Thoreau's "hell-dogs." We learn that "solitude will not be solitude, nor poverty poverty, nor weakness weakness." In the real world these denizens of the actual world are seen as they really are, and by this means are banished to their caves.

Thus Thoreau's trip to Walden may be called an experimental journey into a world of play. Within this context, he uses metaphors involving work and leisure, play and sport. Thoreau delights in reversing the values he finds in the ordinary world. Thus he is able to speak of "luxurious and idle work" (p. 46) when discussing his neighbor's efforts and to remark that what he is doing must seem in their eyes to be "sheer idleness." (p. 92) He is, in fact, able at one point to announce that sometimes, for him, "idleness was the most attractive and productive industry" (p. 160) available. That he, like Carlyle, has a vision of work removed from its industrial context is underlined by the following quotation. "As for *work*, we haven't any of any consequence. We have the Saint Vitus' dance, and cannot possibly keep our heads still." (p. 76)

And genuine work tends to be described in terms of play and sport, though Thoreau is not always consistent in his use of these words. For instance, he says of college students "that they should not *play* life, or *study* it merely, while the community supports them at this expensive game, but earnestly *live* it from beginning to end." (p. 41) Here the word play connotes frivolity, childishness, irrelevance to the important concerns of life. It is the use of the word we would expect from an earnest Victorian. However, metaphors from the world of sports tend to appear when Thoreau needs a metaphor to embody the idea of earnest endeavor. Consider, for instance, the noble exercise of reading books. "It requires," according to Thoreau, "a training such as the athletes underwent, the steady intention almost of the whole life to this object." (p. 82)

Thoreau's consideration of sport in *Walden* appears to pave the way for the emergence of a new meaning of the word play. He considers sports in a number of contexts. For instance, he contends that "to maintain one's self on this earth is not a hardship but a pastime, if we live simply and wisely"; and then gives this abstraction concreteness by adding "as the pursuits of the simpler nations are still the sports of the more artificial." (p. 58) If this is so, artificial America should look to its sports for clues as to how life should be lived. Indeed, later in *Walden*, Thoreau insists that life ought to be lived as sport, not as trade. "Let not to get a living be thy trade, but thy sport." (p. 173)

In the chapter "Higher Laws" he discusses the role of sports in the development of the individual. "They mistake who assert that the Yankee has few amusements, because he has not so many public holidays, and men and boys do not play so many games as they do in England, for here the more primitive and solitary amusements of hunting, fishing, and the like have not yet given place to the former." (p. 177) America is not, apparently, as artificial a society as England. He considers it good that young men hunt and fish, even though he himself has given up these sports. He feels that "there is a period in the history of the individual, as of the race, when the hunters are the 'best men'."

> Such is oftenest the young man's introduction to the forest, and the most original part of himself. He goes thither at first as a hunter and fisher, until at last, if he has the seeds of a better life in him, he distinguishes his proper objects as a poet or naturalist it may be, and leaves the gun and fish-pole behind. (p. 178)

Thoreau here concurs with Thomas Hughes in that both see a positive value in sports as an instrument by which earnest young men are created. But sports here perform another function: they bring one back into touch with "the most original part of himself." They operate as a kind of purifying device through which one enters the real world where "solitude will not be solitude" etc.

All this leads us to a new version of play, far different from the one Thoreau articulated in speaking of students above. Instead of being irrelevant and frivolous, play is the gateway to an understanding of the real world. "Children," insists Thoreau, "who play life, discern its true law and relations more clearly than men, who fail to live it worthily, but who think that they are wiser by experience, that is, by failure." (p. 78) Thoreau here articulates a principle that had been stated some years before by his mentor Ralph Waldo Emerson in an address to the students of the Harvard Divinity School. It contradicts the idea of play implicit in his other use of the word and it tends to suggest an even more positive value for play than his use of the metaphor of sport will admit. Emerson too suggested that life might be better if one played at it. Though he too saw it as a stage in human development, this idea is muted in the following passage.

The sentiment of virtue is a reverence and delight in the presence of certain divine laws. It perceives that this homely game of life we play, covers, under what seem foolish details, principles that astonish. The child amidst his baubles is learning the action of light, motion, gravity, muscular force; and in the game of human life, love, fear, justice, appetite, and God, interact.[36]

VI

Disciples of Thomas Carlyle continued to be optimistic about seeing a value for play as an idea which would help render the shape of the human condition more intelligible than it seemed to be, though Dickens and Thoreau could be said to be more optimistic; Hawthorne less. Thomas Hughes's novel, *School Days at Rugby*, can also be considered the work of a disciple of Carlyle in this respect.

School Days at Rugby, while not as powerful a piece of writing as *Hard Times, Walden* or "The Maypole of Merry Mount," nevertheless contains a more fully articulated social theory. This is, as Walter Houghton describes it, the tradition "of the English Squirearchy, both at home and at the public schools and universities, with its cult of games and field sports, and its admiration for physical strength and prowess."[37] *School Days at Rugby* is best understood as a kind of utopian novel, with Rugby School providing the physical setting. Hughes himself regarded his novel as an excuse for expounding his beliefs. In the preface to the sixth edition of *School Days at Rugby* he exclaimed "Why, my whole object in writing at all, was to get the chance of preaching!"[38] And it is not the society that lives the creed but the community that inculcates it that is the utopian community for Hughes. In the concluding pages of *School Days at Rugby*, a Rugby master tells Tom Brown: "perhaps ours is the only little corner of the British Empire which is thoroughly, wisely, and strongly ruled just now." (p. 382) Rugby approaches the ideal of life more truly than life itself for Hughes, in that it is more explicitly a preparation for the "life to come."

Rugby School, isolated from but at the same time a preparation for the real world, is best represented by its sports. "Rugby football was," say his biographers, "the heart of public school life for Hughes. 'This is worth living for; the whole sum of schoolboy existence gathered up into one straining, struggling half-hour, a half-hour worth a year of common life.' "[39] Tom Brown's first experience at Rugby is a football match and the match itself is presented as an initiation into the community. The goals, which Tom and his friend East encounter on the way to the match, are seen as "a sort of gigantic gallows." (p. 110) At the end of the match there is a great pile-up, at the bottom of which, "Tom is discovered a motionless body." (p. 126) Tom awakes from this into a new world, the world of Rugby School. He hears the elder Brook rationalize their victory at football. "It's because we've more reliance on one another, more of a house feeling, more fellowship than the school can have. Each of us knows and can depend on the next hand man better—that's why we beat 'em today." (p. 136) This is a statement of the kind of community which might result from the application of Carlylian principles of work: each member does his part in the contest, the group benefits. This is the lesson to be gained from playing football. But Hughes sees some limitations in this.

Tom has learned the lesson of play, but not that of work. A

wonderful fellow on the field of play, he is something of a terror elsewhere. To teach Tom a sense of responsibility, Thomas Arnold, Rugby's headmaster, assigns the frail boy Arthur to Tom as a roommate and Arthur becomes Tom's "work." Hughes tells us that through his association with Arthur, Tom

> increased his consciousness of responsibility; and though he hadn't reasoned it out and made it clear to himself, yet somehow he knew that this responsibility, this trust which he had taken on him without thinking about it, head-over-heels in fact, was the centre and turning point of his school life, which was to make him or mar him; his appointed work and trial for the time being. And Tom was becoming a new boy, though with frequent tumbles in the dirt and with perpetual hard battles with himself, and was daily growing in manfulness, and thoughtfulness, as every high-couraged and well-principled boy must, when he finds himself for the first time consciously at grips with self and the devil. (pp. 274-275)

Tom enters a new life here through his work with Arthur. Through Arthur Tom becomes a more religious and responsible citizen. But it is more important to note here that it is Tom's work to introduce Arthur to play. Arthur is introduced to Tom as a boy who "wants some Rugby air, and cricket." (p. 234) After two years at Rugby, Arthur, we are told, "is still frail and delicate, with more spirit than body; but thanks to his intimacy with them [East and Tom] and Martin, has learned to swim, and run, and play cricket, and has never hurt himself from too much reading." (pp. 325-326) After recovering from his illness, Arthur himself thanks Tom.

> My mother brought our old medical man, who attended me when I was a poor sickly child; he said my constitution was quite changed, and that I'm fit for anything now. If I hadn't I couldn't have stood three days of this illness. That's all thanks to you, and the games you've made me fond of. (p. 338)

Play has been a necessary element in Arthur's very survival.

His learning to play is a necessary prelude to his vision of life after death. In a dream he sees "a multitude which no man could number, and they worked at some great work; and they who rose from the river went on and joined in the work. They all worked, and each worked in a different way, but all at the same work." (p. 341) He "longed to see what the work was, and could not." Then, "I saw myriads on this side, and they too worked, and I knew it was the same work. . . ." Arthur feels himself one with the human race: "I saw myself too, and I was toiling and doing ever so a piece of the great work." (p. 342)

Arthur's sense of embarkation on the work of the human race anticipates Tom's consideration of the same subject at the end of the book. A cricket game, in which Arthur also participates, represents the end of Tom's Rugby career. Afterwards he has tea with a master of the school. Tom resents having to go to Oxford, rather than entering the service: "If I can't be at Rugby, I want to be at work in the world and not dwelling away three years at Oxford." At the request of his master, he tries to explain what he means. "Well, I mean real work; one's profession; whatever one will have really to do, and make one's living by. I want to be doing some real good, feeling that I am not only at play in the world." (pp. 389-390) Tom here has transcended play, knows he can remain at Rugby no longer. But play has been one necessary step in preparation for the work of the world. Play has taught Tom the very thing the master underlines for him, that to "make one's living" and "to do some real good" are not the same thing. Rugby football is an important ingredient in Thomas Hughes's formula for setting the industrial world right, a necessary step in the process of understanding one's work in the world.

VII

During the 1880's and 1890's public advocates of the importance of play began to appear. These men (Herbert Spencer was the most famous) argued that if play was not always the means of producing earnest young men that institutionalized sport was, it at least functioned as a "safety valve" in an urban, industrialized society.[40] Neither point of view could be considered optimistic in tone and while Spencer and the disciples of Frederick Jackson Turner lectured on the new frontier of play, literary men, Mark Twain among them, were reexamining the whole pattern of individual development from innocence to experience, to which the experience of play was supposed to contribute so much. This reexamination constitutes the substance of the first twenty chapters of *Life on the Mississippi.*

The theme of initiation gives unity to the first twenty chapters of *Life on the Mississippi.* Initiation can be understood as a change in one's mode of perceiving the world, and, coming as a result of this change, a realization of the nature of one's involvement in a human community. Work and play are important in this realization because Mark Twain's narrator identifies himself with his profession in the same way that Thoreau and Tom Brown identify themselves with sports as a stage in their development. Mark Twain, however, comes to different conclusions as to the value of this temporary reliance on one's profession to provide meaning than do Thoreau and Hughes as to the value of sports. The narrator of *Life on the Mississippi* enters "upon the small enterprise of 'learning' twelve or thirteen hundred miles of the great Mississippi river,"[41] and the author's central purpose is to describe the learning process. More specifically, the reader is to become acquainted with the "curious and wonderful science of piloting," to which the narrator is attracted. (p. 77) Why did the narrator choose the profession of piloting? "The reason is plain: a pilot, in those days, was the only unfettered and entirely independent human being that lived on the earth." (p. 107) But how does one become a pilot? The pilot must learn to perceive the river in a certain way. He must learn which things are significant to his profession; ignore those which are not. The moment during which the narrator first understands this occurs fairly early in the book. He has just failed to distinguish between a "wind reef" and a "bluff reef" and been told by the pilot Bixby that only experience will enable him to distinguish between them. Directly after this, the narrator meditates:

> It turned out to be true. The face of the water, in time, became a wonderful book—a book that was a dead language to the uneducated passenger, but which told its mind to me without reserve, delivering its most cherished secrets as if it uttered them with a voice. . . . In truth, the passenger who could not read this book saw nothing but all manner of pretty pictures in it, painted by the sun and shaded by the clouds, whereas to the trained eye these were not pictures at all, but the grimmest and most dead-earnest of reading matter. (pp. 74-75)

Here the narrator describes two ways of perceiving the river: that of the professional pilot and that of the spectator, the passenger. The process of his initiation into the secrets of his profession carries the narrator into a peculiar community; he is removed from the ordinary world. His way of perceiving the river distinguishes him from rather than binding him to the rest of humanity. He finds the universe meaningful only to the extent that he has learned his trade. His profession provides the means by which he can best perceive reality, understand the meaning of the world. Though his world is a restricted one, the narrator mourns not a loss of freedom but the loss of the ability to appreciate appearances. "I had lost something too," he says, "I had lost something that could never be restored to me while I lived. All the grace, the beauty, the poetry, had gone out of the majestic river!" (p. 75) His initiation has turned him from a frivolous, idle passenger, who sees nothing but pretty pictures in the river, to the properly earnest professional man imagined by Carlyle and Hughes, seeing life as "the grimmest and most dead-earnest of reading matter." As a professional, he must get down to work. This professional world, nevertheless, resembles a world of play as we have discovered it in other nineteenth century authors. It is removed from the ordinary world; it generates its own meaning; it is restricted in time and space.

Mark Twain, however, does not celebrate this movement into the play-world of one's profession. His understanding of the value of his narrator's initiation into the professional community of piloting does not necessarily coincide with the narrator's, as the chapters that follow the narrator's initiation show. In fact, there is an incongruity even within the narrator's meditation in which he first discovers the pilot's mode of perceiving the river, a time when he is supposedly viewing the world clearly for the first time. He first disparages the passengers' way of perceiving the river; they see nothing "but all manner of pretty pictures in it." Then he turns around and regrets the loss of this kind of vision: "all the grace, the beauty, the poetry, had gone out of the majestic river."

The initiation also seems to continue long after the narrator considers himself initiated into the profession. In the very next chapter after the revolution in his mode of perception the pilot demonstrates that the narrator is unable to read the river, which is just what he thought he had learned. (p. 78) Later, in the chapter on the "peculiar requirements of the science of piloting" (p. 97) he again proves himself unable to perform a pilot's duties. His imagination begins to construct dangers out of nothing. (p. 105) He learns from Mr. Bixby's demonstration that he will have to have more confidence in himself.

We should consider also the structure of the book in understanding Mark Twain's relationship to his narrator's changing values. *Life on the Mississippi*'s first twenty chapters are not even half over when the change in the narrator's way of perceiving the river takes place. The narrator's account of his professional education continues through chapter fifteen. A chapter on river people at play (steamboat racing) follows. The next chapter concludes with a seemingly irrelevant anecdote involving Stephen W. and the "innocent Yates." (p. 140) This anecdote serves a serious thematic purpose: it foreshadows another stage in the development of the narrator. Yates, we find, has professional status; he has been graduated as a pilot and gotten a berth. Yet because of his continuing innocence he is made the butt of Stephen's joke. Thus, we learn that initiation into the profession of piloting has nothing necessarily to do with one's relation to the human race at large. Directly following this anecdote, the narrator informs us of another aspect of his own education.

> . . . it was not always convenient for Mr. Bixby to have me with him, and in such cases he sent me with somebody else. I am to this day profiting somewhat by that experience; for in that brief, sharp schooling, I got personally and familiarly acquainted with about all the different types of human nature that are to be found in fiction, biography, or history. (p. 143)

In the process of learning to read physical nature, the narrator has also been exposed to human nature, and it is this, rather than his professional training, which is to be of final importance to him. This leads him to a consideration of the character Brown and the decisive moment in his own development.

The narrator has been made the butt of jokes in order to further his education, but Brown makes his corrections and gives his instructions out of sheer malevolence. He wants the narrator to do something wrong so that he can have the pleasure of reprimanding him for it. This situation reaches its climax in chapter nineteen when the narrator's brother, on orders from the captain, tells Brown to stop at the next plantation and Brown doesn't hear him. Brown becomes incensed with both the narrator and his brother when they insist that Brown was told to stop. He orders the narrator's brother out of the pilot-house and tells the narrator he will attend to him in a minute. The narrator thinks: "It was pilot law, and must be obeyed." The action continues.

> The boy started out, and even had his foot on the upper step outside the

> door, when Brown, with a sudden access of fury, picked up a ten pound lump of coal and sprang after him; but I was between, with a heavy stool, and I hit Brown a good honest blow which stretched him out.
>
> I had committed the crime of crimes—I had lifted my hand against the pilot on duty! I supposed I was booked for the penitentiary sure, and couldn't be booked any surer if I went on and squared my account with this person while I had the chance; consequently I stuck to him and pounded him with my fists a considerable time. (p. 151)

The narrator has developed enough as a human being to understand, in this instance, that there are other loyalties which take precedence over loyalty to a professional code. As a member of the piloting profession he has committed the crime of crimes: as a member of the human race, he has been motivated by the generous impulse to come to his brother's aid. By discarding the code of his professional group he rejoins the humanity out of which the initial stage of his initiation took him. In doing so, he steps out of a play world and into a humanly mature one.

Paradoxically, it is by doing this that he also gains a more lofty independence and freedom than the one he idealizes as the condition of the river pilot in chapter fourteen. This change gives the following comic passage an extra dimension.

> Brown gathered up the big spy-glass, war-club fashion, and ordered me out of the pilot-house with more than Commanche bluster, but I was not afraid of him now, so, instead of going I tarried, and criticized his grammar. I reformed his ferocious speeches for him, and put them into good English, calling his attention to the advantage of pure English over the bastard dialect of the Pennsylvania collieries whence he was extracted. (p. 152)

The narrator has here acquired a certain autonomy for the first time in the book. As he says, "during the brief remainder of the trip I knew how an emancipated slave feels, for I was an emancipated slave myself." (p. 154) Unlike Tom Brown, the narrator has arrived at manhood in spite of the kind of limited world his professional code offered him. The pattern of events in *Life on the Mississippi* specifically rejects the narrator's attempt to view the world as a meaningful entity through his professional code. It is not until he has broken it that he attains manhood and independence.

VIII

Like Mark Twain, Thorstein Veblen had difficulty regarding human development as a harmonious progression from stage to stage, with sports contributing to that harmony. Veblen saw no positive value in sports at all and deplored their popularity in nineteenth century America. Like most other earnest Victorians, he viewed work with a kind of reverence but it may be that, like Carlyle, he reverenced work because it had, among other things, the effect of creating a play world.

Veblen's 1899 *The Theory of the Leisure Class* considered at some length the value of sports in modern society under the heading "Modern Survivals of Prowess." Other modern survivals included were the institution of the duel, patriotism, and certain aspects of adolescent behavior, particularly in boys, which he described as the "aimless and playful, but more or less systematic and elaborate, disturbances of the peace in vogue among schoolboys."[42] Veblen suggests, with this last, an analogy, borrowed in all probability from biology, between the development of an individual and the development of civilization. Thus childhood and the state of savagery had essential qualities in common, as did adolescence and barbarism, adulthood and the state of the modern world. (pp. 168-169) In the context of this scheme "the ground of an addiction to sports is an archaic spiritual constitution–the possession of the predatory emulative propensity in a relatively high potency" and this addiction "in a peculiar degree marks an arrested development of the man's moral nature." (p. 170) Veblen felt that the interest in sports, being left over from the barbaric stage of civilization, would eventually die out. Real interest in sports, he felt, was confined to the leisure class and to the lower-class delinquents. And though he could not deny the common man's interest in sports, he did his best to minimize it and to distinguish it from that of the leisure class.

> . . . the predilection for sports in the commonplace industrial classes is of the nature of a reminiscence, more or less diverting as an occasional interest, rather than a vital and permanent interest that counts as a dominant factor in shaping the organic complex of habits of thought into which it enters. (p. 180)

Veblen insisted on distinguishing sports from play and work, activities we shall find him identifying as dominant in the first and third stages of civilization; the savage and the modern world. Surprisingly, he resists identifying sports and play. He does suggest that sports differ from "other expressions of predatory emulation" in that "the temperament which inclines men to them is essentially a boyish temperament." He speaks particularly of the quality of "make-believe" (p. 170) which seems to pervade games. In his scheme this remark would seem to suggest that sports might better be seen in terms of his first stage of civilization. Though he might thus have connected sports and childhood play, Veblen does not do so explicitly.

The relation Veblen saw between sports and work is somewhat more consciously explored than the relation between sports and play in *The Theory of the Leisure Class.* Veblen speaks twice of the relation of sports to what he calls "the instinct of workmanship." In the first instance he evokes "the instinct of workmanship" as something basic to man which runs counter to the conventions of the leisure class.

> In order to be decorous, an employment must conform to the leisure class canon of reputable waste; at the same time all activity, in order to be persisted in as an habitual, even if only partial, expression of life, must conform to the generically human canon of efficiency for some serviceable objective end. The leisure-class canon demands strict and comprehensive futility; the instinct of workmanship demands purposeful action. (p. 172)

The question now becomes how to resolve the stated purpose of sports, that of "reputable waste," with the instinct of workmanship, an instinct which, according to Veblen, must manifest itself in all human activity. Veblen considers this question in the following quotation.

> The ulterior norm to which all appeal is taken is the instinct of workmanship, which is an instinct more fundamental, of more ancient prescription, than the propensity to predatory emulation. The latter is but a special development of the instinct of workmanship, a variant, relatively late and ephemeral in spite of its great absolute antiquity. The emulative predatory impulse—or the instinct of sportsmanship, as it might well be called—is essentially unstable in comparison with the primordial instinct of workmanship out of which it has been developed and differentiated. Tested by this ulterior norm of life, predatory emulation, and therefore the life of sports, falls short. (p. 179)

Veblen here suggests that the relation between sports and work suggested most clearly by Hughes is a forced and unnatural one. Sports are, to Veblen, what industrial work is to Carlyle; a manifestation of human instinct which needs to be liberated from its contemporary context.

Thus Veblen emphatically divorced sports from work and play, yet he continually uncovered similarities between them that he would not let himself see. Likewise, when he came to develop a theory of play he did not label it play, but called it "idle curiosity" instead. This notion is most fully developed in his 1906 essay "The Place of Science in Modern Civilization." In it, Veblen suggested that "this idle curiosity is, perhaps, closely related to the aptitude for play observed in man and in lower animals. Aptitude for play, as well as the functioning of idle curiosity, seems particularly lively in the young, whose aptitude for sustained pragmatism is at the same time relatively vague and unreliable."[43]

Idle curiosity he defines in biological or chemical terms. Essentially, Veblen feels that the human organism responds pragmatically to outside stimuli. "But that is not all," he continues,

> The inhibitive nervous complication may also detach another chain of response to the given stimulus, which does not spend itself in a line of motor conduct and does not fall into a system of uses. Pragmatically speaking, this outlying chain of response is unintended and irrelevant. (p. 6)

Human responses are of two kinds, then; pragmatic and idle. In the modern world, Veblen tells us, idle curiosity "is often spoken of as the scientific spirit." (p. 12) The scientific spirit is divorced from the ordinary world in that it is not interested in the practical consequences of its findings. "It is a wholly fortuitous and insubstantial coincidence that much of the knowledge gained under machine-made canons of research can be turned to practical account. . . . This employment of scientific knowledge for useful ends," Veblen continues, "is technology, in the broad sense in which the term includes, besides the machine industry proper, such branches of practice as engineering, agriculture, medicine, sanitation, and economic reforms." (p. 16) Technology actually acts to purify idle curiosity, in its modern form of the scientific spirit, of certain inherent defects. In addition to allowing it to be divorced from all practical ends by dealing with them itself, technology, because it proceeds "on an interpretation of . . .

phenomena in mechanical terms, not in terms of imputed personality nor even of workmanship" (p. 18) cuts idle curiosity off from the religious tendencies it had during the savage state of civilization.

Modern science is, for Veblen, a "latterday faith." (p. 27) The ancestors of science, in that they proceed from the same idle curiosity, are the folklore and mythology of savage culture. "This genial spinning of apocryphal yarns" is like science

> in that it has no ulterior motive beyond the idle craving for a systematic correlation of data; but it is unlike science in that its standardization and correlation of data run in terms of the free play of imputed personal initiative rather than in terms of the constraint of objective cause and effect. (pp. 25-26)

The scientific spirit, for Veblen, like play for Huizinga, is self contained. Ideally it does not affect anything outside its own sphere. It is, like play, intimately related to religion. Though Veblen himself only distantly related it to play, the instinct of workmanship which formed the basis of his understanding of the 'real' world may be seen as equally related to the play world.

Though it operated in Veblen's thinking at all times Veblen did not publish a full-length consideration of his notion, "the instinct of workmanship," until 1914 when his book *The Instinct of Workmanship and the State of the Industrial Arts* appeared. This book contains the most systematic positive exposition of his thought that he ever wrote, and it needs to be compared, in terms of the notion of work contained in it, with Carlyle's *Past and Present.* Veblen may be said to have attempted to save Carlyle's idea from the inferences of his successors.

For Veblen, as for Carlyle, human nature consists of certain changeless, eternal qualities which sometimes dominate and sometimes are suppressed by the culture in which they appear. For both, it is institutions that change. Veblen, for instance, says that "changes in the institutional structure are continually taking place in response to the altered discipline of life under changing cultural conditions, but human nature remains specifically the same."[44] For Veblen, as for Carlyle, the institutional structure must be changed to permit human nature to operate freely. This is the nature of reform. Veblen reveals this in the tone of the following.

> But history records more frequent and more spectacular instances of the triumph of imbecile institutions over life and culture than of peoples who have by force of instinctive insight saved themselves alive out of a desperately precarious institutional situation, such, for instance, as now faces the peoples of Christendom. (p. 25)

Human nature best expressed itself in the savage mode of culture, and Veblen looked there to show how human nature operated in its freest form.

> This savage mode of life, which was, and is, in a sense, native to man, would be characterised by a considerable group solidarity within a relatively small group, living very near the soil, and unremittingly dependent for their daily life on the workmanlike efficiency of all members of the group. (p. 36)

Work is, then, an integral part of human nature for both Carlyle and Veblen, but in looking back into history they find the best expression of work occurring in different times. While Carlyle looked to the middle ages and felt that man in the modern world was unable to truly work, Veblen's attitude was different. He saw the middle ages as the time when the instinct of workmanship was in eclipse and felt that forces in the modern world were continually operating to free the instinct of workmanship again.

As Veblen defines the instinct of workmanship, it comes to seem quite similar to his idea of idle curiosity, but with one difference. "The instinct of workmanship . . . occupies the interest with practical expedients, ways and means, devices and contrivances of efficiency and economy, proficiency, creative work and technological mastery of facts." (p. 33) It is not, as idle curiosity is, an end in itself but works toward goals outside its own operation.

> It does not commonly, or normally work, to an independent, creative end of its own, but is rather concerned with the ways and means whereby instinctively given purposes are to be accomplished. According, therefore, as one or another of the instinctive dispositions is predominant in the community's scheme of life or in the individuals' every-day interest, the habitual trend of the sense of workmanship will be bent to one or another line of proficiency and technological mastery. (pp. 34-35)

In the modern world, idle curiosity, in the guise of science, provides these goals. Idle curiosity and the instinct of workmanship, *taken together*, seem to constitute a world like Huizinga's world of play for Veblen. We should note finally that the giving of free play to the combined instincts of idle curiosity and workmanship will also result in the banishment of the Veblenian hell-dogs; animistic, anthropomorphic, or teleological habits of thought, which, in the modern world are being driven to their caves by the instincts of idle curiosity and workmanship.

IX

Both Dickens and Hughes, as disciples of Carlyle, embodied their notion of work in an image of play. Veblen's analysis of the leisure class suggested another way of applying Carlyle's gospel of work to modern society. Robert Frost's "Two Tramps in Mud Time" embodies a notion of play in an image of work, and by doing so offers what seems both an extension and a clarification of Carlyle's understanding of the nature of work. Frost's definition of poetry itself, as a "temporary stay against confusion," has the same basic principle as Carlyle's "genuine work" and of Huizinga's definition of play, the bringing of a temporary and limited perfection into an imperfect world.

Carlyle's statement, then, that "a small poet every worker is" seems particularly applicable to this poem. Frost probably wants his readers to identify the woodchopper and his defense of his actions with the poet and his business in the modern world. As the poem opens two tramps come upon a man splitting wood in his front yard.[45] The word "caught" is the key word in the first stanza. It conveys the impression that the strangers are imposing on the world of the narrator and also that he is embarrassed by this. The narrator describes his task in the first lines of the second stanza, then reveals the source of his embarrassment.

> The blows that a life of self-control
> Spares to strike for the common good
> That day, giving a loose to my soul,
> I spent on the unimportant wood.

Here he sees himself blamed for what Tom Brown learned never to do: separate his task from the "common good." The narrator lays the groundwork for a defense of the position that this is not actually the case with him. The next three stanzas are concerned with the deceptiveness of appearances in various aspects of the natural world. In the sixth stanza the narrator meditates on how the tramps' request to do his woodchopping for pay has influenced his attitude toward doing the job himself. He finds he loves his task all the more. He recognizes the tramps as lumberjacks, professional woodchoppers, and decides that he has "no right to play / With what was another man's work for gain." If his right stems from the love of doing it and theirs from the need for sustinance, then he feels, theirs is the greater right. That he does not feel this to be the case in this particular situation is the statement of the last stanza, quoted here in full.

> But yield who will to their separation,
> My object in living is to unite
> My avocation and my vocation
> As my two eyes make one in sight.
> Only when love and need are one,
> And the work is play for mortal stakes,
> Is the deed ever really done
> For Heaven and the future's sakes.

This is a clear statement of Carlyle's position, and the use of the word "play" is consistent with Huizinga's definition. The narrator has transcended industrial work and has become a genuine worker by "playing" at his task. Chopping wood has become an activity of the spirit. The narrator is able to chop wood with the kind of freedom of one who plays. Both physically and spiritually he is removed from the actual world the tramps represent. The fact that he can love woodchopping in itself justifies his action. It also imposes order, at least temporarily, on his activity, and we may assume that, while the woodchopping goes on, those Carlylian hell-dogs, Doubt, Desire, Sorrow, Remorse, Indignation, Despair itself have been banished to their caves.

X

The hell-dogs return in the work of Robert Lowell. His 1965 play "Endecott and the Red Cross" lists as its sources both Thomas Morton's *New English Canaan* and Hawthorne's "The Maypole of Merry Mount" as well as the story by Hawthorne which gives the play its title. Lowell's "Endecott and the Red Cross" bears a fairly direct relation to Hawthorne's "The Maypole of Merry Mount." Hawthorne suggested that the revelers of Merry Mount and the Puritans were engaged in a struggle to determine the shape of the new world. Rather than carry this theme through his story, Hawthorne chose to make it a sort of allegory of the journey of the human soul through life. Lowell's play is more centrally concerned with the conflict between the two groups, which come to represent England and America, or the old, medieval world, and the new, modern one. The idea of Merry Mount as a paradisaical play world is thrust into the background. Lowell uses the same materials as Hawthorne, but he uses them to dramatize other conflicts. The Maypole is still an important symbol in the play, but mainly of the medieval world Endecott and the Puritans feel is corrupt and wish to leave behind them. Thomas Morton uses the image of the family to describe the community he heads. "I call these people my family, I am their father." He gives his opinion of May Day to Mr. Blackstone, an Anglican priest.

> There's no harm in our traditional May Day,
> it comes down to us, I guess from King Arthur.
> It's one of those things that makes England England
> and survives a hundred civil wars and rulers.[46]

Later Morton's opinions are juxtaposed with those of Endecott.

> ENDECOTT:
>
> I am here to enforce moral decorum.
> Your May Days are a horror,
> your diseased men drink themselves insensible
> and live with Indian women.
>
> MORTON:
>
> Our May Days are lovely and human,
> they are a beautiful old English custom
> practiced by your ancestors and mine, Mr. Endecott. (p. 44)

The fact that Endecott can feel this way about May Day and still remember the past when his wife "used to enjoy maskers like these in England," (p. 29) points to the central conflict of the play. Thomas Morton and Mr. Blackstone represent old England, and the fact that a royal governor has been appointed who will come and impose English royalty and bishops on the Puritans.

Endecott must use his power either to destroy his own past or to destroy the Puritan vision of utopian future, and rejoin the corrupt medieval community. That he will choose the former is foreshadowed by the nature of his reflections on his wife. He first speaks of his wife in describing his becoming a Puritan.

> When my wife died, I went into the army,
> as you know. I soon found I couldn't go on fighting
> without an iron religion.
> I found our iron religion. (pp. 29-30)

Thus the Lord raised him up out of his troubles and made him a Puritan soldier. But in America he was elected governor, became an administrator. Consequently

> I found I was becoming like myself in the old days,
> when I was a worldling and a courtier of King James,
> and wooing my wife. (p. 31)

The kind of power wielded by soldiers is more congenial to the Puritan mind than that of the administrator. Instead of destroying the enemy evil wherever he sees it, Endecott as an administrator has to deal with it in other ways, in order that the state may continue to function.

When Endecott decides to let the Lord and Lady of the May join the Puritan community and thus escape punishment, it is because "this girl reminds me of my wife." (p. 39) He tells the girl he became a Puritan as a consequence of his wife's death. (p. 40) After he has ordered the razing of Merry Mount and thus cut the Puritan community off from its English past, the maskers make him think of his youth in England again. (p. 57) Palfrey counsels him: "Don't look backward. Remember . . . Lot's wife. . . ." (p. 58) Endecott decides that the past must be destroyed:

> and I will crown my speech with some outrageous act
> that will mean there's no turning back for us,
> that England will no longer exist for us.
>
> . . . .
>
> everything here will be Bible, blood and iron.
> England will no longer exist. (pp. 36-37)

Endecott's "outrageous act" is the tearing of the Red Cross from the flag of England, but first he speaks to his soldiers on the subject of England. He first paints it as their homeland, in which they have dwelled and for which they have fought.

> think of the country we left.
> It is crowded and complicated,
> everything time and tradition could give a country is there.
> We learned its customs in order to exist,
> our ancestors were born and died there,
> our kinsmen still live there,
> my own wife and child are buried there. (p. 51)

He then addresses himself to the question of why he and his soldiers left England to come to America. Morton interrupts at this point to remind him that freedom for their worship is all the King and Bishop ask for. Endecott brushes him aside.

> we have come here to make a new world for ourselves.
> I might almost say,
> we have painfully cleared the path to heaven. (p. 53)

Endecott finally demands that his followers cut themselves off from the past.

> We shall make a stand in this land,
> we shall stand on this land,
> that we have brought our possessions to,
> that we have cleared with our axes,
> that we have broken with our plows,
> that we have pacified with our guns,
> that we have sanctified with our prayers.
> God brought us here, shall man enslave us?
> What have we to do with mitred bishops?
> What have we to do with annointed kings?
> What have we to do with England? (p. 54).

The irony of this passage reaches beyond Lowell's play to Hawthorne's short story. Lowell has reversed Hawthorne's symbols. Lowell's Endecott rejects his past and identifies himself instead with the sanctified timelessness of the natural world, which is, for Hawthorne, the world of the revelers of Merry Mount.

Lowell does not use the metaphor of play to indicate the nature of Endecott's dream, and there is no reason he should, concerned as he is with the ironic relation of Endecott's dream with the reality of his existence. Lowell's play involves no value distinction between a realm of work and a realm of play at all. Hawthorne's characters moved from a timeless world of play to a timeful world of love and responsibility. For Lowell, the world is wholly timeful. He does not suggest that the pleasures of Morton's May Day festival are more innocent than Endecott's destruction of them. Endecott's instituted innocence, if it can be called that, is terrifying rather than idyllic. Neither Morton's nor Endecott's settlement represents a good life to the reader. One destroys the other in order to pursue a new world even its leader realizes is unattainable, but would have last forever.

Because it neglects the ideas of work and play utilized by previous authors who used the same subject matter, Lowell's work suggests that we are again in a period in history when men disagree, not only on the relative value of such abstractions as work and play, but also as to which among the many possible abstractions are meaningful in describing the human condition. It may be that we are at the point where we have, as John Dewey would say, "gotten over" the problems posed in defining human activity as either work or play and are beginning to formulate new terms which, as they resolve some of the old problems, present new ones.

II

HOW TO LIVE IN IT

IN THE WORK OF ERNEST HEMINGWAY, THE IMPULSE TO UNDERSTAND human activity in terms of work and play is intense and develops through the course of his writings. His work, in general, seems a long search for a setting within which human action might seem meaningful. The most important manifestation of this impulse is Hemingway's frequent use of the sporting world in the settings of his novels and stories. Joseph Warren Beach has suggested that "manly sports," a category in which he included war, have been "the principal subject in Hemingway."[1] Carlos Baker lists "four subjects which have always fascinated Hemingway," and, of these, three (fishing, hunting, bullfighting) could be classified as sports.[2] In sports, or in activities which have some of the same basic qualities as sport, Hemingway's characters create their own meaningful world within a world essentially meaningless. This created world can usually be described as a world of play.

Perhaps the best descriptions of the meaningless world within which Hemingway's characters are sometimes able to build meaning come in two short stories: "A Clean, Well Lighted Place," and "The Gambler, the Nun, and the Radio," both of which appear in his 1933 collection, *Winner Take Nothing*. "A Clean, Well Lighted Place" provides the perfect image of Hemingway's universe. The old waiter reflects on why he and the old drunk enjoy sitting alone at cafes late at night.

> What did he fear? It was not fear or dread. It was a nothing that he knew too well. It was all a nothing and a man was nothing too. . . . Some lived in it and never felt it but he knew it all was nada y pues nada y nada y pues nada.[3]

The old waiter continues in this vein, reciting the Lord's Prayer and then a Hail Mary, substituting "nada" for all the important words. In such a world, the clean, well-lighted places function to fend off the nothingness which threatens to envelop them as it has the conventional gestures of piety. In them, a man may find peace and even a little dignity. For those whose fear of nothingness results in a need for the cafe "light was all it needed and a certain cleanness and order." (p. 383) This refuge is temporary, but it enables one to face the world with dignity. When the old drunk leaves the cafe "the waiter watched him go down the street, a very old man walking unsteadily but with dignity." (p. 381)

These clean, well-lighted places could be physical settings or they could be mental states. "The Gambler, the Nun, and the Radio" contains a suggestion as to their ultimate value. At the end of the story Frazer, the writer, lies listening to the music the Mexicans are playing and finds he can "not keep from thinking."

> Religion is the opium of the people. . . . Yes, and music is the opium of the people. . . . And now, economics is the opium of the people; along with patriotism the opium of the people in Italy and Germany. What about sexual intercourse; was that an opium of the people? Of some of the people. Of some of the best of the people. But drink was a sovereign opium of the people, oh, an excellent opium. Although some prefer the radio, another opium of the people, a cheap one he has just been using. Along with these went gambling, an opium of the people if there ever was one, one of the oldest. Ambition was another, an opium of the people, along with a belief in any new form of government. . . . But what was the real one? But what was the real, the actual, opium of the people? He knew it very well. . . . Of course; bread was the opium of the people. Would he remember that and would it make sense in the daylight? Bread is the opium of the people. (pp. 485-486)

This passage demands that all conventional ways of understanding the universe be considered illusions which operate temporarily to shield the individual from the true nature of the world around and within him. We see this happening to Frazer even within the meditation quoted above.

> What was the real, the actual, opium of the people? He knew it very well. It was gone just a little way around the corner of that well lighted part of his mind that was there after two or more drinks in the evening; that he knew was there (it was not really there of course).

The story, however, is not essentially concerned with ways of understanding the universe so much as it is with the problem of how to live in it. Each individual must create the world over again, if he is to live well. Jake Barnes announces this most clearly in *The Sun Also Rises.*

> I did not care what it was all about. All I wanted to know was how to live in it. Maybe if you found out how to live in it you learned from that what it was all about.[4]

It is interesting to note that writing does not appear on the list of opiates given by Mr. Frazer, a writer. That his profession, and Hemingway's, does not have the effect of opium, can be seen if we glance at Hemingway's understanding of himself as a writer which comes through most clearly in his posthumous book, *A Moveable Feast.* "Work," he says there, "could cure almost anything, I believed then, and I believe now."[5] This attitude toward work resembles that of Carlyle. Ivan Kashkeen cites it as the source of Hemingway's greatness as a writer. Speaking of Hemingway's selection of the attainment of "Craftsmanship" as his goal in life, he says,

> Still it is a good sign that in working for the sake of work, in fulfilling the prisoner's task he set himself, he remains the ever scrupulous professional. And it is this honest attitude towards his work, blind though it may appear to us, that has earned Hemingway the right to be classed among the masters.[6]

Seeing other professionals at work clearly inspired Hemingway. The section of *A Moveable Feast* on "People of the Seine" gives proof of this. Hemingway speaks of the "serious and productive fishing" on the Seine and tells us that "it was easier to think if I was walking and doing something or seeing people doing something that they understood."[7] Clearly, this activity gives a certain limited order to an otherwise chaotic universe.

In fact, Hemingway seems to have had difficulty making his leisure time meaningful. Like Carlyle, he assigned to his work the task of making life meaningful. In an interview with George Plimpton published in 1958, when Plimpton wondered if financial security (and the kind of leisure it makes possible) might be a detriment to good writing, Hemingway replied:

> If it came early enough and you loved life as much as you loved your work it would take much character to resist the temptations. Once writing has become your major vice and greatest pleasure only death can stop it.[8]

Here a conflict is suggested, the attempts to resolve which constitute Hemingway's central theme. "How to live in it" is the problem to be solved and in trying to solve it Hemingway came to define work as play and to image this in the sporting life, both professional and amateur. The dichotomy of life and work suggested in the above quotation contains all his major subject matters. Writing was work for Hemingway, and as a worker he was interested in his fellow professionals, those who derived their lives' meaning from their work. But, like Hawthorne apparently, Hemingway also considered writing a "major vice," and through it he examined, and identified himself with, the other spectators of the world. In *A Moveable Feast* he identified himself finally, in the following passage, as a professional rather than as a spectator.

> When they said "It's great, Ernest. Truly it's great. You cannot know the thing it has," I wagged my tail in pleasure and plunged into the fiesta concept of life to see if I could not bring some fine attractive stick back, instead of thinking, "If these bastards like it, what is wrong with it?" That was what I would think if I had been functioning as a professional although, if I had been functioning as a professional, I would never have read it to them.[9]

Hemingway clearly reflects back on the nineteen twenties here. This period is generally regarded as one in which many Americans revolted against the traditional values of America. One of these was that hard work would bring one worldly success, and eventually salvation. In the twenties, it was challenged by an idea of play. Hemingway's writings can be considered part of this challenge. We will find that the way Hemingway uses sport undergoes significant changes after the twenties which I believe can be accounted for in terms of the ability of a society based on work to assimilate an ideal of play. The ethic presented in *The Sun Also Rises* can best be described as a spectator ethic. Thus this book challenges directly the predominant work ethic of the older twentieth century society. By nineteen fifty two, the ethic presented in *The Old Man and the Sea* is certainly not a spectator ethic at all, but what we have come to call the professional ethic. Play, then, originally a challenge to work as an ideal, becomes a new concept of work, or at least has been made to operate within a context of work. We shall try to uncover some of the details of this movement between spectator and professional ethic in Hemingway.

For Hemingway, this essentially moral ideal of professionalism was also an esthetic ideal. Thus, in the twenty-six years between *The Sun Also Rises* and *The Old Man and the Sea,* we can see in him not only the evidences of cultural change in general but a change in the conception of the artist and his relation to the world in which he creates. First, we can see the artist as spectator, forfeiting his participation in life in order to observe it the better. Later, we see the artist as professional, creation being his own kind of participation in life; his work-play, his calling.

I

Hemingway's sports stories are central to an understanding of his writings and the vision of man they present is of man at play, in the sense that Huizinga defines it. Our consideration of Hemingway's short stories begins with "Cross County Snow." In this story Hemingway shows us what is important to him about skiing and dramatizes the place of sport in European and American society. We find Nick Adams and a friend skiing in central Europe. We are first presented with the ideal sensations to be realized from skiing.

> The rush and sudden swoop as he dropped down a steep undulation in the mountain side plucked Nick's mind out and left him only the wonderful flying, dropping sensation in his body. (p. 183)

Huizinga has suggested that play is non-rational, and here we have Nick glorying in the denial of mind. Mind is something to be mistrusted. It comes between man and his experience, between man and nature. This quality of mindlessness is what Nick likes about skiing. Nick sees the life he has led skiing in Europe as idyllic and is discouraged about going back to the United States where his pregnant wife awaits him. He finds fault with the mountains in America. "They're too rocky. There's too much timber and they're too far away." (p. 187) One suspects that what really bothers Nick is that the attitude toward sport in a society with an ideal of work is rocky, with many impediments. Sport has been pushed to the far corners of the American mind, and is certainly not identified with play. But even Nick's skiing in Europe is only temporarily proof against pregnancies and their consequences.

The sport which, initially, for Hemingway, removed him from the rational world, and from the dominant ethic of post World War I America, was fishing. In the Toronto *Star Weekly* in 1922 he spoke of tuna fishing as having the same effect as skiing.

> . . . if you land a big tuna after a six-hour flight, fight him man against fish when your muscles are nauseated with the unceasing strain, and finally bring him up alongside the boat, green-blue and silver in the lazy ocean, you will be purified and be able to enter into the presence of the very elder gods and they will make you welcome.[10]

Here fishing is, for Hemingway, a sacred sport. Fishing is here, in itself, a way to give meaning to the world. And in "Big Two-Hearted River," the religion's ritual is developed, and the possibility of a new world opens up.[11]

We may consider Hemingway's two-part story "Big Two-Hearted River" as representing a young man's view of the cultural and moral situation in the United States after World War I and his reaction to it. Nick Adams is returning to Seney, for what purpose we are not told immediately. The opening description of the town is significant.

> There was no town. Nothing but the rails and the burned-over country. The thirteen saloons that had lined the one street of Seney had not left a trace. The foundations of the Mansion House hotel stuck up above the ground. The stone was chipped and split by the fire. It was all that was left of the town of Seney. Even the surface had been burned off the ground.

There is something worth human attention though.

> The river was there. It swirled against the log spiles of the bridge. Nick looked down into the clear, brown water, colored from the pebbly bottom, and watched the trout keeping themselves steady in the current with waver-

ing fins. As he watched them they changed their positions by quick angles, only to hold steady in the fast water again. Nick watched them a long time. (p. 209)

The imagery of this situation is interesting. We are presented with a scene of desolation, yet the enumeration of the thirteen saloons that had lined the one street suggest that it is just as well that the town burned down. In this respect the town represents pre-war America, and we must acknowledge the advent of prohibition. Society, as represented by the saloons, has been obliterated. What appears as desolation, can also be seen as purgation. The river replaces the saloon as the essential element in the setting. The basis of the new civilization will be nature. A kind of apocalypse has occurred. Man must begin to create a new society in a new world. What better or older symbol for the capacity to create than the fish? Ancient mythologies have portrayed men in search of the revitalization of civilization as fishing. If they can catch a fish, fertility will return to the land. Nick Adams, however, fishes for sport, for play. The new civilization will be based on play.

Everything Nick does has the effect of imposing order on a chaotic world. In the first part of the story Hemingway concentrates on Nick's setting up camp and making himself supper. The word "made" seems to have special significance in the following quotation, especially in the context of "homelike" and "the good place." By setting up camp, Nick orders his universe.

Already there was something mysterious and homelike. Nick was happy as he crawled inside the tent. He had not been unhappy all day. This was different though. Now things were done. There had been this to do. Now it was done. It had been a hard trip. He was very tired. That was done. He had made his camp. He was settled. Nothing could touch him. It was a good place to camp. He was there, in the good place. He was in his home where he had made it. (p. 215)

His making supper has a ritual quality to it which is particularly evident in the making of the coffee. He remembers having had an argument with a friend, Hopkins, about how to make coffee but cannot remember which side he took. He finally decides he has made "the coffee according to Hopkins," a phrase with a decidedly religious flavor. (p. 218)

"Big Two-Hearted River: Part II" concentrates on Nick's fishing. As befits the creator of the bases of a new civilization,

"Nick was excited. He was excited by the early morning and the river." (p. 221) As he heads out toward the river for fishing,

> Nick felt awkward and professionally happy with all his equipment hanging from him. The Grasshopper bottle swung against his chest. In his shirt the breast pockets bulged against him with the lunch and his fly book. (p. 223)

As he fishes, he considers the various secrets of trout-fishing.

> He had wet his hand before he touched the trout, so he would not disturb the delicate mucous that covered him. If a trout was touched with a dry hand, a white fungus attacked the unprotected spot. Years before when he had fished crowded streams, with fly fishermen ahead of him and behind him, Nick had again and again come on dead trout, furry with white fungus, drifted against a rock, or floating belly up in some pool. Nick did not like to fish with other men on the river. Unless they were of your party, they spoiled it. (p. 225)

Here some of the characteristics of play as Huizinga defines it reveal themselves. In the first quotation Nick is happy in the *profession* of play, likening himself to the professional fisherman. In the second quotation, Nick distinguishes himself from those who do not know the rules of the game. By the nature of the bait they use, they are differentiated from Nick. Though he does carry a fly-book Nick uses grasshoppers, a natural bait, while the fly fishermen use artificial bait. It is Nick's comparative closeness to nature which enables him to understand both these things. Fishing had definite rules: some know them and some do not. Thus in the two parts of "Big Two-Hearted River" we have first the symbolic renewal of civilization. This civilization is to be based on the natural environment rather than any cultural tradition (the burnt-out town). Secondly, it is a civilization to be based on play, represented by the sport of fishing.

At the other end of the sporting spectrum in Hemingway's short stories are those stories involving sports like boxing and horse racing. If fishing stands for the possibility of an alternative to modern civilization, then these sports are representative of modern civilization itself and the characters in them meant to be admirable are so in spite of their connection with their particular sport. If fishing has renewed Nick Adams, boxing seems to have driven Ad Francis mad, destroyed Ole Andreson and made Jack Brennan a disagreeable and penurious man.

Hemingway's presentation of Ad Francis in "The Battler" emphasizes the man's physical and spiritual grotesqueness:

> the man looked at Nick and smiled. In the firelight Nick saw that his face was misshapen. His nose was sunken, his eyes were slits, he had queer shaped lips . . . the man's face was queerly formed and mutilated. It was like putty in color. Dead looking in the firelight . . . he had only one ear. It was thickened and tight against the side of his head. Where the other ear should have been there was a stump . . .

Through most of the story, we are left to assume that both Ad's appearance and his madness, which he immediately confesses to Nick, were acquired in the course of a "successful" (he is an ex-champion) boxing career. His claim that "I could take it" rings ironically through the story. (p. 131) But Hemingway has Bugs, Ad's friend and keeper, suggest another cause when he tries, near the end of the story, to account to Nick for Ad's condition. "He took too many beatings, for one thing," says Bugs, "but that just made him sort of simple."

> Then his sister was his manager and they was always being written up in the papers all about brothers and sisters and how she loved her brother and he loved his sister, and then they got married in New York and that made a lot of unpleasantness. . . . Of course they wasn't brother and sister no more than a rabbit, but there was a lot of people didn't like it either way and they commenced to have disagreements and one day she just went off and never came back. . . . He just went crazy. (pp. 136-137)

Here the evils of the institution of boxing, the physical and mental destruction of a man, pale beside the personal problem that makes Ad insane. Boxing, finally, is Ad Francis's refuge from the actual world he cannot bear facing. When he attacks Nick, Ad clearly believes himself champion again. "The little man came toward him slowly, stepping flat footed forward, his left foot stepping forward, his right dragging up to it." (p. 135) Unfortunately for Ad, the very world that protects him from the horrors of the actual world makes him, in the eyes of Nick Adams, a horror.

It is difficult to say whether the fate of Ole Andreson is more or less unfortunate than that of Ad Francis. If Ad Francis is still "the battler," Ole Andreson has given up fighting a long time before we meet him in "The Killers." We can only speculate, as the other characters do, about what happened to Ole Andreson when he was fighting that brought down on him in the form of two gunmen, the wrath of the syndicate. While Bugs explains Ad Francis to Nick, Ole Andreson tells nobody anything. Consequently the other characters must decide for themselves what has happened to him. When Ad Francis seems spoiling for a fight, Nick reveals the fact that Ole Andreson was a prizefighter in observing that he "was lying on the bed with all his clothes on. He had been a heavyweight prizefighter and he was too long for the bed." (p. 287) Andreson has clearly been fighting for his life and has given up the fight. He tells Nick that "I'm through with all that running around." (p. 287) His own explanation for the fix he is in is the statement "I got in wrong." Nick leaves and "as he shut the door he saw Ole Andreson with all his clothes on, lying on the bed, looking at the wall." (p. 288) It is not even clear that what he did has anything to do with boxing. It may be that he simply "got mixed up in something in Chicago." On the other hand, common sense suggests that the problem was a fixed fight, and that Andreson had double-crossed the fixers. When Nick wonders what he did, George replies "double-crossed somebody. That's what they kill them for." (p. 289)

All of which brings us to Jack Brennan and the story of "Fifty Grand." This story might be said to be Hemingway's only boxing story, since it is only here that he focuses the story on the boxer himself. "The Battler" and "The Killers" are better understood as chapters in the initiation of Nick Adams than as stories of ex-prizefighters. Hemingway seems more interested in Ad Francis and Ole Andreson as people whose lives have been destroyed by the social environment of prizefighting. His interest in Jack Brennan in "Fifty Grand" is in the athlete, not the human being.

In "Fifty Grand" two worlds definitely emerge, the one dominated by chance, filled with gamblers and wise guys who don't know anything, a chaotic world, the other a world of order, dominated by the "ritual of the professional," inhabited by people who, like the fishermen of the Seine in *A Moveable Feast*, are doing something that they understand. In the chaotic world, as Charles Fenton points out, Brennan is isolated; he is not of it. Hemingway describes him sitting with the gamblers Morgan and Steinfelt.

Jack doesn't say anything. He just sits on the bed. He ain't with the others. He's all by himself. He was wearing an old blue jersey and pants and had on boxing shoes. He needed a shave. Steinfelt and Morgan were dressers. John was quite a dresser too. Jack sat there looking Irish and tough. (p. 309)

What apparently makes Jack Brennan a good professional is revealed in the following quotation.

He was holding himself and his body together and it all showed on his face. All the time he was thinking and holding his body in where it was busted.

Then he started to sock. His face looked awful all the time. He started to sock with his hands low down by his side, swinging at Walcott. Walcott covered up and Jack was swinging wild at Walcott's head. Then he swung the left and it hit Walcott in the groin and the right hit Walcott right bang where he'd hit Jack. (p. 325)

Charles Fenton says of this that "when Jack Brennan was 'holding himself and his body together' he was not merely a muscular lout reacting to agony. 'He was thinking . . .' When he had solved his problem, professionally, he began to act—professionally. . . . 'Thinking' was the operative word in the paragraph we have quoted and examined. This, again, is what distinguishes the professional."[12] Jack Brennan is a professional because he is able to use his head and his hands well in specific situations.

But Jack Brennan's heroic behavior in the ring is in harsh contrast with his character outside of it. In his essay, Fenton attempts to smooth over this problem by showing that "Jack probably never was—nor could be—a good fellow in any conventional sense."[13] This, however, cannot excuse the fact (and Hemingway goes out of his way to insist on it) that Jack is rather parsimonious. He doesn't like to part with money under any circumstances.

In fact, Jack is apparently a capitalist of the most dedicated sort. When asked why he can't sleep, he replies that he worries.

I worry about property I got up in the Bronx, I worry about property I got in Florida. I worry about the kids. I worry about the wife. Sometimes I think about fights. I think about that kike Ted Lewis and I get sore. I got some stocks and I worry about them. (p. 305)

First and last, Jack thinks about his property. His family and his profession come in between. Jack regards himself as a businessman of sorts, too. Convinced he doesn't have it any more, he bets against himself in the fight, feeling sure that he can't fight well enough to win in any case. He explains this to Jerry.

> "Fifty Grand is a lot of money," I said.
> "It's business," said Jack. "I can't win. You know I can't win anyway."
> "As long as you're in there you got a chance."
> "No," Jack says, "I'm all through. It's just business." (p. 315)

The events of the story that follow this dialogue provide Hemingway with many opportunities to show Jack's cheapness, and he takes them all. We find first that Jack writes to his wife instead of calling her because it is cheaper. He undertips Bruce, "the nigger rubber," before boarding the train. At the hotel, he argues with the clerk about the price of rooms and then, having got a double at a reduced rate, induces Jerry to stay with him because "I just want to get my money's worth." Shortly thereafter, an ulterior motive is revealed when Jerry finds he is going to tip the bellboy if the bellboy is to be tipped at all. In the room some cribbage is played, and Jack wins first a dollar and a half, then plays "to see who pays for the meal" and wins and later wins two and a half more dollars. The narrator concludes that "Jack was feeling pretty good." (pp. 316-319) Thus Jack is portrayed as a businessman. His world is circumscribed by his love of money. It's clear, finally, that he doesn't even need the money. With the instincts of a capitalist, he continues to make money long past the time he needs to.

Jack's greed is also, however, the basis of his courage in the ring, though it cannot wholly account for it. Before the eleventh round of the fight he meditates.

> It was going just the way he thought it would. He knew he couldn't beat Walcott. He wasn't strong any more. He was all right though. His money was all right and now he wanted to finish it off right to please himself. He didn't want to be knocked out. (p. 323)

This attitude, at first thought, seems not terribly admirable by most standards. Jack initially denies the possibility of chance interfering in his behalf. Thus he creates an unreal world which justifies his betting on himself. Secondly, he demands the best of all possible consequences stemming from this choice: that he relinquish his championship with dignity. In effect, he transforms a commercial enterprise, making it a spiritual one. Hemingway destroys this world with Walcott's low blow, only to reassert it on a higher level in terms of Jack's reaction to the low blow. Jack is finally admirable because he is able to reassert his simplified world in spite of the low blow Walcott gives him. He has actually transcended the physical realities of the situation. This ability has nothing to do with his greed nor has it anything to do with his "professionalism," the ability to use his head and his hands. He *wills* that he remain standing, and it is for this that we are to admire him.

Hemingway himself does not seem to have been conscious at this time of the central role of will in his own understanding of professionalism. Consider the confusions implicit in the last lines of the story.

> "It's funny how fast you can think when it means that much money," Jack says.
>
> "You're some boy, Jack," John says.
>
> "No," Jack says. "It was nothing." (p. 326)

Here Jack apparently credits his fast thinking and the fact that he would lose the money if he fell for his ability to remain on his feet. Then, in the last line of the story he denies it, indicating that he judges himself by some other standard. Hemingway, perhaps unconsciously, in this story suggests that it is will, and not craft or greed, that makes Jack admirable. He is admirable nowhere but in the prize ring. Perhaps this is why the story, in its initial publication in *Atlantic* in July of 1927, was subtitled "A Story of the Prize Ring."

In an article for the November 1935 edition of *Esquire*, Hemingway made this new dimension of professionalism more articulate. This essay, called "Million Dollar Fright," concerns the Joe Louis-Max Baer championship fight. In the article, Hemingway attacks Max Baer because he feels that Baer acted cowardly during his fight with Louis. Baer, concludes Hemingway, "was paid $215,370.00 for furnishing the fear." He spends a great deal of time explaining this statement.

> Certainly Baer furnished little else. He had never bothered to learn his trade; if he had he would have had something else to think about . . . fighters are trained not to be frightened while fighting. If they know their trade they have something else to think about. If they do not know their trade and are frightened while fighting, they have no business being fighters any more than

a game cock that runs has any business being a game cock.

Here a man's trade protects him from fear, a point of view clearly related to Carlyle's understanding of work. Hemingway goes on from here to speculate on what qualities a great fighter needs. "Strength is what makes a boxer, i.e., boxer vs. fighter, great once the boxer knows everything." (p. 190B) This is undoubtedly what Jack Brennan could feel himself losing. Hemingway turns to other admirable qualities.

Langford was much too easy to hit to beat Louis. But it would be a wonderful fight, and Langford could hit so hard and had such a great heart that he would always be dangerous. (p. 190B)

Here we find a fighter praised for his "great heart" rather than his skill at his trade. Will again appears as a competitor for craft for our admiration. The opening metaphor of Hemingway's article underlines this quality.

There is no money in it for the kingbird when he chases off the eagle. The kingbird is a slate-colored, white-breasted fly catcher, small, trim, neatly built, quarrelsome and a bully; but he likes to bully birds about eight to ten times his size. His only offensive weapon is a small not over-sharp beak to peck with and a heart to back it up. (p. 35)

Here, and in the article as a whole the two qualities are opposed, will against craft. Both are admirable, but both, at least in the boxing world, do not often exist consciously together in the same person. In Hemingway's short stories at least, it is his amateur sportsmen who accomplish the removal of courage (or will) from the everyday world best, his fishermen and his skiiers who succeed in escaping the ordinary world with its hell dogs of human responsibility to a world of play "untainted by ordinary problems and motives." In "Fifty Grand" Jack Brennan successfully discovers this world as he loses his championship. The best indication of this is the fact that, unlike Ole Andreson, he apparently will not have to face the consequences of his double-cross. Brennan, at best, only unconsciously unites the qualities of craft and will that, for Hemingway comprise, when that unity achieves consciousness, the mark of salvation. Nick Adams both in "Big Two-Hearted River," and "Cross Country Snow" is the more successful.

II

Nick Adams' success is due to the fact that he is consciously involved in rejecting the values of his culture, while Jack Brennan clearly accepts them. Hemingway's first novel, *The Sun Also Rises* (1926) was a systematic exposition of a culture formed in opposition to the dominant values of the American culture of the time. Hemingway himself, though he is quoted as saying on one occasion that the book's "only instruction" was to show "how people go to hell," had advised that it be taught in college on the grounds that "It's very moral."[15] The grounds of this morality can, I think, be found in the following quotation from Huizinga's *Homo Ludens.*

> Play cannot be denied. You can deny, if you like, nearly all abstractions: justice, beauty, truth, goodness, mind, God. You can deny seriousness, but not play.[16]

In *The Sun Also Rises,* Hemingway uses the world of sport as a symbolic center for the values by which a man can establish himself apart from society. For Hemingway, at this point in his career, not only is life meaningless but society is corrupt and the construction of meaning must make the individual distinct from society. One of his central themes, during the twenties, according to Reuel Denney, was the development of a "code for spectators." For those who stand aside, Denney sees the whole population of the twenties, and in this respect Hemingway seems representative, as "seeking at once to escape an old morality and to find a new morality, in the play."[17]

Hemingway's characters achieve meaningfulness for themselves in play, as Huizinga defines it, and the setting for this achievement is found in sports, finally and most significantly in the bullfights. First of all, Jake Barnes and his companions are embarked on a way of life which involves a permanent "abolition of the ordinary world," the life of ex-patriates in France. Jake Barnes's distance from the ordinary world of his fellow correspondents is dramatized in the fifth chapter of the first book when he rides home with two of them. When they inquire into what he does nights and he answers that he spends them in the Quarter, one says, "I've meant to get over. . . . You know how it is though, with a wife and kids." The irony of this last statement makes Jake's "distance" a kind of isolation. The talk drifts on, of living in the country and having a little car, far from the world Jake inhabits.[18] Jake's group is highly conscious of being set off from "the ordinary world," witness Brett's judgment of the Count. "He's one of us, though. Oh, quite. No doubt. One can always tell." (p. 32) Thus, even in Paris, Jake is part of a self-conscious group which holds values which distinguish it from society in general. When the setting moves to a festival (an activity found by Huizinga to be a form of play) which is culminated by a bullfight, the code of the group is identified with the art of the bullfighter. It is Robert Cohn, throughout the novel, who preserves our feeling of a "temporary abolition of the ordinary world" by constantly reminding us of that world's existence. Instead of joining in the festival, he prefers to mope along the sidelines, "ready to do battle for his lady love." (p. 178) Robert Cohn is romantically inclined, according to Jake Barnes.

He had been reading W. H. Hudson. That sounds like an innocent occupation, but Cohn had read and reread "Purple Land." "The Purple Land" is a very sinister book if read too late in life. It recounts splendid imaginary amorous adventures of a perfect English gentleman in an intensely romantic land, the scenery of which is very well described. For a man to take it at thirty-four as a guide-book to what life holds is about as safe as it would be for a man of the same age to enter Wall Street direct from a French convent, equipped with a complete set of the more practical Alger books. (p. 9)

What the other characters seem to resent most about Cohn is that he is unable to forget the fact that he has had an affair with Brett and join in the spirit of the festival. In this sense he represents an intrusion of the everyday world that goes on without the festival.

Jake's fishing interlude, with Bill Gorton, is an interlude of a different kind of play. Its function is to show how a state of being at play in the world is achieved. The ordinary world is abolished more by Jake's intense concentration and his enjoyment of what he is doing than anything else. Here he digs a worm.

On the grassy bank where it was damp I drove the mattock into the earth and loosened a chunk of sod. There were worms underneath. They slid out of sight as I lifted the sod and I dug carefully and got a good many. Digging at the edge of the damp ground I filled two empty tobacco tins and sifted dirt into them. The goats watched me dig. (pp. 112-113)

Here he catches a fish:

I did not feel the first trout strike. When I started to pull up I felt that I had one and brought him, fighting and bending the rod almost double, out of the boiling water at the foot of the falls, and swung him up and onto the dam. He was a good trout, and I banged his head against the timber so that he quivered out straight, and then slipped him into my bag. (p. 119)

This fishing interlude provides a contrast in mood from the scenes in Paris and the scenes to come at the festival. Though it does this, Hemingway is still intent on dealing with meaning in terms of play, represented in this instance by the solitary sport of fishing. Fishing gives Jake an order and purpose to the day, a purpose partly achieved by the intense concentration with which he goes at digging his worms and catching his fish. Nothing else exists, everything else is blocked out of Jake's world for the moment. He wills that only these things exist. He is at play.

But it is the bullfights that provide Hemingway with the principal setting in which to demonstrate the values by which his characters can establish themselves apart from society. Early in the book Jake refers to bullfighters as living the ideal life; saying, "Nobody ever lives their life all the way up except bullfighters." Robert Cohn's answer establishes his role as representative of the "ordinary world." He says, "I'm not interested in bullfighters. That's an abnormal life." (p. 10)

The bullfight has religious significance. As Jake and the others arrive at the hotel, the hotel-keeper greets them:

He always smiled as though bullfighting were a very special secret between the two of us; a rather shocking but really very deep secret that we knew about. He always smiled as though there were something lewd about the secret to outsiders, but that it was something that we understood. It would not do to expose it to people who would not understand. (p. 131)

This religion has its own laying on of hands.

When they saw that I had aficion, and there was no password, no set questions that would bring it out, rather it was a sort of oral spiritual examination with the questions always a little on the defensive and never apparent, there was this same embarrassed putting the hand on the shoulder, or a "Buen hombre." But nearly always there was the actual touching. It seemed as though they wanted to touch you to make it certain. (p. 132)

The ultimate meaning to be derived from bullfighting comes from the way the bullfighter handles the bull. Hemingway derives from this first a system of behavior, then a moral basis for it. He has

Jake explain the sport to Brett "so that it becomes more something that was going on with a definite end, and less of a spectacle with unexplained horrors. (p. 167) The esoteric aspect of sport and play is seen here. Hemingway constructs his ideal out of Romero's bullfighting. "Romero never made any contortions, always it was straight and pure and natural in line . . . (his) bullfighting gave real emotion, because he kept the absolute purity of line in his movements and always quietly and calmly let the horns pass him close each time. He did not have to emphasize their closeness." (pp. 167-169)

The ethic expressed in these lines is, in part, a stoic ideal. Romero doesn't make any contortions. He keeps, at all costs, purity of line and deals with the horns quietly and calmly. Cohn, in a lesser way a sportsman, proves incapable of dealing in this way with his horns. Mike Campbell doesn't handle his much better but it seems to be to his credit that he can say "it was a damned fine fiesta," despite the fact that Brett has run away with the bullfighter. (p. 231) Jake comes closest to meeting the ideal set by Romero. When Bill makes an inadvertent remark about his impotence during a carefree conversation, Jake reflects:

> He had been going splendidly, but he stopped. I was afraid he thought he had hurt me with that crack about being impotent. I wanted to start him again. (p. 115)

Again, when Jake sets Brett up with the bullfighter, he is able to assimilate the knowledge that he is playing the pimp and live with it.

> He sat down and looked at her across the table. I went out. The hard-eyed people at the bullfighter table watched me go. It was not pleasant. (p. 187)

Thus the bullfighters' actions in the bullring set the standard of behavior in an otherwise meaningless world.

The ethical standard also has a moral basis, "a morality that has no reference to good or evil." This is roughly equivalent to Huizinga's finding in play "an ethical value insofar as it means a testing of the player's prowess. . . ."[19] Hemingway's characters don't ordinarily care to speak of morality and the only time Jake does he seems to regard his speaking of it as a weakness.

> I liked to see him hurt Cohn. I wished he would not do it, though, because

afterward it made me disgusted at myself. That was morality; things that made you disgusted afterward. No, that must be immorality. That was a large statement. What a log of bilge I could think up at night. (pp. 148-149)

For Jake morality consists here in a person's ability to absorb sensory impressions without disgust. One's "prowess" is being tested, but not by any standard of good or evil. The expression "rather good" seems to be one moral approval throughout the book. For instance, when Romero and Cohn have their confrontation:

The bullfighter fellow was rather good. He didn't say much, but he kept getting up and getting knocked down again. Cohn couldn't knock him out. It must have been damned funny. (p. 202)

It is Romero's will power or "prowess" which is praised here. Brett's conversation with Jake and the end of the book relates her to this standard. Rather than follow her natural inclinations, she wills herself into a higher state of being.

"You know it makes one feel rather good deciding not to be a bitch."
"Yes."
"It's sort of what we have instead of God." (p. 245)

Brett judges herself on the basis of her feelings. She doesn't want to be "one of those bitches that ruins children." (p. 243) She is left feeling "rather good," not righteous. In *The Sun Also Rises* Hemingway used a style of bullfighting to give concrete expression to an ideal way of behaving. His spectators learned from this. But Hemingway proved more interested in the bullfighters than the spectators. In 1932 he published a full length study of the community of bullfighting, *Death in the Afternoon.*

Hemingway describes bullfighting in *Death in the Afternoon* as a kind of ultimate sport, where elements of ritual and contest together form a religious atmosphere.

The bullfight is not a sport in the Anglo-Saxon sense of the word, that is, it is not an equal contest or an attempt at an equal contest between a bull and a man. Rather it is a tragedy; the death of the bull, which is played, more or less well, by the bull and the man involved and in which there is danger for the man but certain death for the animal. [20]

Later Hemingway tells us what "sport in the Anglo-Saxon sense of the word" is. He speaks of aspiring bullfighters fighting bulls which have been fought before in the small towns of Spain.

> It is a sport, a very savage and primitive sport, and for the most part a truly amateur one. I am afraid however due to the danger of death it involves it would never have much success among the amateur sportsmen of England and America who play games. We, in games, are not fascinated by death, its nearness and its avoidance. We are fascinated by victory and we replace the avoidance of death by the avoidance of defeat. It is a very nice symbolism but it takes more cojones to be a sportsman when death is a closer party to the game. (p. 22)

Here Hemingway makes an interesting distinction between the real and the actual which is not unlike the one Carlyle made between true work and industrial work. Games, he points out here, are actually sublimations of encounters with death. Real sport, on the other hand, is an encounter with death itself on equal terms. Bullfighting thus has its essential qualities in common with real sport and both are contrasted with the games Englishmen and Americans ordinarily play. Bullfighting is civilized, i.e. the encounter is ritualized, and "real" sport less so. Games are civilized too, but in the wrong way. The essential quality of the encounter is hidden by the event rather than revealed by it.

Bullfighting has the essential qualities Hemingway respects in sport and the central image of the matador that emerges in his writings is that of an athlete. Even when he is referred to as an artist, athletic images are present. In an early article Hemingway described the bullfighters as athletes.

> The bullfighters march in across the sand to the president's box. They march with easy professional stride, swinging along, not in the least theatrical except for their clothes. They have all the easy grace and slight slouch of the professional athlete. From their faces they might be major league ballplayers.[21]

This kind of identification becomes much more complex in *Death in the Afternoon.* Here Hemingway speaks of the preparation of the bull for the kill.

> . . . when I learned the things that can be done with him as an artistic property when he is properly slowed and still has kept his bravery and his strength I kept my admiration for him always, but felt no more sympathy for him than for a canvas or the marble a sculptor cuts or the dry powder snow your skis cut through. (pp. 98-99)

Here bullfighting is identified with both sport and art.

Death in the Afternoon is not an important book, though, because it is a treatise on sport, or because it identifies the practitioners as athletes. It is an important book because it presents a vision of a temporary social order which is created in the course of the bullfight and which Hemingway seems to suggest would be an ideal order for the whole human race. This I take to be the significance of the last words of the book.

The great thing is to last and get your work done and see and hear and learn and understand; and write when there is something that you know; and not before; and not too damned much after. Let those who want to save the world if you can get to see it clear and as a whole. Then a part you make will represent the whole if it's made truly. (p. 278)

Hemingway has tried to get the whole world imaged in a bullfight. What, then, is the shape of that world?

There are three classes of people in it. The matadors are its rulers. The artist-sportsman is right at the center of this community. The banderilleros and the picadors represent the professional classes, particularly the army. Lastly the spectators comprise the working class, here stood on its head to become a leisure class, somewhat as the working class has in America during the course of the twentieth century.

The picadors and banderilleros are the least important part of this world in any spiritual sense, though their function is still important. In describing the matador as "living every day with death" Hemingway distinguished him from the banderilleros and picadors.

The banderilleros and picadors are different. Their danger is relative. They are under orders; their responsibility is limited; and they do not kill. (p. 56)

Hemingway touches on many qualities of the professional in the following description of banderilleros, including the image of the businessman and the professional baseball player.

Banderilleros are sometimes lean, brown, young, brave, skillful and confident; more of a man than their matador, perhaps deceiving him with his mistress, making what seems to them a good living; enjoying the life; other times they are respectable fathers of families, wise about bulls, fat but still fast on their feet, small businessmen with bulls as their business; other times they are tough, unintelligent, but brave and capable, lasting like ballplayers, as long as their legs hold out; others may be brave but unskillful, eking out a

> living, or they may be old and intelligent but with their legs gone, sought out by young fighters for their authority in the ring and their skill at placing bulls correctly. (p. 202)

These professionals, by the time the climactic moment of the bullfight has arrived, have, in effect, joined the ranks of the spectators.

The spectators too are a select group of people. Hemingway defines the aficionado as a "lover of the bullfight . . . one who has this sense of the tragedy and ritual of the fight so that the minor aspects are not important except as they relate to the whole. Actually, the spectators take a rather active role in bullfighting, as Hemingway says that "if the spectator did not impose the rules, keep up the standards, prevent abuses and pay for the fights there would be no professional bullfighting in a short time and no matadors." (p. 164)

The spectator's most important function is best seen though after we take a preliminary look at the matadors. Hemingway bemoans the fact that in 1932 matadors had become specialists.

> For, now, certain matadors are only capable of certain things. They have become as much specialists as doctors. In the old days you went to a doctor and he fixed up, or tried to fix up, whatever was wrong with you. So in the old days you went to a bullfight and the matadors were matadors; they had served a real apprenticeship, knew bullfighting, performed as skillfully as their ability and courage permitted with cape, muleta, banderillos, and they killed the bulls. It is of no use to describe the state of specialization doctors have reached, nor speak of the aspects of this which are most repellent and ridiculous because everyone has some contact with them sooner or later, but a person who is going to the bullfights does not know that this malady of specialization has spread to bullfighting so that there are matadors who are only good with the cape and useless at anything else. (p. 85)

Specialization in matadors is bad primarily because the sense of wholeness the matador presides over is lost when the matador cannot perform every part of the complex ritual. Hemingway uses some messianic imagery in describing what is necessary.

> What is needed in bullfighting today is a complete bullfighter who is at the same time an artist to save it from the specialists; the bullfighters who can do only one thing, and who do it superlatively, but who require a special, almost made-to-order bull to bring their art to its highest point or, sometimes, to have any art at all. What it needs is a god to drive the half-gods out. But waiting for a messiah is a long business and you get many fake ones. (p. 86)

The complete bullfighter is to restore wholeness and meaning to the bullfight, to get the spectators' minds off the sometimes by themselves messy details of the fight and onto the sublime significance of the fight as a whole. This is the traditional function of the heroic figure. And the material this hero must work with is clearly the modern commercial, industrial world with its made-to-order bulls and its specialist bullfighters. Finally, the matador must communicate with the spectators the wholeness of the bullfight, and the best metaphor Hemingway has for this is the creative relationship between the artist and his audience.

> If the spectators know the matador is capable of creating a complete, consecutive series of passes with the muleta in which there will be valor, art, understanding and, above all, beauty and great emotion, they will put up with mediocre work, cowardly work, disastrous work because they have the hope sooner or later of seeing a complete faena; the faena that takes a man out of himself and makes him feel immortal while it is proceeding, that gives him an ecstacy, that is, while momentary, as profound as any religious ecstacy; moving all the people in the ring together and increasing in emotional intensity as it proceeds, carrying the bullfighter with it, he playing on the crowd through the bull and being moved as it responds in a growing ecstacy of ordered, formal, passionate, increasing disregard for death administered to the animal that has made it possible, as empty, as changed and as sad as any major emotion will leave you. (pp. 206-207)

Though some of the content of this passage may seem obscure, the form the activity described takes is not. This is a peculiar kind of play. Huizinga would have, I think, to say that it is a combination of both the social manifestations of play; the ritual and the contest. In addition to this, the spectators are drawn into the play and receive as much spiritual reward from it as the players. This is a new understanding of the role of the spectator that makes of him a kind of participant. The event has all the qualities of play. It is limited both in terms of time and space. Hemingway's sentence structure conveys especially well the sense of its limitedness in time, even while he speaks of immortality. It is certainly set apart from the actual world; the matador and the aficionados are a special class, apart from the ordinary workaday world. The activity transcends the normal activity of the bullfighter as "professional." By fighting a successful bullfight he succeeds in transforming his work into a voluntary activity. He makes his trade an art voluntarily. For Hemingway, even the bull fights because he wants to, not because he has been goaded into it.

The really brave bull welcomes the fight, accepts every invitation to fight, does not fight because he is cornered, but because he wants to and this bravery is measured, and can only be measured by the number of times he freely and willingly, without pawing, threatening, or bluffing, accepts combat with the picador and whether, when the steel point of the pic is sunk in his muscles of neck or shoulder, he insists under the iron and continues his charge after he begins to really receive the punishment, until man and horse are thrown. (pp. 141-142)

Because of the Spanish Civil War and World War II, Hemingway did not return to bullfighting until the 1950's. His *The Dangerous Summer*, excerpts of which were published in *Life* magazine in the fall of 1960 but which remains unpublished as a whole in the United States, records his experiences of that time. Hemingway himself gave another reason for his having neglected bullfighting for so long at the outset of the first excerpt in *Life*.

So for many reasons, especially the fact that I had grown away from spectator sports, I had lost much of my old feeling for the bullfight but a new generation of fighters had grown up and I was anxious to see them.[22]

Here he suggests that he is no longer interested in being a spectator and is clearly more interested in watching and identifying with the matador himself. Though the bullfight is clearly a sport, the bullfighter, in these excerpts, is clearly an artist and this is the basis of Hemingway's identification.

The bullfighter is the same sort of artist as Nick Adams is a fisherman. He creates new things out of the ruins of the old. Hemingway spends some time describing the conditions of bulls in modern bullfighting, then describes a bullfighter dealing with a poor bull.

Antonio saved the corrida from being a disaster and gave Madrid the first view of what he had become. His first bull was worthless. He was hesitant with the horses and did not want to charge frankly but Antonio picked him up with the cape delicately and suavely, fixed him, taught him, encouraged him by letting him pass closer and closer. He fabricated him into a fighting bull before your eyes. Antonio in his own enjoyment and knowledge of the bull seemed to be working in the bull's head until the bull understood what was wanted of him. If the bull had a worthless idea Antonio would change it for him subtly and firmly.[23]

Here the bullfighter, like Nick Adams, creates order from unworthy materials. The matador resembles the fisherman.

He is not as alone, though, as Nick Adams or, as we shall see, Santiago was. Hemingway describes the peculiar community the world of bullfighting comprises.

> Everyone in bullfighting helps everyone else in bullfighting in the ring. In spite of all rivalries and all hatreds it is the closest brotherhood there is. Only bullfighters know the risks they run and what the bull can do with his horns to their bodies and their minds. Those who have no true vocation for bullfighting have to sleep with the bull every night.[24]

In these articles, Hemingway has moved from identifying with the spectator to identifying with the professional. We can see how this change, Hemingway's growing away from spectator sports, occurs, if we consider other writings about the participatory sports of hunting and fishing, principally *Green Hills of Africa,* "The Short, Happy Life of Francis Macomber," and *The Old Man and the Sea.*

III

Green Hills of Africa, at the time he wrote it, pleased Hemingway. Carlos Baker reports that "in quality, he [Hemingway] thought, it was more like 'Big Two-Hearted River' than anything else he had ever done."[25] In *Green Hills of Africa* the world of sport is suggested as a meaningful alternative to commercial civilization and it is apparently meaningful because it has the qualities of play as Huizinga defines them. The book is ostensibly the narrative of a month's hunting in Africa. It is evident from the construction of the book that Hemingway uses the hunting world the way he used the bullfight; both are formulated in opposition to the values of commercial, industrial America. It is divided into four parts entitled "Pursuit and Conversation," "Pursuit Remembered," "Pursuit and Failure" and "Pursuit and Happiness." Pursuit, then, is obviously the common element; and by pursuit Hemingway means the play or sport of hunting. The first three parts merely provide a background for the fourth, which presents the qualities of the ideal life. Hemingway, however, presents them as not only attainable but as having been attained. Let us consider first the background he provides for his "Pursuit as

Happiness."

Hemingway prepares for his presentation of the good life by setting down certain attitudes about the nature of reality throughout the first sections of the book, three of which we will be concerned with here. The first concerns the experience of war. Hemingway says:

> . . . I thought about Tolstoi and about what a great advantage an experience of war was to a writer. It was one of the major subjects and certainly one of the hardest to write truly of and those writers who had not seen it were always very jealous and tried to make it seem unimportant, or abnormal, or a disease as a subject, while, really, it was just something quite irreplaceable that they had missed.[26]

Why should war be "an experience quite irreplaceable?" Hemingway does not tell us in this passage. The only clue is a reference to "one fine description of fighting" Hemingway finds in Tolstoi's *Sevastopol.* Explicit in the above passage itself is the notion that the experience of war, like the experience of play, sets one off from his fellow men, as he ordinarily encounters them, and puts him in a special world. Consider the following quotation from *Green Hills of Africa.*

> Now, going forward, sure he was in here, I felt the elation, the best elation of all, of certain action to come, action in which you had something to do, in which you can kill and come out of it, doing something you are ignorant about and so not scared, no one to worry about and no responsibility except to perform something you feel sure you can perform. (p. 116)

Is this the experience of hunting or that of war? The two have something in common. Both occur in a world in which certain rules are absolute, a world in certain ways restricted but which in certain others allows absolute freedom.

A few pages later in *Green Hills* Hemingway makes a commitment in another direction, defining work, not hunting, war or play, as the supremely meaningful activity in life.

> What I had to do was work. I did not care, particularly, how it all came out. I did not take my life seriously any more, any one else's life, yes, but not mine. They all wanted something that I did not want and I would get it without wanting it, if I worked. To work was the only thing, it was the one thing that always made you feel good, and in the meantime it was my own damned life and I would lead it where and how I pleased. (p. 72)

Here the Carlyle in Hemingway moralizes on the "idler" in Hemingway. There is an unconscious disparagement of hunting in this attitude. Hemingway attempts to resolve the resultant problem in self-identification by suggesting that he leads two lives. In the first sentence of the quotation Hemingway the sportsman is not entirely repudiated, even though sports are not guaranteed to make one feel good. Play, perhaps, is merely the best substitute for work. Hemingway is defining himself as a professional. He works at work, he plays at play. This tends, however, to jar with the tone of the rest of the book, which proceeds on the assumption that the sport of hunting is intensely meaningful. This conflict within the book is indicative of the process of change in Hemingway's self definition from spectator of life to professional, a change he seemed to recognize in a passage quoted earlier from *A Moveable Feast.*

The book's great statement of the nature of reality comes during a meditation on the Gulf Stream. In this is foreshadowed the quality of life we will find in his ideal world. The passage is worth extensive quotation.

> . . . This Gulf Stream you are living with, knowing, learning about, and loving, has moved, as it moves, since before man and . . . it has gone by the shoreline of the long, beautiful, unhappy island since before Columbus sighted it and . . . the things you find out about it, and those that have always lived in it are permanent and of value because that stream will flow, as it has flowed, after the Indians, . . . after . . . all the systems of governments, the richness, the poverty, the martyrdom, the sacrifice and the veniality and the cruelty are all gone as the high piled scow of garbage, bright-colored, white-flecked, ill-smelling, now tilted on its side, spills off its load into the blue water, turning it a pale green to a depth of four or five fathoms as the load spreads across the surface, the sinkable part going down. . . . All this which still floats well shepherded by the boats of the garbage pickers who pluck their prizes with long poles, as interested, as intelligent, and as accurate as historians; they have the viewpoint; the stream, with no visible flow, takes five loads of this a day when things are going well in La Habana and in ten miles along the coast it is as clear and blue and unimpressed as it was ever before the tug hauled out the scow; and the palm fronds of our victories, the worn light bulbs of our discoveries, and the empty condoms of our great loves float with no significance against one single, lasting thing—the stream. (pp. 149-150)

In this passage the temporal is opposed to the eternal, the natural to the artificial. Hemingway's choice between the two is clear from the images he uses. He chooses the water, "clear, blue and unimpressed" rather than the garbage of history. He chooses the eternal: reality to him is that which endures, not that which changes; time "but the stream he goes fishing in" for reality, truth, significance. This eternal world is natural, everything man-made is "naturally" temporal, perishable. Since man's existence is limited in time, his task is to decide how best to live and create as close to the natural as possible.

After a week of particularly bad hunting, Hemingway is accosted by a native who speaks to him excitedly. The guide translates:

"He says . . . they have found a country where there are kudu and sable. He has been there three days. They know where there is a big kudu bull and he has a man watching him now." (p. 208)

This comes as the promise of heaven on earth to the hunters. The last third of *Green Hills,* "Pursuit as Happiness," follows. The concept of a special place is elaborated at great length. We remember that it is one of the characteristics of play that it stands quite consciously outside of ordinary life and that one manifestation of this is that it occurs in a special place. The ordinary world is temporarily abolished physically as well as mentally.

I could not believe that we had suddenly come to any such wonderful country. It was a country to wake from happy to have had the dream. . . . This was a virgin country, an unhunted pocket in the million miles of bloody Africa. (p. 218)

We are as close to nature here as a man can possibly get. This special land soon becomes the whole world to the hunting party. Hemingway thinks:

. . . sure enough we put up partridges and, watching them fly, I was thinking all the country in the world is the same country and all hunters are the same people. (p. 249)

Hemingway later considers again the presence of virgin land and the presence of the corruptive factors of society. He considers the possibility of a guide he dislikes bringing all his other customers in.

But if he did I'd go on down beyond those hills and there would be another country where a man could live and hunt if he had time to live and hunt.

They'd gone in wherever a car could go. But there must be pockets like this all over, that no one knows of, that the cars pass all along the road. They all hunt the same places. (pp. 282-283)

Thus the virgin land operates as a perpetual frontier, on which a man can continue to exist in a real world, and not an illusory one. Hemingway's final statement of the nature of the virgin country reproduces the frontier exactly:

Our people went to America because that was the place to go then. It had been a good country and we had made a bloody mess of it and I would go, now, somewhere else as we had always had the right to go somewhere else and as we had always gone. You could always come back. Let the others come to America who did not know that they had come too late. Our people had seen it at its best and fought for it when it was well worth fighting for. Now I would go somewhere else. We always went in the old days and there were still good places to go. (p. 285)

For Hemingway, the only significant movement, in time or in space, is towards a special place.

As the sport of hunting has a special place, so it has a special language. This also serves to remove it from the ordinary world, to give it the quality of play. The hunting party confers on how it will deploy itself.

You ask how this was discussed, worked out, and understood with the bar of language, and I say it was as freely discussed and clearly understood as though we were a cavalry patrol all speaking the same language. We were all hunters except, possibly, Garrick, and the whole thing could be worked out, understood, and agreed to without using anything but a forefinger to signal and a hand to caution. (p. 251)

We might note initially another case of the congruence of war and sport in Hemingway's mind in the phrase "cavalry patrol." The major thrust of the passage indicates that the hunters are all so familiar with the rules of the game as to have developed a complex sort of shorthand with which to discuss them.

Garrick is the representative of the "outside world" unable to participate in the world of play created by the others. He is not a hunter, but, as his nickname indicates, a showman. His romantic posturing reminds one in some ways of Robert Cohn's in *The Sun Also Rises.* His presence, like Cohn's, serves to highlight the commendable qualities of those about him. He operates outside the rules of the game and his presence makes the players nervous.

Then Garrick again, "Piga, Bwana, Piga!" I turned on him as though to slug him in the mouth. It would have been a great comfort to do it. I truly was not nervous when I first saw the sable, but Garrick was making me nervous. (p. 255)

Gradually the hunting party is divided into two groups, with Garrick symbolizing those human beings in general who will not play the game. Hemingway describes this split.

Garrick had given up tracking seriously and was only contributing theatrical successes of discovering blood when M'Cola and I were checked. He would do no routine tracking any more, but would rest and then track in irritating spurts. The Wanderobo-Masai was useless as a blue-jay and I had M'Cola give him the big rifle to carry so that we would get some use out of him. The Roman's brother was obviously not a hunter and the husband was not very interested. He did not seem to be a hunter either. As we trailed, slowly, the ground, hard now as the sun baked it, the blood only black spots and splatters on the short grass, one by one the brothers, Garrick, and the Wanderobo-Masai dropped out and sat in the shade of the scattered trees. (p. 268)

This passage serves as an introduction to the figure of the true hunter, the professional ideal. As they track the animal Hemingway recognizes in M'Cola his professional ideal:

We went on slowly. I had always sworn to Pop that I could out-track M'Cola but I realized now that in the past I had been giving a sort of Garrick performance in picking up the spoor when it was lost and that in straight, steady tracking, now in the heat, with the sun really bad, truly bad so that you could feel what it was doing to your head, cooking it to hell, trailing in short grass on hard ground where a blood spot was a dry, black blister on a grass blade, difficult to see; that you must find the next little black spot perhaps twenty yards away, one holding the last blood while the other found the next, then going on, one on each side of the trail: pointing with a grass stem at the spots to save talking, until it ran out again and you marked the last blood with your eye and both made casts to pick it up again, signaling with a hand up, my mouth too dry to talk, a heat shimmer over the ground now when you straightened up to let your neck stop aching and looked around, I know M'Cola was immeasurably the better man and the better tracker. (p. 269)

Essentially what we find in this passage is the quality of work blended with the quality of play. M'Cola's total absorption in his work resembles the total absorption of a child's play. He treats his work, as Hemingway treats his play, with absolute seriousness, absolute attention.

But this tentative resolution of work and play in the code of the professional is never completely achieved in the book. Hemingway remarks at the end of the book:

> I would come back to Africa but not to make a living from it. I could do that with two pencils and a few hundred sheets of the cheapest paper. But I would come back to where it pleased me to live; to really live. (p. 285)

It would seem from this quotation that Hemingway makes his final decision in the book for a utopia of play, not work. The book is finally a book with an ideal of play, though there are occasional impingings of an ideal work.

Hemingway's African experience also produced the short story "The Short Happy Life of Francis Macomber." This story moves toward a possible resolution of the conflict Hemingway had in identifying himself in *Green Hills of Africa.* In "Macomber" a sportsman measures himself against a professional's set of values.

We shall find in this story all the qualities of play as Huizinga outlines them. Viewed through the formulations of the spectator ethic and play the three central characters of the story are symbolic. Wilson, the guide, is the professional, the man who provides the ideals which are sought by Macomber. He lives in a special world, with values of its own. Macomber himself represents the spectator who is eventually able to define himself meaningfully in terms approaching those of the professional. Macomber's wife symbolizes the "outside world," the actuality which man is able to abolish temporarily by transcending it in play.

The story is about the possibility of salvation. It is a recounting of the necessary steps one must take to be saved. Hemingway himself has seemed to reject the idea of salvation. He says:

> Only suckers worry about saving their souls. Who the hell should care about saving his soul when it is a man's duty to lose it intelligently, the way you would sell a position you were defending, if you could not hold it, as expensively as possible. Trying to make it the most expensive position that was ever sold. It isn't hard to die.[27]

Hemingway seems to mean death when he says salvation here, but salvation turns out to mean the same thing it always has except for the original repudiation of it. Man must do certain things in order to be able to die properly just as he must do certain things in order to be saved. The moral underpinning of the story is suggested by the word "happy" in its title.

The story is structured so that we get Wilson's opinion of Macomber first and through this we get an indication of what the ideals of the world of the story are. Out first indication of this comes when Macomber asks Wilson not to talk to anyone about his panicking at a lion's charge. Wilson replies,

> "I'm a professional hunter. We never talk about our clients. You can be quite easy on that. It's supposed to be bad form to ask us not to talk though." (p. 7)

Thus Macomber is informed of the existence of a professional ethic. When the scene shifts back to the event of Macomber's panicking, this code is elaborated. The lion is lying wounded in the long grass and Macomber suggests that they just leave it there rather than going in and getting it.

> Robert Wilson, whose entire occupation had been with the lion and the problem he presented, and who had not been thinking about Macomber except to note that he was rather windy, suddenly felt as though he had opened the wrong door in a hotel and seen something shameful. (p. 17)

The fact that Macomber doesn't realize that the lion is suffering and that he is a potential danger to anyone else passing that way nauseates Wilson. As a final test of Wilson's eventual moral ascendance in the story Macomber's wife sleeps with Wilson, thereby designating him as the first male in the area and relegating her husband to a lower status. Wilson is prepared for this. As a man who has guided for the "international, fast, sporting set" he is aware of the needs and morals of his employers, "and their standards were his standards as long as they were hiring him." However, Wilson reserves for himself an area of purity which he will not let anyone unworthy violate.

> They were his standards in all except the shooting. He had his own standards about the killing and they could live up to them or get some one else to hunt them. He knew, too, that they all respected him for this. (p. 26)

It is in this area of purity that Francis Macomber is to join him to live out his short happy life.

Macomber himself is developed first in opposition to this ideal, then in congruence with it. What he must overcome is fear.

> It was there exactly as it happened with some parts of it indelibly emphasized

> and he was miserably ashamed of it. But more than shame he felt cold, hollow fear in him. The fear was still there like a cold slimy hollow in all the emptiness where once his confidence had been and it made him feel sick. It was still there with him now. (p. 11)

The next day the three go out shooting buffalo, and Macomber anticipates a recurrence of the same fear. However, he finds himself caught up in the excitement of the hunt.

> He expected the feeling he had had about the lion to come back but it did not. For the first time in his life he really felt wholly without fear. Instead of fear he had a feeling of definite elation. (p. 31)

What seems to have happened, is that the action of the hunt has moved Macomber from the province of the mind to the province of emotion, or pure exhilaration. He experiences the same emotions Nick Adams does while skiing. It is a world of pure action, pure impulse. The intellect has no place in it. "Something happened in me after we first saw the buff and started after him. Like a dam bursting. It was pure excitement," says Macomber. As he communicates these sentiments to Wilson, he gains his understanding. Wilson shares with him his philosophy of life.

> He [Wilson] was very embarrassed, having brought out this thing he had lived by, but he had seen men come of age before and it always moved him. It was not a matter of their twenty first birthday. (p. 32)

Macomber's experience resembles in many ways a religious conversion. As he moves from fear to the realm of pure excitement, he becomes initiated. Hemingway describes this feeling of salvation by describing Macomber as "exploring his new wealth." (p. 33)

We have Macomber's wife to thank for the fact that the time elapsed between the attainment of spiritual bliss on earth and the actual passage beyond life is, as the title of the story indicates, "short." When Macomber finds salvation in the realm of play he becomes unavailable to her in the ways he formerly was, and this frightens her. She is finally the unconscious agent of her husband's destruction. Macomber has simply moved outside the realm of ordinary experience, has been absorbed utterly in the play of hunting in the process of becoming a man. Wilson has set down the rules of this play and Macomber has met them. This world is unavailable and intolerable to his wife, who remains a member of the "international, fast, sporting set" that Macomber, however briefly, transcends.

IV

Hemingway was less explicit about the roles of work and play for almost fifteen years after "Macomber." His Nineteen Fifty novel, *Across the River and Into the Trees,* can be considered an attempt to reopen the question. In this as in other respects, the novel seems a failure. The professional soldier does not make an adequate symbol for the idea Hemingway wants to portray. All through the book, Hemingway shows concern about his choice of the professional soldier as a kind of representative man, and in one passage suggests a better figure, better because the symbols of his humanity are more naturally visible. Colonel Cantwell wonders to himself, having frightened off two young men who have been insulting him.

But couldn't those badly educated youths realize what sort of animal they were dealing with? Don't they know how you get to walk that way? Nor any of the other signs that combat people show as surely as a fisherman's hands tell you if he is a fisherman from the creases from the cord cuts.[28]

Hemingway comes to the figure of the fisherman Santiago in *The Old Man and the Sea* more as a result of the failure of *Across the River* than from his learning of the actual event, recorded in a 1936 *Esquire* article. The fisherman of the following quotation has qualities rather different from the ones Santiago shows, though the situation remains the same.

Another time an old man fishing alone in a skiff out of Catabanas hooked a great marlin that, on the heavy sashcord handline, pulled the skiff far out to sea. Two days later the old man was picked up by fishermen sixty miles to the eastward, the head and forward part of the marlin lashed alongside. What was left of the fish, less than half, weighed eight-hundred pounds. The old man had stayed with him a day, a night, a day and another night while the fish swam deep and pulled the boat. When he came up the old man had pulled the boat up on him and harpooned him. Lashed alongside the sharks had hit him and the old man had fought them out alone in the Gulf Stream in a skiff, clubbing them, stabbing at them, lunging at them with an oar until he was exhausted and the sharks had eaten all that they could hold. He was crying in the boat when the fishermen picked him, half crazy from his loss, and the sharks were still circling the boat.[29]

Santiago goes out, himself, under his own volition, to the fish and his response to the events is somewhat more stoical than this fisherman's. The setting of the Gulf Stream here is more important than the figure of the fisherman for Hemingway. It had become the last frontier. In that same letter to *Esquire* Hemingway had written of the Gulf Stream that it "and the other ocean currents are the last wild country there is left. Once you are out of sight of land and of the other boats you are more alone than you can ever be hunting and the sea is the same as it has been since before men ever went on it in boats."[30] On this last frontier Hemingway set his Cantwell-like figure, some years older. There was no woman this time, for the chief female character in *The Old Man and the Sea* is the sea itself, or herself, as Santiago would say.

> He had always thought of the sea as *la mer* which is what people call her in Spanish when they love her. Sometimes those who love her say bad things about her but they are always said as though she were a woman. Some of the younger fishermen, those who used buoys as floats for their lines and had motor-boats, bought when the shark livers had brought much money, spoke of her as *el mer* which is masculine. They spoke of her as a contestant or a place or even as an enemy, but the old man always thought of her as feminine and as something that gave or withheld great favors, and if she did wild or wicked things it was because she could not help them. The moon affects her as it does a woman, he thought.[31]

Hemingway himself was very excited about *The Old Man and the Sea.* According to Carlos Baker, "his enthusiasm was so great that Ernest sent a copy of the story to Wallace Meyer, a quiet and scholarly man who was now his point of editorial contact with Scribner's. He told Meyer that he would not try to point out the story's 'virtues or implicaciones.' All he knew was that it was the best he had ever done in his life. It could well stand as an epilogue to all his writing and to all he had learned or tried to learn, while writing and trying to live."[32]

Hemingway has been known to many critics primarily as a stylist, and in this respect *The Old Man and the Sea* has seemed a disappointing book, not worthy of Hemingway's enthusiasm. The aspect in which the book is successful is the thematic, for Hemingway had finally seen his ideal man clearly and as a whole, something he had not been able to do before even (maybe especially) while looking in a mirror. It is important, I think, to understand the public image of the man who meant so much to Santiago, for this is presumably what Hemingway had to work with when he began the book. Seeing what DiMaggio meant to the popular press should tell us much about what Hemingway felt he meant to Santiago.

Hemingway has not been alone in recognizing heroic qualities in the person of Joseph Paul DiMaggio, New York Yankee centerfielder between 1936 and 1951. A recent use of his image occurred in a 1968 popular song, the concluding stanza of which goes as follows,

> Where have you gone, Joe DiMaggio?
> A nation turns its lonely eyes to you
> . . . .
> What's that you say, Mrs. Robinson?
> "Joltin' Joe" has left and gone away.[33]

Here he appears as a charismatic leader, the presence of whom will abolish loneliness and whose absence creates a kind of wasteland.

Naturally, the public image of DiMaggio had been built up over a long period of time and contained many other elements than this. We will begin our consideration with DiMaggio's 1946 autobiography (probably ghostwritten) *Lucky to be a Yankee.* This book, thoroughly noncontroversial in nature and apparently directed at fourteen-year-olds, should give us some idea, by reason of its very nature, of what values and human characteristics DiMaggio (or his ghostwriter) wished to inculcate in the book's readers. James A. Farley gives the reader an "only in America" introduction. DiMaggio is a true son of Benjamin Franklin.

> (DiMaggio's) is a story that could have happened only in America, the story of Joe, the son of immigrant parents, of a boyhood which was far from luxurious, and his rise to national eminence on the strength of his baseball ability.
>
> I believe Joe's story . . . the story of a boy's life. I hope it will prove of interest to many other American boys, for it is really a story of our times.[34]

As "a story of our times" *Lucky to be a Yankee* then, as Farley and others read it, is to be taken allegorically, as a blueprint for human action as well as the story of an unusually talented athlete. Thus when Grantland Rice says in his foreword to the text that "Joe DiMaggio possesses that magic gift of perfection in his swing at the plate. If ever an athlete was meant for a sport, DiMaggio was meant for baseball," the reader is supposed to regard the ball-player's life as a process of getting in the right relation to fate, of being able to do what one is born to do.[35]

DiMaggio himself stresses three things in accounting for the shape of his career: his "God-given gift," the positive influence of "harmony and good-fellowship," and the adversity against which he struggled, which he calls at one point "the DiMaggio jinx." The first of these he describes early in the book.

> It has always been a theory of mine that hitting is a God-given gift, like being able to run fast or throw hard. Later on, I intend to discuss ways and means players can take to improve their hitting, but I know that I'm a professional ball player today because at the age of 18 I had a natural gift for hitting and for no other reason whatsoever.[36]

Natural genius, then, got him where he was. But DiMaggio found it necessary to develop other qualities in order to achieve his goal. He defines this goal as playing for the New York Yankees, "the greatest professional team in the world." (p. 45) Reporting as a rookie to the Yankees, he discovers the secret of the successful professional team.

> Joe McCarthy (the Yankee manager) greeted me with a warm sincerity that made me feel good and told me to take it easy and not to worry about anything. He introduced me to those whom I hadn't already met, and it was easy to see why the Yankees had such a great reputation as a winning team. There was harmony and good fellowship there such as I didn't believe could exist among professional athletes. (p. 51)

What this means to DiMaggio is made clearer by his description of how he felt on returning for his second year with the Yankees.

> I realized, of course, that by now I was an accepted member of the organization. . . .
>
> Already we were being compared with the great Yankee teams of the past. Our long distance hitting reminded writers of the Murderer's row of other years. Eddie Brannick, secretary of the Giants, called us "a gang of window breakers" because of the frequency with which we hit baseballs out of the ball park.
>
> What nobody outside our tight-knit circle could know, however, was

> that we hit so hard because we were happy about playing ball together. Everybody was interested in the welfare of everybody else. And ball players do their best under those conditions. A player doesn't hit or play too well unless he's happy. (pp. 72-73)

Harmony is necessary to the proper functioning of the community as a whole. In order to fulfill himself, the individual must submit to the welfare of the whole community. Thus while Farley gives us in his foreword the rhetoric of capitalistic individualism, the work ethic, the formula for success in an open society, DiMaggio tells the story for his initiation into a society of a very different sort. He goes on to say: "the thing which pleased me most was the rapidity with which I had been accepted as one of the family." (p. 73) This interesting remark suggests a tension between libertarian and organic views of society within the book. DiMaggio, unlike the man Farley describes, is extremely conscious of his relation to the community.

The major theme of the book, though, is DiMaggio's fight against adversity, "The DiMaggio jinx." A bad knee injury almost prevents him from getting to the major leagues at all. (p. 43) His second day in the Yankee training camp he burns his foot badly while using a diathermy lamp. Reflecting on this, he says, "I wasn't going to be fit in time to be in the lineup when the Yankees opened in Washington, with President Roosevelt throwing out the first ball. I was on the shelf before I was even a fullfledged Yankee." (p. 56) In 1940

> The warning that the DiMaggio jinx was still at work should have been apparent to me when Dom [his brother] pulled a tendon in spring training and had to sit it out on the Red Sox bench. I got through the exhibition season without a hitch but in the last game at Ebbets Field against the Dodgers, I injured my right knee sliding into second. For the fourth time in my five years with the Yankees, I missed the opening game. (p. 91)

Adversity is terribly real in DiMaggio's world: one must always be ready to fight it. Natural calamities can be overcome, he feels. Natural gifts are good, but do not make up the whole self. In order to utilize them best, one must be integrated socially, develop a sense of relation to one's teammates, that one's natural gifts may be used to the fullest potential allowable in an adverse universe. This sums up the message of DiMaggio's life as summarized in his 1946 autobiography. His image as it appeared in the New York newspapers in 1949 and 1950 probably influenced Hemingway's use of him as heroic figure in *The Old Man and the Sea.*

The 1949 season breaks down neatly into two periods as regards DiMaggio's public image. The first is the period between March first and April fifteenth, when it is discovered that he will be out of action indefinitely. The press reaction during this period takes two interrelated forms: worry about DiMaggio's future and an articulation of the qualities that made him great. The second period extends from the end of July to the end of the season in October and during this period his essential qualities are further defined and come to characterize the whole team. DiMaggio himself (or a ghostwriter) suggests the depths of worry that beset everyone after his injury when he says, in a *Life* article written after his return to the lineup, that "after the first dozen times I heard that question—was I going to quit?—I began to think it was like asking a man with a bad heart, 'When do you expect to die?' "[37] Initially, the worries are mainly personal. The *World-Telegram* reports DiMaggio as saying the following:

> "If that piece of bone gets back in there, I will be wrecked." DiMaggio said. "Sure, I played with the spur in my heel through the 1948 season, and hit .320 with 39 homers and 155 runs driven in."
>
> "But what happened to my legs while I was favoring the heel, because of intense pain? I got that terrible charley horse in my left thigh. My knee swelled. My ankles buckled. I figured I had ruined my career. Apart from injuries and the pain, imagine what that sort of thing does to me mentally."[38]

The team's fortunes without him are also a source of worry. He is referred to as the "key man of Yankee fortunes." It becomes "a matter of speculation whether DiMaggio ever will play again." The writers feel sure that "DiMaggio will never again be the DiMaggio of old."[39] Joe Williams of the *World-Telegram* took a more financial view of the situation.

> DiMaggio is trying to be as philosophical as an outstanding star can be who faces the possibility of losing his business, which is an extremely high talent for playing baseball at $100,000 a year . . . the uncertainty of the situation is beginning to depress DiMaggio, as it would anyone in like circumstances.[40]

DiMaggio faces loss of his earning power: he will be out of work. But he is not to be considered a rich man. He must be identified with the common man. Dan Daniel shows us why.

> There is a widespread impression that Joe is a rich man. That is founded on a fallacy. In the first place, he did not hit the high brackets until 1948, and then there are the terrific bites by the income tax. For three years he was in the army. His matrimonial venture cost him plenty too. Now he faces the chance to start laying by some dough, if he can keep on playing for a few more years.[41]

Like the rest of us, Joe is just trying to get along. What, though, are the qualities for which he is admired? DiMaggio has great spirit and great pride. Arthur Daley speaks of "the tortures he went through last September" when "only his blazing competitive spirit kept him—and the Yankees—going."[42] Joe Williams adds this on the subject of DiMaggio's condition: "If he can't give it the old matchless DiMaggio treatment he'll step down."[43] On April first, a *World-Telegram* writer concluded, after watching a DiMaggio work-out, that "Joe has a tremendous lot of pride, and to be remiss in so elementary an essential [after his lay-off he hadn't much wind], even without fault of his own, hurts him."[44] DiMaggio's spirit and determination are seen again in the March 28th *Times.* "Still taking things easy but reporting a lessening of pain in his right ankle, D. said today he would be in the season's opener April 19, 'with or without the pain.' "[45] But on April thirteenth he was declared out of action indefinitely and on April fourteenth Arthur Daley offered a summary appraisal of DiMaggio's qualities in his "Sports of the Times" column entitled "Say It Ain't So, Joe." According to him, DiMaggio was

> "one of the truly great ballplayers of all time" . . . "a fierce competitor of such flaming intensity that he has virtually carried the Yankees on his back since 1936." . . . "he did it by example" . . . "The Jolter . . . a restless seeker for perfection" . . . "his work an all consuming passion" . . . "did everything so easily, so effortlessly, so gracefully" . . .
>
> ". . . it's to be doubted whether he ever was greater than he was in September last season when he almost single-handedly kept the Yankees in the pennant battle right up to the end.
>
> He was a cripple. His heels pained in agonizing fashion . . . Every game was a torture and a torment. . . ."[46]

All the earlier themes are covered here: his immense ability which is quickly brushed aside in favor of his competitive spirit, his leadership by example, his grace, his ability to transcend adversity even when going down to defeat.

DiMaggio's dramatic return to the Yankee lineup in a three

game series at Boston the last three days of June stirred the imagination of the entire country. Headlines from the New York *Times* tell the story while those of the *World-Telegram* describe the shape of DiMaggio's greatness.

June 29: *Times*; DiMaggio's Two-Run Homer Helps Yanks Win

World-Telegram; Our Joe Shows Yankees They Can Stand on His Own Two Feet

June 30: *Times*; DiMaggio Hits Two Homers As Yanks Win

World-Telegram; The Bambino's Flare For Drama Lives Again in Joe

July 1: *Times*; DiMaggio's 4th Homer Beats Red Sox Again

World-Telegram; At This Pace DiMaggio is $100,000 Bargain

On August first *Life* magazine printed an article by DiMaggio entitled "It's Great to be Back" the introduction to which suggests the quality of the country's response to these events.

During the week of June 26th a $100,000-a-year baseball player named Joe DiMaggio, a shy and retiring young man who up to then had been noted chiefly for his easy grace in the outfield and his mechanical efficiency at punching out base hits—suddenly became a national hero. After being out for nearly half the season with a bad heel that threatened at times to end his career, he got back into uniform and—in perfect fairy-tale fashion—began breaking up game after game by hitting the ball out of the park.

It was one of the most heartwarming comebacks in all sports history and from one end of the country to the other it became the summer's prime topic of conversation, even among people who never saw a game in their lives. DiMaggio had always been a great player, and now he took his place in that select circle of athletes, like Babe Ruth and Jack Dempsey, who are not only admired but also beloved.[47]

For what qualities was Joe DiMaggio now beloved? For the most part they are those for which he was formerly admired. But they cohered under the pressure of the events in such a way that sportswriters would be meditating well into the next year on how best to describe what Joe DiMaggio represented to them. Accounts of the games themselves in the *Times* stress the inspirational quality of DiMaggio's leadership. Phrases such as "he carried his team," "a tremendous night for the returning hero," "aroused his mates," "the situation was desperate, but before long DiMaggio asserted himself" dot the accounts of the first two games.[48] Later in the season, after a game in which DiMaggio had contributed little, the *Times* nevertheless praised him for "giving his colleagues the life they invariably derive from his appearance on the battlefront."[49] After the season had been concluded and the pennant won, DiMaggio's contribution was that he "was ever an inspiration for the others. . . ."[50] A leader by example and by inspiration, DiMaggio had charismatic qualities.

> Only Babe Ruth had as acute a sense of the dramatic, and perhaps not even he, fighting Joe's handicaps in condition and vulnerability of that right heel, would have been able to come up with the show that DiMaggio put on Tuesday night, and those two terrific drives with which he made it two straight over Boston.[51]

This "sense of the dramatic," the idea of giving the customers the maximum in thrills, is something new in the writers' projection of DiMaggio's qualities, brought on undoubtedly by the situation. It takes its place along with the others: spirit, ability to triumph over adversity, in this summary statement from the *World-Telegram*:

> Once more Joe's flaming spirit, his flair for coming through against odds, his penchant for the dramatic achievement and consummate showmanship, were stressed as he drove the ball for three runs, and won for the Yankees by 6 to 3.[52]

The writers had difficulty finding a single concept-embodying word to describe him. The most common one was "professional." *Newsweek* reported that "The performance released a flooding appreciation of the great professional."[53] The *World-Telegram* reported that "yesterday the customers in the Fens shouted themselves hoarse for the pro . . ."[54] And on the next day, then Commissioner of baseball Ford Frick was quoted as saying: "However, what DiMaggio has done in the last few days has been a tremendous thing, not only for the Yankees and the American League, but for all baseball. That man is a real pro."[55] This word, however, wasn't entirely satisfactory to some sportswriters. It needed to be redefined. Arthur Daley, for instance, in his

"Sports of the Times" column, found himself saying, "yes, he's a professional, all right, but he's an amateur at heart. The love of the game comes first. . . ."[56] Grantland Rice commented on this same phenomenon: "it should be kept in mind that DiMaggio has suffered more than anyone else through his absences as baseball has been his life's occupation and recreation combined."[57] Here Huizinga's categories help us to understand the idea these writers are digging at. DiMaggio, apparently because of his natural talents, is able to transcend the workaday world in which he operates as a professional. As the professional as *amateur,* he is operating in a world of work. Like that of Robert Frost's wood chopper, his work is play, for mortal stakes. As the season progresses, the whole team is embued with the same quality. Witness this statement by Joe Williams.

> One of the main factors in the Yankees' stirring campaign has been their admirable spirit. Ordinarily I leave this subject for the young romanticists in the press box. Why shouldn't professional ballplayers play with spirit? It's their bread and beef isn't it? But I sincerely believe the spirit here is of a higher quality. I think they've run into so many bad breaks that they have developed an angry determination to prove that nothing can stop them.[58]

Here again the really admirable quality transcends the professional spirit. I think we can conclude that a new kind of meaning is being given the word professional. It now includes the best qualities hitherto associated with amateurism. This is the sum of DiMaggio's newspaper image, and is probably what Hemingway had in mind when he used "the great DiMaggio" as a symbol in *The Old Man and the Sea.*

The central question Hemingway dealt with in *The Old Man and the Sea* is the question of how one plays the game, the same question that interested sportswriters when they talked of DiMaggio. What qualities enable one to live the good life, regardless of the outcome of events? Our first question about the book ought to be, what relation does Joe DiMaggio hold to the central theme and the central character of the book?

The old man is a baseball fan. His attitude toward the sport seems to be one of reverence. He reveres particularly "the great DiMaggio" and the New York Yankees. His first mention of DiMaggio comes in conversation with the boy. The boy says:

". . . When I come back you can tell me about the baseball."
"The Yankees cannot lose."
"But I fear the Indians of Cleveland."
"Have faith in the Yankees my son. Think of the great DiMaggio."[59]

DiMaggio here is the man whose presence assures victory and inspires confidence. This is underlined in a later conversation.

"Tell me about the baseball," the boy asked him.
"In the American League is the Yankees as I said," the old man said happily.
"They lost today," the boy told him.
"That means nothing, the great DiMaggio is himself again."
"They have other men on the team."
"Naturally, but he makes the difference. . . ." (p. 23)

As well as emphasizing the old man's initial convictions about the stature of DiMaggio, this conversation foreshadows the action and meaning of the book. The boy's simple "they lost today" can be seen as a foreshadowing of what will happen to the old man. His reply "that means nothing" suggests a way of finally evaluating the events of the story. The old man will find out that the whole meaning of his life is circumscribed by the statement. Later in the same conversation the old man says "I would like to take the great DiMaggio fishing." (p. 23) This is, in effect, what he does, and the image of DiMaggio expands as the old man's consciousness of what is happening to him expands.

After he hooks the fish and sees how big it is, the old man thinks of DiMaggio again. The image of DiMaggio is somewhat different. He is more clearly the old man's ideal. "Do you believe the great DiMaggio would stay with a fish as long as I will stay with this one? he thought. I am sure he would and more since he is young and strong." (p. 75) This statement is preceded by the old man's charge to himself concerning his ideals. He says "I must have confidence . . . ," evoking again the image of DiMaggio as one who inspires confidence and assurance. And continues: ". . . and I must be worthy of the great DiMaggio who does all things perfectly even with the pain of the bone spur in his heel." (p. 75) It is significant that DiMaggio's name appears here in conjunction with the following new qualities. We are to think of him as one "who does all things perfectly" and who is bothered by "the pain of the bone spur in his heel." How he plays the game is now the important thing, and the obstacles he has to overcome are now important things.

The obstacle of pain is foremost in the old man's mind as he fights the fish and finally kills it. He thinks "the great DiMaggio would be proud of me today. I had no bone spurs. But the hands and the back hurt truly." (p. 107) Later, he makes the same consideration more specifically: "I wonder how the great DiMaggio would have liked the way I hit him [the first shark] in the brain? It was no great thing, he thought. Any man could do it. But do you think my hands were as great a handicap as the bone spurs? I cannot know." (p. 114) Here pain is the factor that links the two. The ability to operate under a handicap finally seems more important than the actual operations themselves. This is the last mention of DiMaggio in the book save one. This one occurs at a place of such great thematic importance that it seems best to go back now and consider the book as a whole in terms of the work-play, or professional-amateur antithesis.

Let us consider the old man's character. It consists almost entirely of virtues. "Everything about him was old except his eyes and they were the same color as the sea and were cheerful and undefeated." (p. 10) Aside from this, he also has great humility and "he was too simple to wonder when he had attained humility. But he knew he had attained it and he knew it was not disgraceful and it carried no loss of true pride." (p. 14) He also considers precision an asset. "It is better to be lucky. But I would rather be exact. Then when luck comes you are ready." (p. 36) Despite his bad luck, he still holds great hope for the future. He makes a statement of faith when he says "my big fish must be somewhere." (p. 38) But then he, like the average baseball player, is also somewhat superstitious. When the fish is playing with his bait, he thinks, "then he will turn and swallow it . . . He did not say that because he knew that if you said a good thing it might not happen." (p. 47) He is also a man of great will power, a fact to which the whole book bears witness.

Besides these personal characteristics he has the tools of his trade, both physical and traditional. When the boy asks him "but are you strong enough now for a truly big fish?" the old man answers, "I think so. And there are many tricks." (p. 15) Later, he says almost the same thing. "I may not be as strong as I think . . . but I know many tricks and I have resolution." (p. 25) These tricks, we assume, are the time-tested methods of expert fishing, the rules of the game, though his "resolution" may turn out to be more important to the old man than they are.

The old man moves outside the ordinary world to do his fishing. He goes out to sea. He meditates on the sea, distinguishing his conception from that of others.

> He always thought of the sea as *la mer* which is what people call her in Spanish when they love her. Sometimes those who love her say bad things of her but they are always said as if she were a woman. Some of the younger fishermen, who used buoys as floats for their lines and had motorboats, bought when the shark livers had brought much money, spoke of her as *el mar* which is masculine. They spoke of her as a contestant or a place or even an enemy. But the old man always thought of her as feminine and as something that gave or withheld great favors, and if she did wild or wicked things it was because she could not help them. The moon affects her as it does a woman, he thought. (p. 32-33)

We assume that the old man shares the sea, as a place and as a vision, with other true professionals, those who preserve the sport of fishing, the play of fishing, while attending to the business of fishing. But on this particular trip the old man doesn't just go out to sea, he goes way out to sea.

> He looked across the sea and knew how alone he was now. But he could see the prisms in the deep dark water and the line stretching ahead and the strange undulation of the calm. The clouds were building up now for the trade wind and he looked ahead and saw a flight of wild ducks etching themselves against the sky over the water, then blurring, then etching again and he knew no man is ever alone on the sea. (p. 67)

Here we can see him moving from one world to another. Like Thoreau, the old man passes "an invisible boundary." He has moved entirely out of the social realm in first discovering his aloneness and has acknowledged his entrance into the natural realm by discerning again that he is not alone. The natural world has traditionally been a world of struggle for existence. Hemingway transforms it into one of play in its more formal manifestation of sport. Let us look at the relationship between the old man and his opponent in this game, the fish.

Having hooked it, the old man begins to analyze the fish's movements:

> Then he began to pity the great fish that he had hooked. He is wonderful and strange and who knows how old he is, he thought. Never have I had such a strong fish nor one who acted so strangely. Perhaps he is too wise to jump. He could ruin me by jumping or by a wild rush. Perhaps he has been hooked many times before and he knows that this is how he should make his fight. He cannot know that it is only one man against him, nor that it is an old man. But what a great fish he is and what he will bring in the market if the flesh is good. He took the bait like a male and he pulls like a male and his fight has no panic in it. I wonder if he has any plans or if he is just as desperate as I am. (pp. 54-55)

Initially he pities the fish. The keynote of the meditation is the suggestion that the only reason that the old man still has the fish hooked is that the fish is playing by the rules of the game. He knows the best way to relieve himself of the situation he is in and he is doing that, not being able to know that almost any unorthodox move would be enough to upset the old man. Finally the old man sees the fish as a worthy opponent, and wonders what his next move will be.

The old man considers the place in which he hooked the fish and why the fish would be in this particular place. He and the fish have this in common.

> His [the fish's] choice had been to stay in the dark deep water far out beyond all snares and traps and treacheries. My choice was to go there to find him beyond all people. Beyond all people in the world. Now we are joined together and have been since noon. And no one to help either of us. (p. 55)

Both opponents, then, have moved beyond the ordinary world and here like the bullfighter and his bull they are engaged in a test of strength which will prove fatal to one. The fish's condition is a foreshadowing of the old man's. Later the old man begins to feel a certain brotherhood with the fish. As he eats to regain his strength he thinks "I wish I could feed the fish . . . he is my brother." (p. 65) Later still, sorrow is added to this feeling of brotherhood. "Then he was sorry for the great fish that had nothing to eat and his determination to kill him never relaxed in his sorrow for him." (p. 83) Finally, after the old man has won and the struggle between them is over, as the boat, with the fish lashed to the side, is bringing them both back to the distant land, there is confusion in the old man's mind as to who has really won. It does not seem to matter.

Then his head started to become a little unclear and he thought, is he bringing me in or am I bringing him in? If I were towing him behind there would be no question. Nor if the fish were in the skiff, with all dignity gone, there would be no question either. But they were sailing together lashed side by side and the old man thought, let him bring me in if it pleases him. (pp. 109-110)

The most meaningful episode in the book, the contest between man and fish, is over. The point of the passage seems to be that now nothing else matters, once they have played the game.

We get a hint of the nature of the struggle in the old man's first thoughts after having killed the fish. He says to himself "get to work, old man. . . . There is very much slave work to be done now that the fight is over." (p. 106) It does not seem too much to assume that Hemingway is setting up a distinction between the contest and work here. The old man is out of the world of play now and there is work to be done. Later, after the sharks have begun to do *their* work he thinks "man is not made for defeat. . . . A man can be destroyed but not defeated." (p. 14) This describes exactly the condition of his opponent, the fish.

The struggle between the old man and the fish is foreshadowed within the book when the old man remembers "the hand game." Younger then, he was known as Santiago *El Campeon* and he was challenged by "the great negro from Cienfuegos who was the strongest man on the docks." (p. 76) The old man had then the same respect for his opponent that he had for the fish. "He was sure then that he had the negro, who was a fine man and a great athlete, beaten." (p. 77) Also, the loser in this contest had not just been beaten, but destroyed.

. . . there had been a return match in the spring. But not much money was bet and he had won it easily since he had broken the confidence of the negro from Cienfuegos in the first match. (p. 78)

The thematic climax of the book comes when the old man makes a statement of the essential nature of his contest with the fish. He has been meditating on the possibility that his action may have been sinful. "Do not think of sin," he tells himself, ". . . there are people who are paid to do it . . . you were born to be a fisherman as the fish was born to be a fish. San Pedro was born to be a fisherman as was the father of the great DiMaggio." (p. 116) The implication here is that people who were born to be something live in a fundamentally different universe than those who are merely paid to do something. DiMaggio here is connected with those who are born into their professions. This quality enables one to transcend the workaday world where sin is inevitable. The old man describes the difference between the two worlds.

> You did not kill the fish only to keep alive and to sell for food, he thought. You killed him for pride and because you are a fisherman. You loved him when he was alive and you loved him after. If you love him, it is not a sin to kill him. Or is it more? (p. 116)

Essentially the distinction is between the world of work and the world of play, a public world and a private one. The professional ethic here includes the peculiar morality of play. The concept of sin does not cover the situation. Both opponents have played the game in the correct manner and this is what gives the situation meaning. The ordinary world has been rejected, the old man has not killed the fish in order to sell him, though this is his ordinary workaday task. Fishing has been both a sport and a profession, the old man has embraced both the sport and the profession but the meaning of his life surely comes from his ability to live in the world of play even though it is circumscribed by a professional world.

In *The Old Man and the Sea* the world of play is tragically temporary. The ordinary world, the real world which has been temporarily abolished, returns with a vengeance in the form of sharks who devour the fish, leaving the old man impoverished again in the actual world. Even the world of play is made up largely of the endurance of pain and the only way of enduring the ordinary world is in the knowledge that one has played the game well. The ordinary world constantly circumscribes the world of play. Throughout the book the old man has lived in a world where victory means destruction of the opponent. In the end, though, he himself is not destroyed, but beaten.

> "They beat me, Manolin," he said. "They truly beat me."
> "He didn't beat you. Not the fish."
> "No. Truly. It was afterwards." (pp. 136-137)

The old man has demonstrated how to endure defeat and to maintain his dignity in spite of the outcome. He can distinguish between a world which has meaning for him and one which the sharks inhabit. Defeated in the workaday world, he triumphs in a world of play, and by this triumph, is able to endure his actual defeat.

V

Hemingway never wrote a book about a professional baseball player, though he might well have. We must turn to another writer to see how the contemporary world of professional sports offers an equally ideal setting for the kind of story Hemingway wanted to tell, and had at least imagined in *The Old Man and the Sea.*

Mark Harris's *The Southpaw,* published a year after *The Old Man and the Sea,* demonstrates how clearly the distinction between the worlds of work and play can be dramatized in fiction utilizing a sports setting. This novel is centrally concerned with the problem of the individual's relation to society and it uses the form of the novel of initiation to tell this story. During the course of the novel Henry Wiggin, a boy, grows up, becomes a man.

As Hemingway has done so many times, Harris includes a romantic ideal which must be overcome before maturity is attained. Since the reader is always conscious of Henry Wiggin writing a book, it is fitting that this romantic ideal also be embodied in a book, which is a parallel of Henry's own: *Sam Yale—Mammoth.* The inspirational message next to Sam Yale's photograph reads:

> This book was written in the hope that every American boy now playing the great game of baseball in his home town, wherever that may be, will take inspiration from my straight forward story. Some of my readers, in the not-too distant-future, will be wearing the uniform of one of the big-league clubs. His success or failure in reaching that goal, and in remaining there once he has reached it, depends on him and him alone.[60]

After this there are some simple rules to be followed; take the game seriously, live a clean life, listen to your high school coach, and have faith in yourself, in that order. Paradoxically, when Harry does meet Sad Sam for the first time, Sam gives him some more rules to be followed.

If you ever get anywheres in this game remember that a good pitcher can kill himself in the winter time. I put on 15 pounds this winter and killed my damn self and maybe took 3 years off my playing days as well. I am an old man rushed in my grave by women and liquor. Give them the wide go-around and keep in the out of doors all winter. (p. 86)

These however are offered in an entirely different spirit from those in Sam's book. When Henry reports to the major league club, he is warned to have nothing to do with Sam Yale because "everything he touches turns to shit." (p. 118)

Later Henry loans Sad Sam a copy of his book to read and Sam offers the definitive judgment of it: "this book is all horse-shit." (p. 239) Sam expands on this theme.

If I was to write a book for kids I would not write such trash as this. . . . This is a good book and teaches them all the right things about smoking and going to church and such. For most kids that is all right. It will get them where they wish to go. They never aim very high. Those that aim high when they get there finds out that they should of went somewheres else.

When Henry tells him he is right, Sam asks him how he should know anything about it, being only a rookie.

It will take you 15 years to find out. You get so you do not care. It is all like a ball game without nobody watching and nobody keeping score and nobody behind you. You pitch hard and nobody really cares. Nobody really gives a f____ what happens to anybody else. (pp. 238, 239)

Sam also tells Henry that Krazy Kress, not he, authored the book. Henry has a showdown with Kress after the pennant has been clinched. He tells him "I could write a book better than that lefthanded." (p. 336) Henry makes one of his statements of identity to Kress as author of *Sam Yale–Mammoth,* a book he finally outgrew. He says "I bust my ass for no man."

I have really learned a lot this year, and it never really added up until this afternoon. But I will tell you 1 thing, Krazy. You have f_____ed up the game of baseball. You have took it out of the day time and put it in the night. You have took it off the playground and put it in the front office. (p. 337)

Krazy is representative of the corrupt society which is destroying the game of baseball and from which Henry must be able to distinguish himself if he can be said to be a mature human being. The place where he can do this is the baseball field, the ultimate region of meaning in this book.

The first climax of the book comes when Henry and his girl friend, Holly, have an argument about the kind of person Henry is becoming. Holly feels that he is losing his manhood and is simply an "island in the empire of Moors." (p. 306) Holly goes on to point out where Henry's true being lies:

> You will go on playing baseball till your feet trip over your beard. It is a grand game. I love to see it, and I love to hear you talk about it. It is a beautiful game, clean and graceful and honest.
>
> . . . .
>
> You are a lefthander, Henry. You always was. And the world needs all the lefthanders it can get, for it is a righthanded world. You are a southpaw in a starboarded atmosphere. (p. 307)

Holly sees baseball as an island of cleanness in a corrupt world, a place where innocence and integrity are still possible. She is trying to revert Henry to his original view of baseball, this time unromanticized. Baseball is "a beautiful game, clean and graceful and honest." One is reminded by this of Hemingway's ideal bullfights, and by the following passage, of Jake Barnes's fishing trip.

> It was a beautiful sight to see a good outfielder gather in a fly ball, moving over graceful as you please while from 250 to 300 feet away someone has tossed the ball up in front of himself and laid into it and sent it upward in a high arc until the ball is just a white speck against the blue sky, and then it hits its highest point and begins to drop, and you look down and there is a player loping over, moving fast or slow, depending on how he sizes up the situation, and he moves under the ball and it zooms down in his glove . . . when a big-league ball player does it, it looks easy because he is so graceful, and he gathers it in and then runs a few steps on his momentum and digs his spikes in the ground and wheels and fires that ball back where it come from, and it hops along, white against the green grass. (p. 51)

The concentration involved here, both on the part of the ballplayer and the spectator, operates to abolish the workaday world in the same way that Jake Barnes's concentration on his fishing does.

Holly also calls Henry a lefthander in a righthander's world; thus he must identify himself as distinct from the dominant social values. Indeed Henry in the end adopts a rather antisocial attitude when he finally comes into manhood. Henry's movement into manhood is symbolized in the book by a vulgar gesture he makes to 35,000 fans in the stands and millions more on television during the World Series. Henry tries to tell exactly what he meant by it.

> It really wasn't supposed to be vulgar, though. I don't know what it *was* supposed to be. I guess all I was saying was they could go their way and I could go mine, and some folks is born to play ball and the rest is born to watch, some folks born to clap and shriek and holler and some folks born to do the doing. I was born to do the doing and know nothing of wars and politics. All I know is what I like and what I do not like. But I did not know how to say all this. So I said it in the best way I could. (p. 346)

What this amounts to is a declaration of independence on Henry's part. He is now strikingly similar to Hemingway's bullfighter; a sort of non-rational artist in a world absolutely circumscribed by rules, beyond which lies a corrupt society and further a meaningless universe. Holly sums up Henry's achievements for the year.

> . . . you growed to manhood over the summer. You will throw no more spitballs for the sake of something so stupid as a ball game. You will worship the feet of no more Gods name of Sad Sam Yale nor ever be a true follower of Dutch Schnell. And you will know the Krazy Kresses of this world for the liars they are. You will never be an island in the empire of Moors, Henry, and that is the great Victory that hardly anybody ever wins any more. (p. 348)

Like Santiago's, Henry Wiggin's "great victory" lies in his ability to distinguish between the various worlds which make up his life. They both rise above the sharks and Krazy Kresses of this world; in effect banish them, Carlylian hell dogs, to their caves. But both their worlds are circumscribed by the fact that this banishment is temporary.

III

PROFESSIONAL SPORTS: THE CASE OF RING LARDNER

WE MUST NOW GO BACK A FEW YEARS TO LOOK AT THE WRITINGS OF RING Lardner, at once a creative writer and a baseball enthusiast and reporter. His writings will show how one sport, professional baseball, was understood in the years before the first World War. That Lardner largely gave up writing about and reporting sports after the first World War indicates a shift in attitudes toward professional sports and what they represent in general.

It was after he moved to New York in the summer of 1919 that Ring Lardner ceased to utilize professional sports, particularly professional baseball, as subject matter as often as he had previously. This sudden shift in subject has been accounted for in two ways. For some people, Lardner was always a writer who simply recorded what was around him. For these, the shift in subject presented no problem, since Lardner ceased to be employed as a sports reporter after moving to New York, except when he was on special assignment. Others felt that the Black Sox scandal, in which certain members of the Chicago White Sox conspired to throw the 1919 World Series to the Cincinnati Reds, and which was uncovered late in the summer of 1920, may have disillusioned him. Neither of these attempts to account for the shift in subject matter seems acceptable. That Lardner continued to write about sports after his move to New York seems to disprove the first. The fact that Lardner seldom spoke, either publicly or privately, about the Black Sox scandal suggests the limitations of the latter. In order to discover why Lardner happened to stop writing about sports, we will have to consider these things; why people have thought the way they did about Lardner's choice of subject matter, how he regarded sports, and whether this changed. Thus, this chapter will have three parts. The first concerns itself with the opinions of earlier critics on the question. The second examines representative examples of Lardner's work, both fiction and non-fiction, before 1919. The third considers representative examples of his fiction and non-fiction written after 1919. What should become clear is that after 1919 Lardner became concerned with two developments that he felt were hurting the quality of professional sports: a new, and, to Lardner, inferior style of play was introduced and this style appealed to the fan's lowest impulses. After 1919, much of his writing that did concern itself with sports was concerned with attacking the new style of play, particularly in baseball, or with attacking the fans for their stupidity in enjoying it. By looking at some of Lardner's writings from this angle we will be able to discover in addition what Lardner himself valued in life, for in attacking one style of play in baseball he defended, at least by implication, another, and we may safely assume that he defended it because he felt it valuable.

I

Most critics seem to agree that Ring Lardner regarded professional baseball as a representative institution in American culture and had no desire to use it as a setting for values alternative to those of the dominant culture, as Hemingway would do in some of his sports stories later. In fact, Henry Wiggen takes pains to distinguish himself from Jack Keefe and his creator. Wiggen comments on Lardner's baseball stories once in *The Southpaw* and this statement serves to distinguish the world of Lardner's baseball stories from the world of *The Southpaw*. This is Henry Wiggen's boyhood judgment:

There was also some books of baseball stories, such as those by Sherman and

> Tunis and Lardner, although Lardner did not seem to me to amount to much, half of his stories containing women in them and the other half less about baseball than what was going on in the hotels and trains. He never seemed to care how the games came out. He wouldn't tell you much about the stars but only about bums and punks and second raters that never had the stuff to begin with.[1]

The essence of this youthful criticism is in the sentence "he never seemed to care how the games came out." Henry's book, on the other hand, is very much concerned with this; he even records the entire box score of his first game in the majors. It is within the matrix of the game that Henry finally finds his manhood. On the other hand, Lardner's concern is with the ballplayer as an ordinary human being. He sees nothing special or redemptive about life on the ball field.

Gilbert Seldes also makes this point in the following quotation:

> . . . Lardner was always writing about human beings; they happened at first to be ballplayers because he knew the diamond and the bull-pen and the bench; but his stories are always about human beings who suffer pride and avarice and love and folly and ambition—as you find them wherever simple people are gathered together, not necessarily in the sight of God.[2]

Clifton Fadiman, in his essay "Ring Lardner and the Triangle of Hate," agrees with Seldes. He argues that "the baser part of the soul of a class or nation is frequently revealed in the sports to which it is addicted." Lardner, he maintains, writes about them, but, unlike Hemingway, "is absolutely never taken in by them." Fadiman goes on to contrast Lardner's sports stories with those of Hemingway on the grounds that Hemingway "sees sport as a human value" and "presents a semi-philosophical apology for sport." Lardner, on the other hand, uses it only as a setting within which to present basic American types.[3]

In an essay entitled "American Fiction," written in 1925, Virginia Woolf also considers the question of the role of sports in Lardner's fiction. In America, she concludes, "there is baseball instead of society."

> It is no coincidence that the best of Mr. Lardner's stories are about games, for one may guess that Mr. Lardner's interest in games has solved one of the most difficult problems of the American writer; it has given him a clue, a centre, a meeting place for the diverse activities of a people whom a vast continent

isolates, whom no tradition controls. Games give him what society gives his English Brother.[4]

For Virginia Woolf, games are the organizing principle in American civilization; they are representative; they function as traditions and institutions do in European society. Baseball, for her, is but the first of a series of games which Lardner will use as a substitute for social order.

According to all these critics, Lardner never intended his sports as a matrix for presentation of a set of values intended as an alternative to those of a commercial civilization, but rather used the setting as representative of that commerical civilization. They themselves saw nothing disharmonious between the values of professional baseball and those of American society at large.

By no means everyone felt that the setting was a satisfactory microcosm for American life, or even, for that matter, humanity in general. F. Scott Fitzgerald, in his memorial article, "Ring," felt that Lardner's early interest in sports had stunted his whole growth as a writer. Fitzgerald saw professional baseball as

> a boy's game, with no more possibilities in it than a boy could master, a game bounded by walls which kept out novelty or danger, change or adventure. . . . However deeply Ring might cut into it, his cake had exactly the diameter of Frank Chance's diamond. . . . It was never that he was completely sold on athletic virtuosity as the be-all and end-all of problems; the trouble was that he could find nothing finer. Imagine life conceived as a business of beautiful muscular organization—an arising, an effort, a good break, a sweat, a bath, a meal, a love, a sleep—imagine it achieved; then imagine trying to apply that standard to the horribly complicated mess of living, where nothing, even the greatest conceptions and workings and achievements, is else but messy, spotty, tortuous—and then one can imagine the confusion that Ring faced on coming out of the ball park.[5]

This paragraph might better apply to Hemingway, for it was Hemingway rather than Lardner who presented the two ways of life in the manner Fitzgerald does here. For our purposes, it is enough to notice that what Fitzgerald conceives as happening to Lardner resembles a kind of loss of innocence. Lardner, he feels, in his interest in professional sports, had isolated himself from "the horribly complicated mess of living" and because of this, was overwhelmed by the confusions he faced "on coming out of the ball park." Clifton Fadiman, too, who has imagined Lardner incapable of any human response except hatred, has to admit that some of the baseball stories do not fit his conception of the man. He finds that

> There are also a number of baseball stories which at times appear to contain a sort of kindly humor. At the risk of being called sentimental, one might affirm that baseball is the only American activity for which Mr. Lardner has any kindness. Although he is well aware that basically the national game is as highly and as spicily commercialized as modern politics, he prefers (and not for merely business reasons) to dwell on its more farcical side.[6]

Even though Fadiman's way of understanding Lardner prevents him from imagining Lardner becoming disillusioned, he still sees baseball holding a special place in Lardner's mind. Many other critics see him as having become disillusioned with professional baseball after 1919, of rejecting the world in which he lived and moving on to another.

John Berryman, for instance, lists the Black Sox scandal of 1919 as being "among the things he never recovered from."[7] Maxwell Geismar's statement of what happened to Lardner after 1919 implies the same trauma.

> After the Chicago White Sox scandal in 1919, he had written those lines—"I'm forever throwing ball games, pretty ball games in the air. . . ."
>
> Only now he was suspicious of the Fix in everything: of the gamblers, the racketeers, the syndicates; of the *professional* corruption in what had been the natural popular entertainment, the source of folk pleasure and legends in the U.S.A. And wasn't he right in believing that a nation's sports (like an individual's humor) was the real key to its character?[8]

This belief, that the Black Sox scandal symbolized for Lardner the fact that an essentially folk community was being replaced by a commercially oriented communtiy, was most fully developed in the criticism of Gilbert Seldes. Seldes combined it with the theme of the loss of innocence.

> In 1910, when Lardner began to write about baseball, it was popular, with a less synthetic appeal. It was still in its romantic era, on the threshold of glorification. . . . Between the time of *You Know Me Al* and Lardner's second baseball series, *Lose With A Smile,* the great baseball scandal broke out. Enough members of the White Sox accepted bribes to throw the 1919 World Series to the Cincinnati Reds. . . . To protect the business, a baseball czar was appointed on the assumption that one could cure the ills of democracy by an appeal to Caesar. But for a long time baseball, as a gambler's paradise, took the sweetness from the sandlots. Heroic publicity and maybe

a faster ball were used to bring the game back. In 1932, when Lardner reverted to his first theme, his heart was not engaged. He was no longer amused, and the book may be funny, but it is not amusing. It is melancholy.[9]

But no more melancholy than his other writing of the time. We should not attribute the tone of that book to Lardner's feelings simply about professional baseball. It is clear from this quotation that Seldes feels that the Black Sox scandal served as a symbol for the growing awareness of Americans of the commerical basis of American society. It is also clear that the event fits the pattern of the loss of innocence. Baseball for Seldes moved from a romantic era to a commercial era. For people who were still young in 1919 and who followed baseball the scandal did amount to a trauma. Ring Lardner, however, was thirty-four years old at the time, had been the intimate of baseball players for some twelve years, and was the author of stories which supposedly divulged the meanness and pettiness of the average ballplayer, whom he also apparently took to be the average American. It is impossible to imagine him being disillusioned by the fact of the scandal. To see what caused him to turn away from professional baseball we ought first to consider what he liked and didn't like about it and the best way to do this is to look at representative writings on sports before 1919. Lardner, we will find, admired a certain style of play in baseball. The values he assigned to this style of play are roughly equivalent to the dominant values of American commerical civilization.

II

It may be that Lardner, by satirizing Jack Keefe, is defending the ideals of the status quo in professional baseball before 1920, and by implication of American society at large. His Jack Keefe stories may be considered the defense of a set of values. To understand them this way, we must look first at the non-fiction he wrote for various magazines between 1912 and 1919. Several scholars have noted the immense growth of articles about baseball and interest on the part of the reading public in baseball during the years in which Lardner produced the "busher" stories.[10] Lardner has commonly been assumed to have written these stories in part to debunk the image of the ballplayer created by this immense coverage. Lardner himself, however, participated in this coverage. During that period he wrote several articles on baseball for both *Collier's* and *American* Magazine which form a part of the image he may also have been debunking.

The first article to appear was called "The Cost of Baseball," published in *Collier's* in March of 1912. The article is written in straight English rather than dialect and is concerned with explaining the more business-like aspects of baseball to the public. Containing neither satire nor humor of any sort, it seeks to explain that "baseball is a business, a mighty big one, and it requires sound business sense of a peculiar kind to be successful in it."[11] In this look at the economics of baseball, there is no hint of dissatisfaction with the status quo and a positive interest in presenting aspects of the game which would probably not have interested many if baseball had at that period really been in the "romantic era" Gilbert Seldes felt it was. Instead, Lardner seemed interested in equating the world of professional baseball with the business world in general, with the mainstream of American society.

In 1915 he published a series of four articles on baseball for *American* Magazine: " 'Braves' is Right," an article in dialect on the 1914 world champion Boston Braves; "Some Team," also in dialect, in which he picks his own all star team; "Tyrus: the Greatest of 'Em All," on Ty Cobb; and "Matty," on Christy Mathewson. In these articles Lardner describes the style of play he regards as ideal in baseball as he analyzes in succession the make-up of a championship team, the ideal team, the ideal ballplayer and the ideal pitcher. These articles deserve consideration one by one.

The focus on the article " 'Braves' is Right" is on the manager of the team, George Stallings. Lardner credits him with inspiring the team to the heights it achieved. The team itself Lardner characterizes in the following manner: "a pretty fair minor league club—that's what I figured 'em when I seen 'em."[12] Even though they are the world champions, Lardner has grave reservations about their talent. "I say the Braves won by hustlin' and fightin' rather than because they was a aggregation o' world-beaters." (p. 22) Later he expands on this.

> The kind o' men that can do their best in a pinch is the kind that's most valu'ble in baseball or anywheres else. They're woth more than the guys that's got all the ability in the world but can't find it when they want it. I say the Braves is the kind that can do things when they've got to. Is that

knockin' 'em?[13] (p. 23)

Less talented than some of their rivals, the Braves still finished ahead of all the rest. Lardner attributes this to three things: their cleverness, luck, and the managerial talents of George Stallings.

The first two come together in the quotation above concerning their ability to do their best in a pinch. The values praised are those of a commercial society. The Boston Braves are the Yankee pedlars of the twentieth century. "A club that's done what the Braves done ought to get full credit. They's no denyin' that they made a sucker out o' the National League, and then went ahead and made a rummy out o' the Athaletics." (p. 22) Any club that wins in this way counts to a certain extent on luck, and Lardner underlines this too. "When they finally busted loose, Old Joe Horseshoes joined 'em and stuck with 'em. . . . O' course that's all right; the luck goes with a winner. But they can't never say they didn't have plenty of it." (p. 21)

The inspiration for the Braves is their manager, George Stallings. His first job is to give the team confidence they can win, a hard job in the case of the Braves, who were in last place as late as Bastille Day. Lardner says that Stallings too had the team doped out as a pretty fair minor league club. His strategy was to make them mad.

> He was pannin' the life out o' them, callin' 'em bushers, and askin' 'em how they come to be tryin' to play ball when they might of got a job drivin' a dray or readin' meters for the gas comp'ny or doin' somethin' they *could* do. . . .
>
> That's the way he was talkin' to 'em, and he meant it, too. But he wouldn't of never give 'em that line o' talk if he hadn't of knew it would wake 'em up. (p. 19)

To inspire them, or "wake 'em up," is Stallings' first purpose, but once awakened they must be kept awake. Stallings does this with praise. "He took that bunch o' no-accounts and goaded 'em into bein' stars, and when he had 'em so that they was playin' way over their heads, showin' him what a mistake he'd made, he says to them: 'Well, boys, you are ball players after all.' And they b'lieved him." In effect, he practices the same deception on them that they practice on the rest of the league. "This gang was willin' to think they could play ball, and when their manager told 'em they could, they fell for it." (p. 20) For this he is praised, not for his magical powers, but for his competitive shrewdness. "I'm givin' Stallin's credit for bein' that smart." (p. 22) Intelligence in the sense of shrewdness is what is praised throughout the article. Like "The Cost of Baseball," it celebrates baseball's integration with the values of the commercial civilization within which it exists.

The most interesting moments in the second article, "Some Team," Lardner's "all star club," come when he feels there might be some opposition to his choice. On choosing the last of his six pitchers, he pauses for effect. "Well, then I'm goin' to hand you another wallop," he says.

> What about Eddie Cicotte? There's one bird that I got the figures on, and they show that it's harder to score off of him than anybody else, that is, the last figures I seen. But a fella don't have to chase up the figures to know he's a whale. He don't look like a pitcher, but stick him with a club that can score a couple of runs for him ev'ry day, and he'll win just as many games as Johnson or Alexander. They ain't a smarter pitcher in baseball and they's nobody that's better all-around ball player, no pitcher, I mean.[14]

Eddie Cicotte is nominated here for his smartness and his ability to do everything that is demanded of a pitcher in professional baseball. But it is smartness or braininess that Lardner admires most in players, as in managers. Here Lardner describes Nap Rucker, another of his pitchers. "Rucker knows what he's out there for. He ain't like a lot o' these pitchers that leaves their brains on the bench, along with their sweater." (p. 21)

Lardner's interest in "smartness" as the most important quality a baseball player can have leaves him in a quandry momentarily in choosing his second baseman.

> You can't get away from Collins at second base. If John Evers could hit and run with him, they might be some argument. They ain't enough difference in their fieldin' to talk about, and they're both smart as whips. It comes down to a question o' mechanical superiority, as the fella says, and you got to give it to Collins 'cause he can hit better and run the bases better. He's speedier 'n John in ev'rything but brains, and it's a toss-up there. (p. 80)

Lardner seems here to bow reluctantly to "mechanical superiority." "Brains," he would like to feel, is a much more important quality.

Lardner's last two articles in the series for *American* Magazine both concerned individual players; Ty Cobb, Detroit outfielder, and Christy Mathewson, New York Giants pitcher.[15] Both are presented as examples of excellence in baseball, Cobb as the greatest ball player of all time. We shall be concerned with how Lardner accounts for their greatness. Lardner uses a different metaphor to describe each man, although both metaphors have been associated with commercial, industrial civilization. Cobb is linked with mechanical energy; he is the motive force behind the team. "Say, he ain't worth nothin' to that club; no, nothin'!" Lardner exclaims . . . "That bunch could get along just as well without him as a train without no engine." ("Tyrus," p. 19) Mathewson is associated with images of money and saving. The metaphor appears several times in the course of the article.

He's just like one o' there here misers. They get ahold of a lot of money and then they don't let none of it go, except just enough to keep 'em from starvin'. Instead o' money, Matty got ahold of a curve ball and this here fade-away and a pretty fair fast one and a slow one and a bunch o' control, and then he locked it all up and took a little bit of it out to spend when nec'sary, only most o' what he's been spendin' is control, which he's got the most of, and which it don't hurt him none to spend it. ("Matty," p. 27)

Comparing him with other pitchers, Lardner says that "he's a tightwad with his stuff, and they're spendthrifts." ("Matty," p. 29) Mathewson is a less dynamic capitalist than Cobb; his chief interest lies in how and when to dispose of his talents.

Lardner stresses Cobb's competitive desire, a quality we never hear of in the article on Mathewson. Lardner tells us that "when he wises up that somebody's got somethin' on him, he don't sleep or do nothin' till he figures out a way to get even." ("Tyrus," p. 19) This quality enables Lardner to get out of the bind he found himself in when he tried to choose between Eddie Collins and John Evers as the second baseman on his all-star team. In the following passage he gives Ty Cobb the competitiveness of Evers and the mechanical ability of Collins.

He's got a pretty good opinion of himself, but he ain't no guy to brag. He's just full o' the old confidence. He thinks Cobb's a good ball player, and a guy's got to think that way about himself if he wants to get anywheres. I know a lot o' ballplayers that gets throwed out o' the league because they think the league's too fast for them. It's different with Tyrus. If they was a league just three times as fast as the one he's in and if he was sold up there, he'd go believin' he could lead it in battin'. And he'd lead it too! ("Tyrus," p. 21)

This intense competitiveness made Cobb a very unpopular player both among his opponents and among his teammates. Lardner softpedals some of the more horrible consequences of this aspect of his personality, though the following sentence may be as true as it is humorous. "He got trimmed a couple o' times, right on his own club, too. But when they seen what kind of a ball player he was goin' to be, they decided they'd better not kill him."[16] ("Tyrus," p. 21)

Luck, apparently, was on Cobb's side. "You say you've heard ball players talk about how lucky he was." Lardner argues that "you got to have the ability first, and the luck'll string along with you. Look at Connie Mack and John D., and some o' them fellas." Cobb, like these men, is successful in that he has "pulled more stuff than any other guy ever dreamed of." ("Tyrus," p. 19) According to Lardner, though, a certain amount of ability is necessary before it can produce luck. And, from the article on Mathewson, we learn that luck does not necessarily follow, for Mathewson has a poor record in World Series play, and, if we are to believe Lardner, this is due to an absence of luck. "Most o' the games he lost was a crime." ("Matty," p. 27)

> . . . that's a fair example o' the luck he's had in all these World's Seriouses except the first one. If a rotten pitcher got a dose like that, I wouldn't slip him no sympathy. But it sure does give me the colic to have them things happen to a guy that don't have to take off his hat to nobody, and then see the bugs run around hollerin' "Well, I guess we can beat the great Mathewson!" Yeh, they can beat him with a whole blacksmith's shop full o' horseshoes. ("Matty," pp. 28-29)

This from a man who has told us of Ty Cobb that "if he's got horseshoes, he's his own blacksmith." ("Tyrus," p. 19)

What unites both Mathewson and Cobb as outstanding players is their intelligence coupled with their capacity and willingness to learn. Of Cobb, we hear that "he's twice the ballplayer now that he was when he came up. He didn't seem to have no sense when he broke in; he run bases like a fool and was a mark for a good pitcher or catcher." ("Tyrus," p. 19) Mathewson proceeds, in his own way, in the same direction. "I s'pose when he broke in he didn't have no more control than the rest o' these here collegers. But the difference between they and him was that he seen what a good thing it was to have, and went out and got it, while they, that is, the most o' them, thought they could go along all right with what they had." ("Matty," p. 27) It is what Cobb learns that makes him great. "Well, he's still takin' chances that nobody else takes, but he's usin' judgment with it. He don't run no more just for the sake o' runnin'." ("Tyrus," p. 19) What this judgment amounts to is described in the following sentence: "They's lots of other fast guys, but while they're thinkin' about what they're goin' to do, he's did it. He's figurin' two or three bases ahead all the while." ("Tyrus," p. 20) Here what might have been called great instinct, is presented as cleverness, figuring, planning ahead of time. Cobb is simply craftier than any of the other players. The same is true of Mathewson, though he is a considerably more genteel figure. In the last passages of the article, Lardner addresses himself to the question "what makes him the pitcher he is?" Immediately we learn that "he's got a lot o' stuff, but so has other pitchers." What counts is his knowledge of the craft of pitching. "But his fadeaway and his curve and his fast one and his control wouldn't none of 'em be worth near what they is worth if he didn't know all they is to know about pitchin'. It's the old bean that makes him what he is." ("Matty," p. 29) This "old bean" tells him that it is important to know how to hit and run the bases and field his position too.

We should turn our attention to Jack Keefe now with these qualities, particularly shrewdness and the ability to learn, in mind. A consideration of the character of Jack Keefe ought to show him to be the antithesis of these qualities, and therefore tell us that what has been known as the debunking of an actual ballplayer, ought also be known as an inverted statement of the qualities of an ideal ballplayer. Lardner is in this sense a conservative, wanting not to change the ideals of the community of professional sports, but to reassert their values. If he also "debunks the stereotyped image of the athlete as a popular idol,"[17] it is not his central purpose.

Jack Keefe is certainly the antithesis of Cobb and Mathewson, and is as certainly calculated to be so. Compared to the sensible competent workmanship of their careers, he continually behaves like a lunatic. In a story written after those which constitute *You Know Me Al*, Jack writes the following to his friend Al, speaking of a conversation with Kid Gleason, whom the manager has assigned to keep him out of trouble. "That's what I would like to be Al," Jack says, "is an aviator and I think Gleasons afraid I'm going to bust in to that end of the game though he pretends like he don't take me in earnest. 'Why don't you?' he said 'You could make good there all right because the less sense they got the better. . . .' "[18] Here Lardner opposes both Jack Keefe and "aviators" (as he will in the future oppose the new style of play in baseball) to common sense. Both, it is implied, are senselessly romantic.

As such, Jack Keefe is incapable of grasping the first principles of the common-sense world of professional baseball. As a soldier in *The Real Dope,* Jack is asked to give "a little talk on baseball." This is later expanded into an article in the regimental newspaper entitled, "War and baseball 2 games where brains wins." In a final metamorphosis, the article reappears in a series of points Jack hopes to give to General Pershing on the "stragety" of conducting a war.[19] Jack is, however, never able to demonstrate how "brain wins," for his talks only demonstrate that he has no "real dope" but is himself, instead, one.

Jack is equally incapable of understanding the world of professional baseball with its common-sense ideals and work ethic. After being told he is to be sent back to the minors, he is unable to accept the White Sox President Comiskey's exhortation to work hard. "Then he patted me on the back and says, 'Go out there and work hard boy and maybe you'll get another chance someday. . . .' I ain't had no fair deal Al and I ain't going to no Frisco. I will quit the game first and take that job Charley offered me at the billiard hall."[20]

Jack is also incapable of learning. Kid Gleason is assigned to try to teach him something. "After supper Gleason went out on the porch with me. He says, 'Boy you have got a little stuff but you have a lot to learn.' He says, 'You field your position like a wash woman and you don't hold runners up. . . .' Then he quit kidding and asked me to go to the field with him early tomorrow morning and he would learn me some things. I don't think he can learn me nothing but I promised I would go with him." (pp. 20-21) Being incapable of learning, Jack is incapable of improvement, a quality Lardner admired in Cobb and Mathewson. Callahan, the manager, is the next to give Jack a lecture. "Callahan and I sat down to breakfast all alone this morning. He says, 'Boy why don't you get to work?' I says What do you mean? Ain't I working?

He says, 'You ain't improving none. You have got the stuff to make a good pitcher but you don't go after bunts and you don't cover first base and you don't watch the base runners.' " (p. 29) Jack's childish ego is, of course, the cause of his lack of progress. It stands between him and any sort of improvement in his profession or for that matter, any sort of meaningful contact with the world.

> They always was good to me here and though I did more than my share I always felt that my work was appreciated. We are finishing second and I did most of it. I can't help but be proud of my first year's record in professional baseball and you know that I am not boasting when I say that Al. (p. 10)

Jack's ego, it seems, is most often an instrument of self-deception. In the quotation above, he takes credit for the team's success. In the quotation below, the situation is more complicated. Jack's manager suggests that he sleep nights instead of keeping a date with his girl.

> He says Go to bed nights and keep in shape or I will take your money. I told him to mind his own business and then he walked away from me. I guess he was scared I was going to smack him. No manager ain't going to bluff me Al. So I went to bed early last night and didn't keep my date with the kid. She was pretty sore about it but business before pleasure Al. (pp. 49-50)

By the end of this passage he has adopted his manager's point of view so completely that he is able to moralize to Al about his off-the-field activities. As Henry Wiggen observed, Lardner takes Jack Keefe out of the realm of sports and brings him back into the realm of ordinary experience, the workaday world. Keefe becomes a working stiff like many of his readers. He is both more and less than a ballplayer. Although he is no Paul Bunyan of the diamond, he does become a universal type. He is, according to Maxwell Geismar, "the average American citizen, or Mr. USA."[21] Basically, though, he is, by Lardner's standards, a lousy ballplayer.

Two early stories preview Lardner's later attitude toward sports: "My Roomy" and "Champion." "My Roomy," Lardner's second published story, is one of his most admired and one of his most enigmatic. Howard Webb places it with Lardner's late stories in which the problem of identity is the central theme: "Mama" and "Poodle."[22] Most critics have wondered about the apparent cynicism of such an early story. Hopefully, our understanding of the style of baseball play Lardner admired will help show how Lardner came to write it when he did.

The narrator of "My Roomy" shows quite early in the story how Buster Elliott, the story's protagonist, deviates from the style of play in the professional baseball of the time. " 'Well,' I says, 'he'd be the greatest ballplayer in the world if he could just play ball. He sure can bust 'em.' "[23] He is simply a slugger, not a complete baseball player at all. If Jack Keefe is a poor ballplayer, largely because his ego prevents him from improving, Buster Elliott is always something other than a ballplayer; he has no idea what a ballplayer is. He is as distant from the actual world as Jack Keefe is, but while Jack is generally persuaded not to carry out his plans of revenge, not to follow his first impulses in reaction to others, Buster apparently cannot help doing so. It is possible to conceive of making Jack into a baseball player, and the team and the coaches continue to try, whereas they give up rather quickly on Elliott. He is, we may suppose, a sort of monomaniac in that he refuses to admit the existence of a point of view other than his own. He appears in the actual world as a kind of madman, never reading his fiancee's letters because "she can't tell me nothin' I don't know already." (p. 208) Perhaps his most characteristic response comes when the narrator asks him if he can play poker; "They's nothing I can't do!" (p. 199)

Unfortunately, there are things that he prefers not to do. These, at first, concern various aspects of the game of baseball other than hitting.

> John ast him what was the matter, and Miller tells him that Elliott ain't doin' nothin' but just standin' out there; that he ain't makin' no attemp' to catch the fungoes, and that he won't even chase 'em.
>
> Then John starts watchin' him, and it was just like Miller said.
>
> Larry hit one pretty near in his lap and he stepped out o' the way. John calls him in and asks him:
>
> "Why don't you go after them fly balls?"
>
> "Because I don't want 'em," says Elliott. (p. 184)

His "business," as he says, "is bustin' things," and because of this he is of limited use to the baseball team. The heavy hitter who does not care for other phases of the game can only function as a pinch hitter in the game of professional baseball as it was played in 1914. Outside this world, Elliott has an even less productive function. Released to a minor league team, he goes home instead, only to find that his girl has married someone else. A friend's letter to the narrator tells of Buster's fate. "The news drove him crazy—poor boy—and he went to the place where they was livin' with a baseball bat and very nearly killed 'em both." (p. 215)

If "My Roomy" presents one different type of person from Jack Keefe, "Champion" presents another, and one definitely more negative. "Champion" is a polemic on the subject of the moral nature of public figures in sports, and on the moral nature of the community which demands them. In his essay on Ring Lardner, Grant Overton juxtaposes "Champion" and the busher stories. Lardner, he contends, liked the busher, Jack Keefe. With Midge Kelly, the champion, the situation was different.

> "Champion," the story of a prizefighter who made his way by knocking down his mother and double crossing his best friends, is something else again. Mr. Lardner got awful tired of seeing a big bum translated into a popular hero. Having been a sport writer himself, he knew all about the methods by which such deification is accomplished, including the press agent and the sporting writer who is on the fight promoter's payroll. The spectacle turned his stomach once too often and "Champion," in the volume "How to Write Short Stories," was written.[24]

What Lardner does in this story is give an inside account of a champion's rise to the top. Midge is more like Buster Elliott than Jack Keefe, and he is in a profession where "bustin' things" is more appropriate. This quality Midge shares with Elliott. He is known, not as a boxer, but as a hitter. Midge is sure to be popular with the fans, according to his manager, " 'cause the people pays their money to see the fella with the wallop."[25]

It is Lardner's insistence on the public's desire to be fooled, to live in a world of illusion, that makes "Champion" interesting to us. This attitude apparently makes its first appearance in "Champion." The last lines of the story convey this sense. "The people don't want to see him knocked. He's champion." (p. 178) "Champion," like Lardner's baseball articles in this respect, is an attempt to educate the public. With regard to boxing, by 1917 when "Champion" was written, Lardner was beginning to lose faith in his ability to educate. After 1920, as we shall now see, he began to lose his faith in the ability of baseball fans to tell good baseball from bad.

III

Sport as a subject was used less and less by Lardner as his life as a professional writer had less to do with it. After he moved from Chicago to New York in the summer of 1919, he was professionally interested in sports only when he was on special assignment from one magazine or another. Though this partially accounts for Lardner's not writing more about sports, there was an element of choice involved in his eschewing sport as a subject.

As we have seen, he began to doubt that sports fans were the kind of people he could respect. They did not seem to be able to tell a genuine sporting event from a farce. What had begun in "Champion," continued in Lardner's other fight stories written during the twenties. "The Battle of the Century," published in the *Saturday Evening Post* in October 1921, resembled "Champion" in that it was another piece of "inside" reporting. Apparently a thinly disguised story of the promotion of the Dempsey-Carpentier fight of July 1921, the story turns on the possibility of gulling a large number of fight fans into thinking the very uneven fight could be a contest. The champion, named Dugan in the story, can find no real competition and, according to his manager, "ain't no matinee idol." The challenger they finally dig up, Goulet, is "a war hero and handsome . . . its making him a popular idol in America."[26] Through shrewd promotion the fight is a financial if not an artistic success, and the narrator concludes the story with this summary.

> The plain fact was this: A good big man was going to fight a little man that nobody knew if he was good or not, and the good big man was bound to win easy unless he had a sunstroke.
>
> But the little man was a war hero, which the big man certainly wasn't. And the little man was romantic, besides being one of the most likeable guys you'd want to meet—even if he did have a Greek profile and long eyelashes.
>
> So they was only one logical answer, namely that Goulet, the little man, would just about kill Dugan, the big man, maybe by a sudden display of superhuman stren'th which he had been holding back all his life for this one fight, but more likely by some more mysterious trick which no fighter had ever thought of before, because in order to think of it you had to have a French brain and eyelashes. If Goulet wasn't going to win, what did him and his manager mean by smiling so much and looking so happy? Of course the two hundred thousand fish [their guarantee] had nothing to do with it. (p. 86)

This appears to be an attack on the fan's romantic inclinations. The fans will not stick to the plain common-sense facts of the situation and, as a consequence, they are taken in by shrewd promoters.

In the late twenties and early thirties, Lardner's quarrel with the insensitivity of the fan deepened. In "The Venemous Viper of the Volga," a story rather similar to the "Battle of the Century" in its portrayal of shrewd boxing promoters, a totally incompetent boxer is by devious means promoted to the rank of challenger. His manager is even afraid to let him box anyone in public, it is so obvious he is not a fighter. But the fans, Lardner tells us, are oblivious to this. "Ivan all but took his first dive while trying to negotiate the unaccustomed ropes, but the fans overlooked his awkwardness and cheered him to the echo because he was new and bore such a striking resemblence to a fight crowd's grandpa, the ape."[27] In an article for *Collier's* in 1921, he speaks of people "with the mentality of an eight-year-old Eskimo, in other words, a great many fans. . . ."[28] This contempt even extends to the "fans" of radio programs. In his *New Yorker* column, "Over the Waves," Lardner wrote in 1933 of "as dumb a drove of oxen as the great invisible audience."[29] These quotations point to an even more unpleasant dimension of the fan's romanticism, at least to Lardner's mind. This he called hero-worship.

Lardner first and most fully developed his idea of hero-worship in his contribution to Harold Stearns's *Civilization in the United States,* "Sport and Play." Probably written in 1921, this essay attacks Americans for their attitudes toward sport and play. He argues that "it is silly—to propound that sport is of mental benefit. Its true basic function is the cultivation of bodily vigour, with a view to longevity."[30] Lardner felt that too few honored this function for two reasons. The first was that people lacked the imagination to see that they could add years to their lives by keeping fit. The second was that "we are a nation of hero-worshippers."

> . . . hero-worship is the national disease that does most to keep the grandstands full and the playgrounds empty. To hell with those four extra years of life, if they are going to cut in on our afternoon at the Polo Grounds, where, in blissful assininity, we may feast our eyes on the swarthy Champion of Swat, shouting now and then in an excess of anile idolatry, "Come on, you Babe. Come on, you Baby Doll!" (p. 461)

The baseball fan is an object of scorn here. That he worships the ballplayer had not always been the case, for the style of play, Lardner felt, had changed, and the new style was particularly conducive to hero-worship. It developed the romantic sensibility of the fan, rather than the common-sense appreciation of the combination of mechanical ability and brains that Lardner liked to see.

Babe Ruth is the symbol of this new style of play and spectator appeal and it is interesting first to note how Lardner presented him in his fiction. Ruth appears in the last series of Jack Keefe stories published in the *Saturday Evening Post* during the summer and early fall of 1919. Ruth had entered the major leagues as early as 1914 and between then and 1919 had enjoyed success as a left-handed pitcher. In 1918, according to Ruth himself, partly because the Boston Red Sox were short of players because of the war, he began to play the outfield regularly in addition to pitching, and in 1919, when the stories were published, was on the way to a new home run record.[31]

Through Jack Keefe's eyes, Ruth appears as Ty Cobb does, another excellent hitter whom he will outpitch. Jack tells Al how Ruth is to be handled. "And another thing Eddie done was to make a monkey out of Ruth and struck him out twice and they claim he is a great hitter Al but all you half to do is pitch right to him and pitch the ball anywheres but where he can get a good cut at it."[32] Unfortunately, Ruth demolishes him so thoroughly that Jack has no alibi. "Well Al I didn't get one anywheres near close for Strunk and walked him and it was Ruth's turn. The next thing I seen of the ball it was sailing into the rightfield bleachers where the blackbirds sets. And that's all I seen of the ball game." (p. 126) Of course Jack has his good days too against Ruth, though they are not often actually as good as he would like them to appear. He writes to Al.

> Well, I suppose you seen in the paper what I done to Babe Ruth yesterday and its no wonder they call him Babe Al as I had him swinging like a baby in a cradle and the only 2 times he ever fouled the ball was when Leibold run back and catched the fly ball and another time when Gandil speared that line drive offin him but he would have struck out on that ball only it was a bran new ball and I tried to curve it and it didn't break like I intend it.[33]

Thus to Jack Keefe Babe Ruth in 1919 promised no revolution in playing styles. Although he is able to hit the ball further, he presents the same problems to a pitcher that Ty Cobb does.

Nevertheless, a revolution did come, spurred, perhaps, by the desire to make the public forget the scandals surrounding the 1919 World Series. Even Ruth, who had had a career in the years before, seemed to feel the quality of play had suffered from the change in style. Lardner quotes him as saying that "I don't need brains in baseball, not against our competition anyway."[34] Lardner's interest in the style of play had always been intense, witness this ancedote his son John tells. The year in which this event occurred would be 1929 or ten years after Lardner is supposed to have lost interest in baseball.

Thirty-odd years ago, my father and mother worried and conferred when I was caught reading a novel about flaming youth called *The Plastic Age*. But my father was even more worried when he caught me reading a baseball novel called *Won In The Ninth*. He didn't take it away from me, but he warned me not to let my mind be soiled by corrupt observation of baseball procedures.[35]

In the early twenties, "baseball procedures" were changing. Lardner was representative in identifying the cause as a change in the manufacture of the baseball itself, causing it to travel further when hit. He described his attitude toward the change in a 1924 newspaper column.

I got a letter the other day asking why I didn't write about baseball no more as I usen't to write about nothing else, you might say. Well, friends, I may as well admit that I have kind of lost interest in the old game, or rather it ain't the old game which I have lost interest in it, but it is the game which the magnates have fixed up to please the public with their usual good judgment.

A couple yrs. ago a ball player named Baby Ruth that was a pitcher by birth was made into an outfielder on acct. of how he could bust them . . . and the master minds that controls baseball says to themselfs that if it is home runs that the public wants to see, why leave us give them home runs. . . .[36]

In "the game which magnates have fixed up" Buster Elliott would be a star. Lardner described in more detail what he disliked in the game in an article in the *New Yorker* in 1930 called "Br'er Rabbit Ball" and privately in a letter to John McGraw, retiring manager of the New York Giants, in 1932. "Br'er Rabbit Ball" begins with a statement of Lardner's lack of interest in baseball.

In spite of the fact that some of my friends in the baseball industry are kind enough to send me passes every spring, my average attendance at ball parks for the last three seasons has been two times per season (aside from World's Series) and I probably wouldn't have gone that often but for the alleged necessity of getting my innumerable grandchildren out in the fresh air once in a while.[37]

In this essay Lardner expresses concern for pitchers in the era of the lively ball. "I mean it kind of upsets me to see good pitchers shot to pieces by boys who, in my time, would have been ushers." (p. 61) What bothers him more is that the fellows doing the damage should not, in his opinion, even be in the league. "It gnaws at my vitals," he continues, "to see a club with three regular outfielders who are smacked on top of the head by every fly ball that miraculously stays inside the park—who ought to pay their way in, but who draw large salaries and are known as stars because of the lofty heights to which they can hoist a leather covered sphere stuffed with dynamite."[38] (p. 61) Again, Lardner's Buster Elliott seems to have returned from the madhouse to which Lardner had consigned him in 1914. Lardner closes his article by quoting Babe Ruth.

Well, the other day a great ball-player whom I won't name (he holds the home run record and gets eighty thousand dollars a year) told a friend of mine in confidence (so you must keep this under your hat) that there are at least fifteen outfielders now playing regular positions in his own league who would not have been allowed bench room the year he broke in. Myself, I just can't understand it, but Brooklyn recently played to one hundred and two thousand people in four games at Chicago, so I don't believe we'll ever get even light wines and beer. (p. 65)

Lardner explains what has been lost for him in a letter to John J. McGraw in 1932. "Baseball hasn't meant much to me since the introduction of the TNT ball" he tells McGraw. The TNT ball, he says, "robbed the game of the features I used to like best—features that gave you and Bill Carrigan and Fielder Jones and other really intelligent managers [Frank Chance, presumably, among them] a deserved advantage and smart ball players like Cobb and Jim Sheckard a chance to do things."[39] Baseball, for Lardner, no longer provided for what Donald Elder called "the triumph of merit." The best man, he felt, should be the most intelligent, not the strongest, and the new game made hash out of this ideal. Lardner remained loyal to the old game, which adequately embodied the ideals of the urban industrial society in which it originally thrived. In a sense, as Fitzgerald had said, Lardner's world "had exactly the diameter of Frank Chance's diamond." The diameter of Babe Ruth's diamond was rather different.

IV

PROFESSIONAL BASEBALL: THE BLACK SOX, JUDGE LANDIS, BABE RUTH

RADICAL CHANGES TOOK PLACE IN PROFESSIONAL BASEBALL BETWEEN September 1919 and June 1922. In its public image during these years, baseball ceased to be a sport explicitly identified with American culture at large, and began, in the values it projected, to be a sport largely associated with anti-democratic values, much like the values embraced by the literary community examined earlier. Where baseball formerly happily identified with commercial values, after 1922 it could no longer do so happily. The new values it embraced made it more interesting to the literary community, and brought it closer to what we have understood as play. It is important to understand that this change is neither particularly abrupt nor is it absolute: the values embraced before 1919 are never consciously discarded, those embraced after 1922 are not taken on to the exclusion of the former. But the new values tend to predominate after 1922, though the old ones continue to be felt.

The events of these thirty-two months and the response of professional baseball to them fall into three categories. The best known event of this period is the famous Black Sox scandal, in which eight members of the Chicago White Sox accepted money from gamblers to throw the World Series of 1919 to their opponents, the Cincinnati Reds. The first section of this chapter will consider the shape of the public response to this event. As one consequence of this scandal Judge Kenesaw Mountain Landis, Federal Judge of the circuit court in Chicago, was asked to become the Commissioner of Baseball, a position especially created for him. The second section of this chapter will recount the political events within the world of professional baseball that brought this about and analyze the nature of the political community which comprised professional baseball after Landis assumed the Commissionership. The third important event in professional baseball during these years was the emergence of Babe Ruth as a new kind of heroic baseball player. Concentrating on his public image, the final section of this chapter will be concerned with radical change in the style of play in professional baseball during these years and the values associated with it.

Before we begin this, however, it may be helpful to take a look at what baseball was thought to be like before the World Series of 1919, as a way of keeping the events that do occur in perspective. Baseball occupied a somewhat anomalous position in the public mind. On the one hand it was a sport: connected because of this with the instinct of play and for this reason commendable. It got people outdoors for recreation or inspired the young to greater heights of character-building endeavor. On the other hand, it was a commercialized amusement, deplored by those custodians of the nation's morals whose concern it attracted, as in the following quotation:

> In realizing that recreation is one of its functions the Church has opportunity for social service which will be of lasting moral benefit to the children, since heretofore "the failure to satisfy the play instinct has left the way open for commercialized amusement to establish itself for profit and with little regard to the moral quality of the recreation offered."[1]

Here baseball joins with other commercial amusements which, because they appeal to the play instinct of children, are apt to mislead them in an industrial society. The instinct of play must, according to the Church, find purer objects for its satisfaction than professional baseball.

The autobiography of Charles A. Comiskey, owner of the Chicago White Sox and one of the pioneers of the American League, was published during the summer of 1919, and in it is reflected a concern for broadcasting baseball's purity and honesty.

He speaks here of the sport as a proper profession for young men.

> Formerly sport was not regarded as a proper calling for young men. It is beginning to assume its rightful place in society. To me baseball is as honorable as any other business. It is the most honest pastime in the world. It has to be or it could not last a season out. Crookedness and baseball do not mix. It has become immeasurably more popular as the years have gone by. It will be greater yet. This year, 1919, is the greatest season of them all.
>
> The reason for the popularity of the sport is that it fits in with the temperament of the American people and because it is on the square. Everything is done in the open. What the magnates do behind the scenes the fans care nothing about.[2]

Here Comiskey makes two separate points. He simply asserts natural incompatibility of baseball and immoral behavior: they "do not mix." In addition, he says that baseball is popular because "it fits in with the temperament of the American people." For Comiskey, baseball reflects positively the character of American society as a whole.

Baseball was interesting to men other than those monetarily concerned with it. In July of 1919, far from the concerns of Charles Comiskey or of any sportswriter, Morris Cohen published a little essay entitled "Baseball," in *The Dial.* In it he considered the significance of baseball as a sport in America. He argued that "by all the canons of our modern books on comparative religion, baseball is a religion, and the only one that is not sectarian but national."[3] In this essay we have a possible response to churchmen who see baseball as a "commercial amusement" opposed to the moral potential of true play. "The essence of religious experience," Cohen continues,

> is the "redemption from the limitations of our petty individual lives and the mystic unity with a larger life of which we are a part." And is not this precisely what the baseball devotee or fanatic, if you please, experiences when he watches the team representing his city battling with another? Is there any other experience in modern life in which multitudes of men so completely and intensely lose their individual selves in the larger life which they call their city?[4]

Cohen cites a function religion shares with play here: the abandoning of the ordinary chaotic world for a transcendent, arbitrarily ordered one. This order, Cohen suggests, functions in more ways than Greek tragedy does.

The truly religious devotee has his soul directed to the final outcome; and every one of the extraordinarily rich multiplicity of movements of the baseball game acquires its significance because of its bearing on that outcome. Instead of purifying only fear and pity, baseball exercises and purifies all of our emotions, cultivating hope and courage when we are behind, resignation when we are beaten, fairness for the other team when we are ahead, charity for the umpire, and above all the zest for combat and conquest.[5]

Cohen ends his essay by proposing a system of "international baseball" as a substitute for "the more monotonous game of armaments and war." He hopes that

National rivalries and aspirations could find their intensest expression in a close international pennant race, and yet such rivalry would not be incompatible with the establishment of the true Church Universal in which all men would feel their brotherhood in the Infinite Game.[6]

Here baseball becomes a local manifestation of the "infinite game." Instead of keeping people from real play, as some churchmen suggested, Cohen feels that viewing the sport will lead people toward a notion of their common humanity in a true religion. The events of the following months were to move the public image of baseball toward Cohen's understanding of it. We will be concerned first with the World Series scandal of 1919, or; more specifically, with the shape of public response to it.

Part 1. The Shape of Scandal

One fact about the scandal is undisputed: that is that eight players on the Chicago White Sox team agreed with gamblers for a sum of money to play in such a way that the Cincinnati team would win the series.[7] Evidences of this agreement appeared even before the series began, in shifts in the betting odds. Many papers noted that "Cincinnati money was more in evidence than White Sox coin yesterday. As a result the odds which had been current around the city, were changed, bringing the Reds nearer to an even money proposition."[8] The New York *Times* suggested a reason for this shift.

The report to the effect that Eddie Cicotte has a sore arm, which was current in New York yesterday, had a material effect on the world series betting. Whereas the White Sox had ruled favorites at odds of 7 to 10 late last week, the quotations suddenly shifted, and last night the best price to be had was

5 to 6. The sudden appearance of thousands of dollars of Cincinnati money no doubt was occasioned by the rumored indisposition of Kid Gleason's star pitcher.[9]

People were generally aghast at the amount of money bet on the series, whereas the shifting odds caused only moderate surprise and were quickly accounted for. The New York *Times* reported on October 6, while the series was still on, that "the revived interest in baseball and other sports this season has also caused a great increase in betting and there has been more wagering on this series than on any baseball games for several years past."[10] Two days later the *Times* quoted "a former National League club magnate" to the effect that "I have been to every world's series since the classic was inaugurated, but I have never seen so much betting as there has been at these games." The *Times* continued, saying that "gamblers from Pittsburgh, Cleveland, New Orleans and other cities have bet heavily on the series; also, all the race horse crowd which is here at the Latonia meeting has gone in heavily for wagering on the series, and the sum of money which will change hands when the clash is over will look like another Liberty Loan."[11] *The Sporting News* editorialized on this phenomenon, treating the presence of so many gamblers as a danger to baseball. After first distinguishing between two kinds of gamblers, those who bet "as sportsmen" and the "hook nosed gentry" who bet "as a business," the editorial got down to the relation of betting and baseball.

> There is not a breath of suspicion attached to any player, or a hint that any effort in any manner was made to influence a player's performance—not a chance for that—but there is repugnance among sportsmen that such organized methods of getting "dope" for gambling purposes should be practiced.
>
> And more than that there is danger. There are no lengths to which the crop of lean-faced and long-nosed gamblers of these degenerate days will go.
>
> It's a hard problem to tackle, too, but we believe the men who are in control of the game can meet the issue, and it is put up to them. It is put up to them to keep baseball clean for Americans—for that kind of American who doesn't organize betting syndicates and make a 'business' of anything there is a chance to filch a dollar out of, however sacred it may be—to Americans.[12]

At the center of this argument lies the idea that professional baseball (and gambling too) is a sport, not a business and that to make it a business is to corrupt it, make it "unclean."

But, as Christy Mathewson put it in a newspaper column written soon after the series, "disgruntled gamblers can start disagreeable rumors."[13] This was one way of explaining the alarming rumors which began almost as the series started. Suggestions that things were not on the level appeared in the accounts of the first game, which the White Sox lost 9-1. The New York *Times* reported that "when the White Sox came out to practice before the game the band played 'I'm Forever Blowing Bubbles,' which may or may not have applied to the world's series ambition of the White Sox."[14] Christy Mathewson added this loaded sentence in his column of the same day. "The White Sox are supposed to be a great ball club, but no team to my knowledge was ever defeated by so large a score in an opening game of the world's series when each contender was trying its best."[15] When the White Sox, after losing four of the first five games, won the sixth game, I. E. Sanborn of the Chicago *Tribune* was moved to include the following in his account of the game:

> Their work in this battle silenced all the dangerous gossip that had been circulated by disgruntled gamblers, and convinced even their enemies that as a team the White Sox take off their lids to no one when it comes to gameness. . . . There was not a man on the Sox team who did not prove, in one way or another, that he was willing to break his neck to win today's game, for there was not a man of them who did not know what some folks were saying about them.[16]

Here the "disgruntled gamblers" appear again, and with them, for the first time, a hint concerning "what some folks were saying about" certain White Sox players.

"What some folks were saying about them" was that "the big gamblers had got to them." Directly after the series Charles Comiskey offered to pay anyone who had concrete evidence of fixing $10,000 or $20,000 reward.[17] The Kansas City *Star* printed a number of specific rumors, one of which was "that Eddie Cicotte was bought by a gambling bunch and that other players were in on the deal to throw games."[18] All these rumors were at first vigorously denied. Even as he offered a reward for information that would prove the players to have been crooked, Comiskey insisted that "these yarns are manufactured out of whole cloth and grow out of bitterness due to losing wagers."[19] Others were quick to explain in some detail why this was so. Christy Mathewson argued that "the rumors and mutterings about the honesty of the series are ridiculous to me. It seems that there are some irrefutable arguments against the possibility of any arrangement being made which would conflict with the natural outcome." He gave three reasons why it would be impossible to fix a game. There would have to be too many men in on the fix for it to be accomplished successfully and, in addition, it would be much too expensive to buy off as many players as seemed to be necessary. Mathewson also felt that "ball players are inherently honest. Only once or twice during long experience with the game have I seen more than one or two players who have made any peculiar looking moves, and they were very quickly detected and the banana peel placed under them. They skidded out of baseball." The act of playing baseball seems to insure this inherent honesty. Mathewson tells a story of a ball player who had made an agreement to lose a game.

> That afternoon this same player went up a bank against the scoreboard and made a circus catch never before pulled off in that orchard. He was probably sore at his manager and, in a minute of anger before the contest, had thought he would throw it, but once out in the field that old winning instinct in the heart of every big league ball player came up. He went back and made the catch, at the risk of breaking an arm or a leg or his neck.[20]

In spite of the faith of Mathewson and others in the players' "inherent honesty," rumors abounded during the fall and early winter in 1919, and they were increasingly specific. The response of baseball people and sporting journalists was to focus away from the players and on a gambling menace originating outside the structure of professional baseball and threatening its purity. Two arguments were presented. First the gamblers must go, and then baseball would be all right. Secondly, betting by the players must be discouraged. Arguments of this sort kept attention away from the fact that players might have played deliberately to lose ball games. In October *The Sporting News* editorialized that "a lot of gamblers, every one of them spotted and known in the ball parks which they frequent, have through their quarrel besmirched baseball. This bunch of parasites has been a growing nuisance. . . ."[21] The New York *Times* pointed out that "it is the professional gambling that causes the trouble in baseball, just as in any other sport. It is the professional element which had tainted the gambling in racing and boxing in the past."[22] Here a certain kind of gambler is specified as a menace. The people who make gambling their profession are the dangerous ones. The following excerpts from another *Sporting News* editorial show how the focus on gamblers helped blur the possibility that players were crooked:

There is only one way to loosen the tightening fingers of the gamblers on baseball and that way is to smash that grip with a club. . . . The ugly stories in connection with the recent World's Series are only a chapter in the history that will be written of the efforts of the gamblers to get hold of baseball. . . . There may be nothing in the World's Series scandal—there has been no evidence, we think we can say, that is positive enough to convict any one of crooked work on the playing field, but it's through no fault of the gamblers that there have not been games bought and sold.[23]

Here the very real possibility of crooked playing is at the same time admitted and passed over by the use of gamblers as scapegoats.

This same editorial made another point that baseball people felt was important. Rumors of scandal were felt to be as bad as the real thing. "We hear magnates decry and denounce because scandal stories are being peddled." The fans might lose interest in the game if there were continued rumors of crooked play. This point is made in a short story by Charles E. Van Loan, published in *The Sporting News.* Here the manager of the team meditates on the influence of professional gamblers on baseball.

When betting is eliminated, most sports remain honest and fair, but when the door is opened to the professional gambler, danger comes with him. Flannery [the manager] knew that the drawing power of his team depended upon the belief, deep rooted in the heart of every bleacher customer, that the games they paid him money to see were 'on the level.' The ethics of the case never bothered Joe, but the business angle of the case appealed to him in an instant.

Commercial motives here are apparently to be admired in baseball people but not in gamblers. We will find that "ethics" become much more prominent in public utterances of baseball people than they are here. Later in the story, when Flannery confronts the crooked players, he tells them that "if it wasn't for stirring up a dirty mess in the papers, I'd have you blacklisted and kicked out of baseball, but I'm not going to ruin the attendance this season, just for a pair of thieving rats like you."[24]

The rhetoric involved in describing the gambling menace

deserves mention. Everyone is willing to admit, as a *Sporting News* editorial does, that there may be "two or three or a half-dozen crooks" among "the thousands of clean, conscientious players who are in the game as a profession, giving it their best efforts to make it the nation's greatest sport." These, in connection with the gamblers, are referred to as "the incipient poison that was getting into its [baseball's] system."[25] John B. Sheridan develops this metaphor most vividly in his column in *The Sporting News*. "For the player who will 'throw' one game," he says, "will infect the entire fabric of baseball. . . . As one bad apple will spoil a barrel of good apples, while a barrel of good apples cannot make a bad apple good, so one crooked player will rot the entire body of Organized Baseball. . . ."[26] All these images are associated in that they imply that the removal of a few "bad apples" will restore the game to health. F. C. Lane delivers the most succinct judgment of the gambling menace. He asserts that "they have no direct influence on the game but their very presence is a contamination."[27]

It was, however, impossible to keep this point of view during the 1920 baseball season. For one thing, specific evidence of player crookedness kept turning up, and the focus shifted to the relation of gamblers and these crooked players.[28] *The Sporting News* called this "a new and unexpected problem" for the leaders of Organized Baseball. The editorial goes on to speak of the fear these men had that the general public might hear "of even one individual case of a crooked player" and as a consequence might "lose faith in the honesty of the whole game." Because of this fear, *The Sporting News* felt, attempts by these crooked players to throw games had initially been hushed up. Now that it was clear, as a result of public knowledge of player crookedness, that the public's faith, as the editorial put it, "was not and has not been shaken in the integrity of baseball," player dismissals could be announced and reasons for the dismissal announced too. The editorial went on to worry over one other thing. Earlier it had been customary, and this is precisely Comiskey's course with the Chicago White Sox after the 1919 World Series, to exonerate players whose guilt was not absolutely clear. Proof, indeed, it was admitted, was sometimes impossible to get. It would now be possible, suggested *The Sporting News,* because of the public's "faith in the judgment and intentions of those who have the game in their keeping," to dismiss players without having "evidence of the same character . . . that might be required in a court of law."[29]

Despite this, officials and writers continued to protest their, or the public's, faith in the honesty of baseball. While the owners were being urged to throw out players under suspicion of crookedness, the public was urged to continue to accept "every performer as an honest athlete until he proves himself otherwise."[30] Harvey Woodruff, sporting editor of the Chicago *Tribune,* felt that "fans, as a general rule, believe in the honesty of baseball." Reports of player crookedness were frightening because they were now undeniable but Woodruff argued that "there probably is not as much crookedness as many persons believe. So many rumors and some circumstantial evidence lead one to believe, reluctantly, that some games may have been 'thrown.' "[31] John A. Heydler, President of the National League, entoned the official viewpoint a few days after Woodruff's column appeared. In statements given out on consecutive days he said first, that "baseball is too big an institution for a few players to wreck, and the game itself will triumph in the long run, backed up by the 98 per cent honest players and the millions of fans."[32] On the next day he made himself clearer by saying that "practically all of the ball players in the profession are honest and Square in every way." In this statement he vowed to run down "to the end every rumor of crookedness from now on," and to do it "openly and above board. It's a terrible thing to allow a few players who may be wrong to cast a cloud over all the others in the game."[33]

Perhaps especially because these "2 per cent crooked" players were around, the professional gamblers continued to come under attack. "Crookedness," as a writer in the Shreveport *Journal* put it, "was creeping into baseball."

> Almost daily, one reads of a baseball scandal precipitated in the majority of cases by the complete sell out of a player to gamblers who are not sportively enough inclined to wager their money and take a gambler's chance of winning. To "cinch" bets, they reach a weak player with a few dollars, gain the latter's promise to "throw" a game, and instead of a gamble, their bets become sure things.

The focus here is on the unsportsman-like gambler, not the "weak" player. Indeed, the *Journal* writer argues that "gambling, in so far as it affects baseball, must die or the game itself will. . . . The gambling scorpion has left an indelible mark on the sport that cannot be erased and must be scotched before the mark becomes a blot."[34] Again, there is a sense only that baseball is being contaminated by forces from outside it. Professional betting creates the cheating, according to John B. Sheridan, *Sporting News* columnist. "When the money bet runs into the thousands, the gamblers are sure to try to reach and to corrupt some of the players."[35] Sheridan, in reporting a conversation he had with an owner on the wisdom of publicly dismissing ball players thought to be crooked, suggests that the crookedness grows from one ball player to another once one is crooked. The owner tells him of a man suspected of crookedness whom he retained because he did not have sufficient evidence and Sheridan asks "was it wise to permit this man, suspected of playing in the interest of gamblers, to remain in Organized Baseball, to proceed unmolested, perhaps to corrupt other players?"[36] Here the crooked ball player is imagined as the tool of the gamblers.

Writers looked to precedents set in other sports when they described what would happen to professional baseball if the gamblers got a foothold. Baseball was called the country's national game when this was discussed. In the Kansas City *Star*, an article on gambling in baseball began "is baseball, America's one national sporting institution, to go the way of horse racing, once the 'sport of kings,' boxing, formerly known as 'the manly art,' and wrestling, 'the glory of old Greece?' "[37] The St. Louis *Star* said very much the same thing, asserting that "it would be a sad blow to American sportsdom in its democratic sense of ranging from bank president to office boys if baseball, proudly acclaimed as America's national pastime, were to follow in the footsteps of horse racing and prize fighting and become primarily a vehicle for the promotion of gambling enterprises."[38] The idea is perhaps best communicated in verse form, as in the following poem by William A. Phelon, printed in *The Sporting News*:

THE "FIXER"

He laid his hand upon the foot race game.
    And in a year, or less, corruption ruled—
So, sprinting died—cast out and thrown away
    by those who had been cheated and befooled.

Wrestling next yielded to the fixers' wiles—
A manly game that once seemed clean as gold,
Became the outcast of the sporting world,
When its great battles had been bought and sold.
Horse racing proved a gorgeous plunder field—
The fixer reaped a harvest, till his play
Became so raw, so coarse, that racing took
A blow that echoes even to this day!
Boxing was "taken" by the fixer's crew—
Bout after bout, for easy money's sake,
Instead of honest tests of fighting skill,
Went into history as fake on fake!
And now—the climax of his countless crimes—
The fixer seizes the Greatest Game,
Befouls it, strives to tear its structure down,
And seeks to cloud it with eternal shame.[39]

This poem dramatizes nicely both the current sense of baseball's position in the sporting world and the power of the image of the gambler to dominate the scene. Since baseball is "the Greatest Game," it is naturally the climax of the gambler's nefarious career. Though the imagery used to describe the gambler is not consistent within the poem, it should be noted. First the gambler is a kind of leper, corrupting everything he touches. After "he laid his hand upon the foot race game . . . corruption ruled . . . sprinting died." In the second part of the poem, on wrestling, we hear only of his "wiles," a world which vaguely associates him with the commercial world, as opposed to the sporting world, as does the concluding phrase of the section, "bought and sold." In the section on horse racing, the gambler is pictured as a farmer, "reaping a harvest" from "a gorgeous plunder field." The word "crew" in the boxing section faintly suggests a gang of brigands. In the last four lines, though, a rather complicated metaphor is partially buried. The fixer becomes especially violent. The word "befouls" seems the key to the image, suggesting the phrase "befoul one's nest." The fixer, then, becomes some sort of bird, who seizes the nest (the Greatest Game), befouls it, then tries to tear it apart and, in an image which is impossible to make intelligible, "seeks to cloud it with eternal shame." This final image of the fixer is clear and clearly terrible, "the Greatest Game" is not clearly imaged at all. The gambler, a force understood to be outside the sporting world and opposed to it, is imagined to be the cause of all of the troubles of the Greatest Game.

Phelon's poem appeared about six weeks after the scandal actually broke in September 1920. Nearly a year after the 1919 World Series, Eddie Cicotte and Joe Jackson confessed that they and six other players had made an agreement with gamblers to lose the 1919 World Series. These confessions were made in the course of a grand jury investigation into the charges of corruption in baseball that had begun early in September under the direction of Judge Charles A. McDonald. We want next to see what effect this grand jury investigation had on the shape of the scandal. As Phelon's poem suggests, one effect of the revelations was to increase the intensity of feeling against professional gamblers as people whose occupation was "befouling" clean sports. On the whole, though Byron Bancroft Johnson, President of the American League, proclaimed that "there was a time the authorities of the game could have controlled the gambling situation, when it was in the spawning period," and that "today it has grown to such proportions that the hand of a stronger and sterner power has been invoked,"[40] those connected with the grand jury investigations sounded just like baseball people in their rhetoric.

Sixteen people were eventually indicted, including eleven ball players and five gamblers. Four of these ball players, Eddie Cicotte, Claude Williams, Joe Jackson and Oscar "Happy" Felsch, confessed to having taken part in the throwing of the 1919 World Series, but in summing up its findings the grand jury minimized the extent of the scandal. It made this the first of two points. "While evidence has been found that some games were thrown by players, the practice was not general," the report says, "and the leaders in organized baseball may be relied upon to keep the game above suspicion." It continues: "Considering the magnitude of the enterprise and the great number of ball players engaged, we believe a comparatively small number of the players have been dishonest. . . ." The report goes on to a statement of the jury's faith in the role of professional baseball in America.

> The jury is impressed with the fact that baseball is an index to our national genius and character. The American principle of genius and fair play must prevail, and it is all important that the game be clean, from the most humble player to the highest dignitary. Baseball enthusiasm and its hold on the public interest must ultimately stand or fall upon this count.
>
> Baseball is more than a national game; it is an American institution, having its place prominently and significantly in the life of the people. In

the deplorable absence of military training in this country, baseball and other games having 'team play' spirit offer the American youth an agency for development that would be entirely lacking were it relegated to the position to which horse racing and boxing have fallen. The national game promotes respect for proper authority, self confidence, firmmindedness, quick judgment and self control.[41]

Baseball, here, is given responsibility for the development of the characters of Americans at large. It produces the qualities that Americans should be proud of, according to the grand jury.

Baseball Magazine, the stoutest of all defenders of professional baseball and attacker of all those who dared insinuate there might be anything crooked about it, applauded this grand jury report and quoted it at some length. "Throughout its laborious and painstaking investigation the Grand Jury showed a full appreciation of the value of baseball and a praiseworthy solicitude over its continued welfare," said a January 1921 editorial. "The tone of its final report was distinctly reassuring and should go far to restore the confidence of the public in the essential honesty of the game, badly shaken as that confidence was by the recent astonishing revelations of corrupt practices."[42] *Baseball* also quoted Ban Johnson's attitude toward the grand jury proceedings. He said, "A man does not like to discover that he has a cancer; but having discovered it nothing remains but to cut it out." This was one way to choose to understand what had happened to professional baseball. *Baseball* seemed to agree, for it continued on after quoting Johnson. "An unseen cancer had eaten into the very vitals of the game. The Chicago Grand Jury exposed this cancer but it did far more. It removed the infected spot and by its heroic treatment, let it be hoped, made any recurrence of the disease improbable, if not impossible."[43] This is only one of several responses to the grand jury hearings which kept people busy in the ten months between the hearings and the trial of indicted players and gamblers of July 1921. We shall turn to these now.

Understanding the hearings through use of medical metaphors such as those used by Johnson and *Baseball* Magazine was quite common. But any investigation of the shape of the response to the grand jury investigation, and to the players' confessions in particular must begin by noting the simple shock registered by many at first hearing of it. People apparently refused to believe it. James T. Farrell recalls in brilliant understatement his own feelings as a boy when the scandal broke. He says that "charges appeared in the newspapers that White Sox players had deliberately thrown games. I recall not wanting to believe this."[44] The now-famous saying "say it ain't so, Joe," apparently actually a cry of small boys of Chicago to Joe Jackson as he left the grand jury hearings after confessing, conveys some of the shock of the event.[45] James T. Farrell tells a version of the event in which attitude is expressed slightly more succinctly; in his version the boys call to Jackson, "It ain't true, Joe."[46] They assert his innocence, rather than asking him to do so. Walter Camp, in an article on the scandal published in the *North American Review,* found the perfect description of "the attitude of the 'fans' of the country when this disclosure burst upon them" in "a story that a small boy, an embyro 'sand lot's player,' was shortly after the scandal, found out in the yard breaking his bat into kindling wood and crying silently."[47]

As the Jackson anecdote suggests, the first wave of shock was accompanied by a concern for the response of "the kids." Jackson himself was reportedly admonished by Judge McDonald for "crabbing the game of the kids."[48] *Collier's*, in its editorial on the scandal, asserted that "the real crime" was that the gamblers and crooked players "destroyed the faith of millions of kids."[49] The Chicago *Herald & Examiner* based its editorial on the Jackson anecdote, and, after recounting it, asked "but what of the kid?"

> Jackson was his hero. It is possible to believe that Jackson's example may outweigh the teachings of his parents, of his Sunday school teacher, all the other good influences in his life, just at this stage of that life. Why should the kid go straight? If the grand jury has him to deal with some day, would it be unfair to Jackson to carry the blame back to the dirty money that sold out Comiskey and the Sox fans?[50]

"Millions of boys" have been threatened and disillusioned by the disclosure of the scandal, according to these responses, but the public response in general indicated that no one was particularly worried about the situation. An article by Billy Sunday, printed in the Kansas City *Star*, among other papers, shows the connection between these two views. He begins

> The heart of the average American boy will cherish bitter enmity toward the dastardly gambling in that it corrupted his baseball idols.

> But no boy will say today he has lost faith in baseball. He is just one more factor of a public eager to repudiate the slightest suggestion of dishonesty and anxious to back up the efforts to maintain for baseball the reputation it has had for years—clean, on the square, wholesome and distinctively American.

Here along with the focus on the American boy appears the assertion that the public will not believe that the game is essentially dishonest; "it ain't true," baseball, the whole community seemed to be saying. Billy Sunday appeared to be stating his faith in the uncorruptibility of the American boy. He went on to say that even the scandal "will not rob the average boy of his interest and love for baseball. Boys go in to win. No suspicion of the crookedness ever enters their heads."[51]

This faith in incorruptibility, which had extended from the American boy to the ball players, made it very hard, even after the confessions, for people to accept the fact that there were such things as crooked players. Most people, like Billy Sunday, tended simply to assert the idea that baseball was fundamentally honest. Some people sensed the contradictions inherent in this attitude more than others. Billy Evans, who was pursuing a dual career as a major league umpire and journalist, wrote

> The 1919 World Series is a nightmare to me, now that I know it was crooked. I hate to think about it. I had such confidence in the integrity of every man connected with baseball that I didn't believe it possible. Anyone who knows baseball knows that to put over a crooked deal it is necessary that most of the team be implicated. I did not think such a thing was possible, yet it seems that the trick was turned.[52]

"Nightmare" seems a good word, because what most people did was assert that the "real" world of professional baseball was not like that.

Two reasons were advanced as a basis for this common faith in baseball's inherent honesty. The first was that it was commercially profitable to be honest. The New York *Times* best expressed this point of view in an editorial just before the confessions were made.

> In the last forty-three years big league baseball has been almost wholly free from serious charges of corruption. Prompt action at almost the very beginning of National League history removed a group of players who made a business of "throwing" games, and ever since then the average American has

been as sure of the purity of the national sport as he was of the corruption of national politics, and as proud. Baseball became a great and profitable industry largely because of that confidence. . . . This keen realization of the financial value of honesty has probably been chiefly responsible for the maintenance of a standard which is amazingly high for a sport which is first of all a business.[53]

These "amazingly high standards" have a commercial basis. Baseball is honest because it is profitable to be honest. Three days after the editorial quoted above, the *Times* suggested another reason for baseball's honesty. The article suggested that "the game itself will suffer temporarily as a result of the public's confidence being temporarily shaken, but the sport will thrive under cleaner conditions. Baseball is too big an institution," the article continued, "to be permanently crippled by the actions of a few players who betray their trust for the sake of money. That the great majority of baseball players, both major and minor leaguers, are honest, will be generally admitted." This is the standard assertion; that, though there may be a few crooks, baseball is fundamentally honest. The article goes on to suggest why. It concludes that "a sport that has honesty of endeavor as its crowning virtue has been contaminated by crooks, but in the main it will be found to have been as honest as the American public has always regarded it."[54] The phrase "honesty of endeavor" suggests the playing field rather than the counting house. The Chicago *Tribune* suggests somewhat the same thing when it editorializes that "baseball and gambling cannot live together. Baseball attracts thousands of spectators daily in the season simply because they delight in watching a contest between highly skilled athletes, with the result in doubt until the last man is out in the last inning. If the fans know before the game that one team is 'fixed' to lose there will be no interest. Baseball will die." Here the sense of the commercial basis of the game is still present, but it is muted and the focus of the passage is on the contest itself.

Perhaps it was *The Nation* whose editorial best combined these two bases for honesty and best indicated the relative importance of each. It said:

Perhaps we had not realized how much the fortunes of baseball hang upon a moral issue. The sport has grown to vast dimensions, involving an amount of money and time and emotion that hardly any other institution in the United States can equal. From the outside it looks like a material enterprise if any thing does. And yet all this investment, all these hours, all this excitement, would fade away if the public could not feel confidence in the integrity of the players. The weather may be tricky or a bat may slip or a ball may bounce in some unexpected way; now and then the best man may go stale or lose his nerve; the professional honor of the player, however, has been taken for granted. . . . There is something about the very nature of the game, played in the bright sunlight with nerves at the very edge of tension, that produces the illusion of cleanness in the characters of the performers more or less comparable to the sharp, clean movements and instinctive responses of their bodies.[55]

Here the commercial basis of professional baseball is acknowledged only to be tossed aside. The fortunes of baseball hang instead on a moral issue. The question finally is one of professional honor of the player. This suggests that the player has abandoned, in the act of throwing a game, his professional honor for commercial purposes.

The comparative honesty of the baseball community was insisted on in most newspaper responses to the revelations of the scandal. *Baseball* Magazine, as might be expected, expressed this point of view most forcefully.

The honesty of baseball has been called in question. Yes, but how seriously? A few individuals have been convicted of crooked work. The vast majority of players are honest. No one doubts their honesty. The game in the main, is honest. The gambling danger then, lies rather in the future than the present. The game has not been greatly injured, yet. It might be, of course, were the gambling evil suffered to progress. But at present baseball is still sound at the core.

Baseball Magazine also quotes Jim Dunn, President of the Cleveland Indians, as saying "don't run away with the idea that baseball is very bad. Admitting the presence of a few grafters and crooked players it is still the most nearly honest institution that I have ever come in contact with. And I have had dealings with good, average, reputable people all my life."[56] The implication here that baseball is an exceptionally honest institution, and that it may provide a standard by which other institutions may be judged, can also be seen in the following excerpt from a Chicago *Herald & Examiner* editorial entitled "Baseball and Banking":

A baseball player is hired by gamblers to throw a game. Does that mean that organized baseball is dishonest?

Well, about once a week some cashier embezzles a few thousand dollars and is caught at it. Does that mean that organized banking is dishonest?

In any big concern there are always some weaklings. Circumstances may make crooks of them. Is the concern, therefore, dishonest? Not as long as the managers are straight.[57]

Professional baseball was in certainly no worse shape than the rest of the community, and may have been in better shape, according to these views.

If this is the case, it should have some effect on the kind of action taken to remedy the situation. Most publicly agreed that no mercy was to be shown offenders. Honus Wagner was quoted as saying that "there should be quick retribution for every player who has allowed himself to be reached while the temptors of the players should be railroaded along with Cicotte and others of the White Sox who have betrayed their employers and fellow players."[58] James Isaminger in *The Sporting News* announced that "the only way baseball can save itself is for the chiefs to take vigorous action and chase every malefactor out of the game. The public is in no humor for whitewashing or timid steps. The baseball chiefs should know of this feeling. They should realize that baseball is on the defensive and they must take a most unrelenting stand to save their faces."[59] Isaminger appears to have written this in fear that the owners might not move vigorously enough. After Charles A. Comiskey, owner of the White Sox, had dismissed the players following the confessions, *The Sporting News* wrote, under a picture of the banished players, that "they have been dismissed from baseball and whether or not they go to jail their punishment will be such that other crooked players, if there be any left in the game, will hesitate to ever again throw down baseball."[60] It is clear that further crookedness is to be prevented by the severity of the punishment. As Harvey T. Woodruff says in "In the Wake of the News," "such a terrible object lesson is enough to keep clean for years to come any other players who might be tempted to similar knavery."[61]

What metaphors these men used to describe the process of getting rid of the crooked element suggest that the community was going through a transformation rather than a reformation. As we have seen, Ban Johnson regarded the crooked ball playing as a "cancer" to be "cut out." Other commentators did not use such extreme imagery. It may be that the closer one was to the structure of baseball, the shriller one's rhetoric got. Many called for a "clean-up" of baseball without developing the metaphoric possibilities further.

Others used the metaphor of "housecleaning." *The Literary Digest* quotes two other sources and uses the metaphor itself in its article on the scandal. It quotes an unnamed sporting writer to the effect that "baseball must be cleaned from cellar to garret," then the Brooklyn *Eagle* that "it is a nauseous mess that for a moment beclouds the greatest professional sport in the world." Summarizing, *The Literary Digest* announces that "the time has come for a thorough housecleaning in the baseball world."[62] The quotation from the *Eagle* suggests that the housecleaning may not be an easy one. *The Sporting News* quotes Fielder Jones as saying that "this nasty mess in baseball" must be cleaned up so thoroughly that it will "be wiped out for all time." He continues, "Baseball must be cleaned up from the bottom to the top. Any hesitation, any deviation, would be fatal to the game. We must have honest baseball or there will be no baseball at all."[63] The Chicago *Herald & Examiner* also focused momentarily on what was to be cleaned up when a letter to the editor expressed the hope that "the present investigation will cleanse baseball of its stain and make it more elevating than ever."[64] Other modifications of the cleansing metaphor were to center more on this aspect.

As Johnson's remark indicates, baseball could also be looked at as an organism to be healed. *The Sporting News* was fond of Johnson's cancer metaphor, using it at least twice more in its editorials. In the middle of the grand jury hearings it suggested that "there are still cancer spots to be reached that so far have not been touched."[65] In March of 1921, still unhappy about the lack of vigor of the owners' prosecution of suspected crooked players, *The Sporting News* said "there are plenty of signs of the sore that was eating into the major leagues. Everybody now knows what a blessing it would have been had the magnates gone right to the core of the cancer at once; events have demonstrated that bold and radical action would have been the best."[66]

Many other references likening the actions taken to the healing of an organism do not refer to cancer specifically. These begin with such phrases used to describe the reform as "how to cure it" and refer to the crooked players in terms such as "any taint of crookedness and graft" or "a possible source of contamination for others."[67] John B. Sheridan wrote that, even if the specific players that were, had not been caught, "still the body of baseball would have been infected." He concludes that "one thing we should have. It is a thorough purging."[68] Here the metaphor is somewhat more developed. The next two examples introduce the figure of the physician. Both suggest that the disease has not been very serious. Early in 1921, Jay E. House, an editorial writer on the Philadelphia *Public Ledger,* suggested that "the prescription for the infection which crept into it and corrupted fewer than twenty players was the knife. Organized Baseball could have cleansed itself; it never was necessary to call a surgeon in outside practice."[69] *Baseball* Magazine reveals a more tolerant attitude toward both baseball and the physician, but says just about the same thing in a June 1921 editorial. "True a certain amount of infection was recently discovered in the baseball body, but heroic remedies were applied and the patient is now convalescing nicely under the care of a competent physician. . . ."[70] This physician was Judge Kenesaw Mountain Landis, in November of 1920 appointed Commissioner of Baseball in a restructuring of baseball's political community. We will deal with him at length in the next section of this chapter. Here it is important to see that the metaphor is closely associated with the choice of policy. The baseball body was to be cleansed of all infectious elements.

An image related to this likened the scandal itself to a natural catastrophe which itself had something to do with the cleansing of baseball. John B. Sheridan remarked, using a somewhat confused metaphor, that "I welcome the earthquake. It will rid us of a lot of rats and barnacles without whom the ship of baseball will be ever so much better."[71] Speaking of an individual who suggested that the grand jury stop investigating the scandal, *The Sporting News* suggested "he could no more stop the house cleaning that baseball is going to get than a village ordinance could check a Mississippi flood."[72] Finally, William L. Chenery in the New York *Times* tells us that "Colonel Jacob Ruppert, joint owner of the New York American League club, is convinced that the present storm which broke over Chicago was the one thing needed to clear the baseball atmosphere and to restore the normal order."[73] It is as if the scandal itself will transform everything, allowing a return to "the normal order." The two villains who make up the cancer baseball would cut out of itself were the professional gamblers and crooked ball players. Though the image of the gambler hadn't changed since the uncovering of the scandal (he was still the root of the evil), that of the player had.

By some standards the crooked players were as bad, or worse, than the gamblers. In a strong editorial written right after the confessions, the Chicago *Tribune* blistered players and gamblers alike, accusing both of a "cringing yellowness."

> Whining, accusing, denying, pleading, the crooks and gamblers seek to crawl out of the mess into which their greed and baseness have led them. Like rats they seek to desert the ship which they fear is sinking. Like rats they seek to climb over each other to the open air, squealing and fighting as they scramble.
>
> Revealing such character in adversity there is little wonder that they were willing to betray employer, fans, and friends and defile their profession for promised dollars.[74]

An article the same day went far to match the *Tribune*'s editorial hysteria. I. E. Sanborn wrote that

> It was so cold that the loyal Sox at one time contemplated burning the uniforms of the disgraced eight, but it was decided it would be preferable to ask President Comiskey to send the baseball suits of the discarded players to some delousing station to be renovated for possible use in the future.[75]

Here the sense of disgust concerning the players' actions in throwing the games is very high. Upon reflection, *The Sporting News* printed an article which suggested that the ball players who became crooked were actually worse than the gamblers, since the ball players' "profession was wholesome, while theirs [the gamblers'] is regarded as being neither clean nor wholesome, morally or legally."[76] Worse than gamblers, according to *The Sporting News*, the crooked players were worse than any other kind of crook also. Verse was written with this as its theme. The last stanza of one printed in *The Sporting News,* "The Unpardonable Sin," states this and manages to imply that professional baseball exists on a higher plane than the other activities mentioned.

> A man may trim a lot of folks
> in trade or politics
> And still the careless human blokes
> Forget his lowly tricks
> But he who throws a baseball game
> Is doomed to everlasting shame.[77]

A long editorial written in March of 1921 when it appeared that the players and gamblers indicted by the grand jury would never come to trial provides a summary of this kind of attitude toward the crooked players.

> The White Sox players go "free," too—the sort of freedom that Judge Landis can give others of their ilk who still are permitted to wear the uniforms they have disgraced. But what sort of "freedom" is it the players are privileged to enjoy? Any self-respecting gun man or porch climber would rather be in jail than have their privilege. Decent men loathe them, ordinary sneak thieves hold them in contempt—one of them does not dare look his own hunting dog in the eye and the story is told he hasn't been able to steel himself to see that dog since his crime. They have paid the price—have paid it to their lawyers, have paid it to the world. Draw the curtain on them.[78]

Clearly, in this view there is no possible sympathy for the crooked players. But another view also held currency at the same time.

This other view held that the players were "the poor pawns" of gamblers and, while they should be punished for their weakness, they already have been punished because they are now "broken and branded for life. Their punishment is already cruelly severe."[79] Indications that the fans felt this way were evident almost immediately after the confessions. The Chicago *Herald & Examiner* printed two letters, one of which spoke of "these poor tools, whose dishonorable retirement from baseball ought to be sufficient punishment," the other of which "would reinstate the players who confessed." The writer of the latter letter, according to the *Herald & Examiner*, "blames Gandil and Risberg [two players who did not confess] for corrupting the others."[80] Even some who felt the severest penalties should be dealt out shared this image of the ball players. Paul Eaton, who argued that "this is a case where organized baseball cannot show leniency," made this comment in the same article in *The Sporting News*:

> This is not written in any spirit of satisfaction over the punishment these players have brought upon themselves. I am sorry for most of them. What is more, I believe that a majority of them would never have gone into such a scheme if they had not been pushed and dragged into it by others, and that some did not realize what they were doing. A lot of persuasion and specious reasoning was required to mislead certain players who were involved.[81]

In general, most writers and baseball officials stuck to the point of view, at least in public, that severe punishment for the players was necessary, whether they felt the players were poor pawns or the deepest villains. The fans, as indicated above, seem to have felt differently. In December of 1920 Harvey Woodruff asked readers to express themselves on the question, "Have the White Sox baseball players who threw the World's Series of 1919 been punished enough for their perfidy, or should they be brought to trial on the grand jury indictments returned and sent to prison, if possible?" Woodruff then proceeded to outline the two possible kinds of answers as he saw them.

> The argument advanced against further action is that these players have been driven out of baseball, have lost their best means of earning a living, are practically social outcasts, and therefore have suffered enough for their mistakes, or crimes, as you please.
>
> The other argument is that no punishment is too severe, and that a prison term would be an even stronger deterrent to any player who might be tempted in the future.[82]

Though the letters Woodruff printed were two to one in favor of the severest punishment, Woodruff had to report that some sixty per cent of the fans favored no further action and, as an indignant editorial in *The Sporting News* said, "a considerable number of votes, mark ye, were for giving the accused players another chance with the White Sox. Reinstate them on probation, said some; it was their first offense and they will never fall again; they have been punished enough by the publicity of the thing, said others."[83]

This was not to be, and the same editorial suggested one reason why.

> Are we going to let baseball go down in the general crash of things? It has been the pride of baseball that it was one thing in our national life that kept straight. It has viewed crookedness in other lines of sports, in politics, and in industry, from that angle. But to hold itself on the pedestal it had to depend on the public as much as on its administration and performance. Now of what use is the effort of administration to maintain the plane if the public is not responsive?[84]

This notion, that baseball is in some way superior to the country at large, took several forms during the months between the grand jury inquiry and the trial itself. Harvey Woodruff noted the following difference between baseball law and criminal law. "The eight indicated White Sox stand indicted on present evidence, so far as baseball is concerned, no matter what the result of their criminal trial. Unlike criminal law, the burden of proof must rest with the defense, rather than the prosecution, before these men could be reinstated to good standing. It would be necessary to show conclusively they were guiltless in the greatest scandal in the history of baseball."[85] The idea here is, as a *Sporting News* editorial put it "that baseball can dispose of the situation more effectively than can any court, with its admitted troubles with perjurers, bribers of witnesses, lawyers without self-respect, political influences and so on."[86] In all these cases, the community of baseball sees itself as distinct from the community at large. The implication seems to be that baseball is also better able to deal with its problems.

Verse published in *The Sporting News* by George Moriarity in October of 1920, can provide a kind of summary to the responses to the scandal between the time of the scandal and the trial of the players and gamblers. Moriarity, an American League umpire, titled his effort "Cheer up, Old Game!" The first stanza

> Come, Father Baseball, lift your weary head,
> And face with hope the sunrise glowing red,
> All is not lost because the tempters' gold
> Has snared the weak and erring from the fold;
> In spite of wayward lads who sold their fame
> Today you are by far the greatest game.

presents the erring players as tempted sheep, straying from the flock because of gamblers' money. Though the gamblers have corrupted a few, baseball is still "the greatest game." In the second stanza we come upon a metaphor of cleansing.

> Yea, lift your head, and once again be proud.
> You're gazing at a disappearing cloud.
> Sometimes the mud is splashed upon the pane
> But when wiped off, we see clear skies again.
> Each army great has traitors, yet we find
> It's honest soldiers on to victory wind.

Here the scandal is imaged as a passing rainstorm, easily gotten over and easily cleaned up after. Things must be seen in their proper relationships. The third stanza contrasts baseball with the rest of the country's institutions.

> Cheer up, Old Game, just think of politics,
> And other earthly games so full of tricks,

The profiteers, a menace to our land—
    If only they were governed by your hand
So Spartan like in seeking out the thief,
    'Twould fetch to this old troubled world relief.

Here baseball as an institution is clearly better able to deal with its problems than the country at large. The last stanza expresses confidence in the future.

Convinced that you are free from grimy stains
    And confident that honest baseball reigns,
The faithful fans have flocked in by the herds
    To see Spoke's Indians fight Robby's birds,
Condemning not the loyal with the few
    Black sheep that strayed and broke their faith with you.

O, Father Baseball, you will live because
    You cherish honesty and rout the flaws.[87]

The final couplet mentions the two main strains of the action which followed the disclosure of the scandal: the assertion of baseball's honesty and the vow to purge the sport of any "flaws." The last full stanza sees the 1920 World Series and the fans' response to it as a sign of hope that "honest baseball reigns."

After many delays, in June of 1921, the trial of the accused players and gamblers began in Chicago. From the beginning the State's Attorney's office, which had, since the grand jury hearings, undergone a changeover as a result of elections, was pessimistic about the possibility of successfully prosecuting the baseball case. It seemed that no Illinois law adequately covered the crime. In addition to this, the scandals in the Pacific Coast League had gone to the courts and the State had been unable to prosecute for the same reason. George E. Gorman, appointed by the new State's Attorney, Robert E. Crowe, to handle the cases, could not say whether or not "the prosecutions would stand under the law on which the indictments were returned."[88] Reports such as these kept appearing in various papers. Later in January of 1921, the Kansas City *Star* reported that "persistent reports from Chicago, indicating that the Cook County authorities have definitely pigeonholed the indictments on the ground that they are worthless and that if brought to trial the men would be acquitted, have reawakened interest in their cases today."[89] One of the prosecuting attorney's assistants was quoted as saying, "It would cost a lot of the people's money . . . to bring the ball players to trial, and the small chance of getting convictions would not justify the expense."[90] Finally, the State's Attorney, Robert Crowe, called all concerned into his office and, as a result, "some of them denied statements they were alleged to have made as to the worthlessness of the indictments and that the whole proceedings of the grand jury that returned the indictments was a 'joke.' "[91]

The reluctance to prosecute was matched by the reluctance of some witnesses to appear. In a long drawn-out court action in New York, Abe Attel, with the legal counsel of William J. Fallon, successfully resisted efforts to bring him to Chicago.[92] These lawyerly efforts on both sides disgusted baseball writers. *The Sporting News,* for instance, editorialized that

> The case has passed out of the hands of the baseball people—even out of the hands of Commissioner Landis—the lawyers are in the saddle and riding their own race. Let them ride it—baseball at least has one privilege left. It can choose the sort of men who can play the game, and the announcement by Landis that he has declared the 'suspended' White Sox to be on the 'ineligible' list is the answer of baseball.[93]

Baseball's response to the idea that the cases might not be prosecuted was clear from the start. After the cases were dropped temporarily in late March (apparently much of the prosecution's evidence had just been discovered to have been stolen), the New York *Times* printed a statement which is representative of baseball's viewpoint.

> The action of the Court, however, will have no effect on the standing of the players in organized baseball. President Comiskey of the White Sox on Wednesday released unconditionally all of the players involved, assuring the south side fans that they would not be allowed to wear Sox uniforms again. Previous to that Commissioner Landis placed the indicted players on his ineligible list, which will prevent their playing with any other club until they convince the Commissioner that their hands are clean.[94]

Though baseball was interested in having the cases prosecuted, the prosecution was essentially irrelevant, since baseball itself had already acted in the case of the players. The disenchantment with the courts themselves made baseball respect its own, less democratic, institutions for the dispensation of justice all the more. Disgust for the courts is reflected by the following verse, which appeared in *The Sporting News* just as the trial finally began:

A smile now wreathes the magnate's face,
His worries are all gone;
Meanwhile the baseball bribery case
Goes on and on and on.

When starting out to right a wrong,
Time has no limitations,
And so the case is passed along
To future generations.

Though evil ways men fall upon
And juries may indict 'em,
Their case goes on and on and on
And so ad infinitum.[95]

However, the trial eventually started, and the strategy of the defense became apparent immediately. Actually, it had been apparent for some months, ever since Cicotte, Jackson and Williams had repudiated the confessions they gave to the grand jury the preceding fall. The Washington *Post* gauged the situation correctly when it told its readers that "indications are that the case may develop into a battle of legal entanglements which will leave the jury deciding not whether there actually was a conspiracy for the series to be thrown, but merely whether such a conspiracy was against Illinois laws. The defense tonight was ready to submit half a dozen motions tomorrow, each of which probably will further entangle the legal aspects of the trial."[96] And this is the way it worked out. Speaking informally before the defense summarized its case at the end of the trial, Benedict Short, one of the defense lawyers, said the "State has failed to establish a criminal conspiracy and that he confidently expects acquittal."

There may have been an "agreement" entered into by the defendants to take the money offered them by scheming gamblers . . . but it has not been shown the players had any intention of defrauding the public or of bringing the game into ill repute. They believed, we contend, any arrangement they may have made was a secret one, and would, therefore, reflect no discredit on the national pastime, as it would never be disclosed.

There will be a miscarriage of justice if any of these players are convicted. All of the leading gamblers involved have managed to wiggle out. Certainly these men should not be held.[97]

This defense admits a great deal in presenting its case, and, in the end, the argument says that, though the acts of the players may not be moral, they are not illegal.

The prosecution stated its case in moral terms, in terms of which professional baseball might be proud. "This is an unusual case," Edward Prindeville's summary for the prosecution began, "as it deals with a class of men who are involved in the great national game, which all red blooded men follow." (This remark, in retrospect, does not seem an especially intelligent one, since the jurors were chosen because of their lack of knowledge of baseball.) "This game, gentlemen, has been made the subject of a crime. The public, the club owners and even the small boys playing on the sand lots have been swindled. That is why these defendants are charged with conspiracy."[98] Here Prindeville is relying more on images than arguments. Their "crime" is not legally defined, and is less prominent than "the small boy playing in the sand lots." Prindeville continued to stress this dimension of the event in the conclusion of his statement. "The crime strikes at the heart of the red blooded citizen and every kid who plays in a sand lot."[99] The jury had to choose between the defense's legal definition of the situation and the prosecution's moral definition of the situation.

Judge Hugo Friend helped them along by adopting the language of the defense in his charge. He "told the jury that the State must prove that it was the intent of the Chicago White Sox players and others charged with conspiracy, through the throwing of the 1919 World Series, to defraud the public and others and not merely to throw baseball games."[100] It took the jury a very short time to decide for acquittal.

The trial itself had not much effect on the shape of the scandal. The reaction of baseball to the acquittals is also entirely predictable. Immediately after the verdict was in, Judge Landis issued a statement barring the acquitted players from any further participation in Organized Baseball.

> Regardless of the verdict of juries, no player that throws a ball game; no player that undertakes or promises to throw a ball game; no player that sits in a conference with a bunch of crooked players and gamblers where the ways and means of throwing games are planned and discussed, and does not promptly tell his club about it, will ever play professional baseball.
>
> Of course I don't know that any of these men will apply for reinstatement, but if they do, the above are at least a few of the rules that will be enforced. Just keep in mind that, regardless of the verdict of juries, baseball is entirely competent to protect itself against crooks, both inside and outside the game.[101]

This verdict was, of course, favorably received within the baseball community. In the next issue of *The Sporting News*, Joe Vila noted that "the prompt ultimatum of the High Commissioner of Organized Baseball made the situation as clear as crystal." He further commended the Judge "for his promptness in chloroforming the 'acquittal' of the Black Sox."[102] A New York *Times* editorial captured the confusions of a moralist understanding of the jury's verdict, saying,

> The court instructed the jury, according to Chicago dispatches, that it had to determine "whether the defendants intended to defraud the public and others and not merely to throw ball games." To the lay mind this sounds very much like asking whether the defendant intended to murder his victim or merely to cut his head off, but the law is a mystery not open to the speculations of the profane.
>
> If the innocence of the ball players is established, in all this labyrinth of subtleties it is rather hard to find out just what the jury decided they didn't do.[103]

It didn't, finally, matter. Many other editorial writers evoked other juries who found the players guilty. The New York *Evening Post* editorialized immediately after the verdict.

> We must accept the acquittal as just under the court's charge to the jury. But the accused players know as well as anyone that they would have to run the gauntlet of two other trials and gain two other acquittals before their admirers could call them, as they did yesterday, "the clean Sox." Could the major leagues acquit them sufficiently to allow them to play again? If they did, could public sentiment acquit the players sufficiently to approve such action? Friends of the sport will trust that the players will never again be admitted to big league baseball. The salutary effect of the scandal upon its standards would be wholly destroyed if they were allowed to return to the game.[104]

This image of multiple juries implies levels of comparative morality. The mention of "the salutary effect of the scandal" suggests that it is because of the scandal that baseball has attained its current high level of morality. Because baseball could attain this level, the Washington *Star* could talk of "a dangerous lesion in the American moral sense" shown by the acquittal.[105] By implication, there was no longer "a dangerous lesion" in the moral sense of professional baseball. *The Sporting News*, a month after the acquittal, editorialized on the saintliness of professional baseball. "Baseball," it said, "is determined to rise to a higher moral plan in all particulars." The editorial contrasted baseball's high moral plane with the generally lower moral plane of the country at large.

> This new moral sense in baseball, when one considers the general let down in morals, is something striking. It encourages us to believe that the game is reaching the plane it should be on, approaching the standard when it can be said of the game as operated and played that it sets an example for politics, business and society generally.[106]

Thomas Rice in *The Sporting News* also made the occasion of the acquittal an occasion for chastising the community at large because it did not meet the moral standards of baseball. He speaks of letters he has received which argue for the return of the Black Sox to baseball and suggests that they "confirm the gloomy view taken of the state of the country when such a thing can be."

> . . . the spectacle of the Chicago jury which acquitted the defendants of a legal crime although three of them confessed to a moral crime, was one of the most astounding illustrations of the tendency of the times ever brought to the attention of the intelligent observer. . . . We would hate to raise a boy to be a juror who would acquit legally certain men who had besmirched the national game, and who would then dine with those men in a public restaurant, holding a jollification the while.[107]

The image of the young boy is particularly compelling in this context, because baseball had been so quick to invoke him in other circumstances. The jurors had not set a good example and this is what baseball had set out to do.

John B. Sheridan had the last word in this. He felt that

> Baseball morals should be, must be, higher than our business, legal or commercial morals. We must have a higher code of honor in sport than in business. Our baseball players must observe a stricter and higher code of morals and of honor than their fathers, brothers, cousins and friends who are merely "in business." It is right that we should preach and practice higher morals in baseball, in all sports, than are preached or, at least, practiced in business. If the morals of sport ever descend to the depths of the morals of business then, indeed, is sport gone to hell in a hand basket.[108]

Here again baseball looks down from a moral plateau onto the rest of society. But Sheridan doesn't say why. In a September issue of *The Sporting News,* in response to a letter asking for the reinstatement of the Black Sox, Sheridan attempted to explain why baseball is now too good for them. He felt it took a different kind of man to protect a society from "crooks, thieves and murderers."

For when the time comes you must have men who can steel their hearts and minds and hands to do execution upon the traitor, the spy, the despoiler of the dead, the deserter and even upon the unfortunate boy who, weary with days of marching and of fighting, sleeps upon sentry duty. When danger threatens there must be men who will sentence their own sons to death if they offend against the laws of the land. The soft-headed, soft-hearted, weak-kneed and the flabby minded won't do then. We must have men of steel.[109]

This passage describes the way a community operates in time of war: all the images are military images. This is the kind of community professional baseball had become. At war with the weaknesses around it, it demanded the sort of man Sheridan described.

In surviving the scandal, baseball had, in its own eyes, undergone a process of purification. Once a sick organism, it had regained its health and, indeed, thought of itself as healthier than the society of which it was a part. It had, in the course of the scandal, successfully articulated its role in the community at large, which was that of moral exemplar. It was, after the scandal, close to presenting itself as an alternative society to the community at large. It was more moral because it had solved the problems posed by pressure groups that too often make a democratic, capitalistic society the prey of its strongest elements. And it had disassociated itself, in so far as is possible, from the taint of commercialism.

Part 2. The Shape of Political Action

Baseball people responded concretely to the fact of the scandal in two ways. In addition to going about "cleansing" or "purifying" the game by banning players for life, they lobbied in state legislatures for the passage of bills to make bribing and bribe taking a felony and were successful in many states. But the most important concrete response to them, and to the public, at least in terms of the press coverage it got, was the impulse to change the political structure of the game. In this section of the chapter, we will see what kind of political structure baseball understood itself to have before the scandal, how it was changed, and the public image of the new structure.

The politics of professional baseball before the scandal revolved very much around the figure of the President of the American League, Byron Bancroft Johnson. Johnson was, and had been for years, feuding with the owner of the White Sox, Charles A. Comiskey and it may be that the scandal became public as a result of this feud. It is apparent, at any rate, that the purpose behind changing the structure of professional baseball was to remove Johnson from the seat of power. The scandal gave Johnson's enemies a public reason for doing this, just as the scandal was, for Johnson, a possible means of solidifying his position. But this battle only occasionally became public, and it is the political rhetoric of the change in the form of baseball's government which is of interest to us here.

In attacking Johnson, even before the scandal broke, many people expressed dissatisfaction with baseball's form of government and made suggestions for its improvement. We shall look at these first and after that turn to the argument that raged, during the grand jury investigation, over a specific proposal to reorganize baseball government called the Lasker plan. Between the proposing of the Lasker plan and the forming of the new government in January of 1921, the new government was formulated and a new head of baseball chosen, Kenesaw Mountain Landis. We will want to see what kind of government baseball people thought they were constructing and what kind of man they had asked to take the new job of Commissioner. Finally, we will look at a specific decision of the new Commissioner, to see how he acted in public. For this we will consider Landis' most famous early decision, the Babe Ruth barnstorming case.

The summer of 1919 found things moving at a placid pace in baseball politics. In Charles Axelson's "*Commy*," it was made evident that, in public, even the famous feud between Ban Johnson and Charles Comiskey was a thing of the past. Axelson wrote of Johnson and Comiskey, who together had organized the American League twenty years before:

> The partnership then formed has never been sundered and the mutual friendship was the basis for the prosperous condition of the sport today. The disagreements which have periodically come to the surface always have been more apparent than real and, regardless of personal differences which have developed, Johnson and Comiskey have stood shoulder to shoulder for the betterment of the game for almost a quarter of a century.[110]

However at midseason war broke out again. Carl Mays, Boston

Red Sox pitcher, quit the team. The Boston owner, Harry Frazee, promptly sold him to the New York Yankees, a club Mays was happy to join. President Johnson chose to suspend Mays indefinitely for jumping his Boston contract. The Yankee owners, Jacob Ruppert and Tillinghast l'Hommedieu Huston, replied by getting a court injunction which enabled them to use Mays.[111] The rhetoric which emerged from this court case characterized Johnson as an "unmolested despot" and a "czar." One of Ruppert and Huston's lawyers found that Johnson's role in professional baseball was making it unAmerican. The Chicago *Tribune* reported that the lawyer "indulged in a lengthy harangue about Americanism and the necessity of making baseball a typical American sport instead of a sort of Russian national pastime with an all-powerful czar in charge."[112]

This kind of language was used often in speaking of Ban Johnson, and it was not always meant to be derogatory. *The Sporting News,* whose editors supported Johnson to the very end of the fight and beyond, made the following statement, which seems more a statement of fact than an attack:

> Although there is hardly any doubt that there is plenty of enmity in the baseball world against Ban Johnson, President of the American League and recognized czar for the past several years of America's national sport, those against him are likely to find it a herculean task to dispose of the big chief.[113]

Later, *The Sporting News* referred to Johnson as "the supreme ruler" of the American League, "its very foundation stone."[114] A later comment in *The Sporting News* seemed to admit that Johnson had autocratic tendencies, but that these, at least at certain times, were if not good then necessary. "Ban Johnson," the article said, "may be czaristically inclined—he probably hasn't outgrown the time when an iron hand was needed to guide the American League through the shoals of its first years—but Ban has done more for the good of baseball than a thousand Frazees, Rupperts or Hustons."[115] *The Sporting News* was also able to mount an argument in Johnson's favor based on democratic principles. The base of his power lay in the fact that he controlled five of the eight club owners of the American League. The owners of the Boston and New York clubs and Charles Comiskey were those consistently opposed to his policy. Because Johnson could always rely on a majority vote, statements like the following were frequently seen in pro-Johnson publications: "The recent war was fought, so we are told, to make the world safe for democracy. Let us believe, if we can, that the object was accomplished. Those who are yelling loudest about autocracy in baseball seem now to desire rule and dominance by the minority, and as between an autocracy and an oligarchy, give us the benevolent despot every time."[116] A later statement pictured Johnson as representing the American way and hinted that the insurgents were anarchists.

> The action of the majority membership of the American League in endorsing Ban Johnson and the principles he stands for in baseball government should be answer enough to those who have howled "czar" and "autocrat." No czar rules by consent of the majority, and the principles that are at the foundation of America's life are enunicated in the action of the American League. The "autocrats" are the rule or ruin minority who refuse to recognize constituted authority and by their insurgency threaten the foundations of baseball—or would if their methods could prevail. That they will not prevail is sure while the game is in the hands of men like Ban Johnson and those who stand back of him.[117]

Baseball Magazine used much the same language to attack him. W. A. Phelon (who also contributed a regular column to *The Sporting News*) described Johnson in less than glowing terms as "more of a dictator than ever" and reported that the majority of the American League club owners had declared him "lord and high mogul forever and a day."[118] A month later the magazine printed a farcical play titled "The Recent American League Meeting," in which Johnson's power was described as "Prussian tyranny."[119] Occasionally, even in *The Sporting News,* some misgivings about Johnson's political power would appear. It is probable, one correspondent wrote, "that the days of President Johnson's autocratic reign are past, as the unrelenting opposition of the insurgents, and the possibility of defections from his at present loyal faction, will serve to keep him within safe and constitutional lines in future. And so some little good may come out of the malodorous Mays case."[120] Johnson emerges from this rhetoric as a kind of czar. While this state is in some ways respectable, both sides rely on democratic principles to make their cases.

While the base of Johnson's power was his control of a majority of club owners in the American League, he had managed to extend that power by gaining sway over the Chairman of the National Commission, baseball's ruling body, August "Garry"

Herrmann, who was also President of the Cincinnati Reds, the National League club who would oppose the White Sox in the 1919 World Series. This National Commission, popularly known as "the supreme court of baseball," was its highest ruling body. It consisted of three members: the Presidents of both major leagues, Johnson and John A. Heydler, President of the National League, and a chairman, to be chosen by the two Presidents, who, since the founding of the National Commission in 1903, had been Garry Herrmann. There is no accounting for how Johnson got control of Herrmann, but since both Johnson and Herrmann had served on the Commission since its inception and Heydler was the latest in a series of National League Presidents, it is not hard to see a possible reason why the two always voted together.

In 1919, while Johnson was facing attacks from within his own league, he was also being attacked by the National League, because of his apparent control of the National Commission. And the Commission itself was coming under attack. In *Baseball* Magazine a former National League club owner, Charles Webb Murphy, argued that "professional baseball needs a different governing body from the one it now has." Murphy called for "a new deal in the conduct of the national game . . . that the autocratic methods of the past in baseball must cease," and concluded that "a new era in the management of the game would undoubtedly be welcomed by the men in both major leagues and in all the so-called minor leagues as well."[121] Murphy did not seem to have objections to the form of the National Commission; it was clear that the basis of his argument was a dislike of the way Ban Johnson ran things. He described Johnson as a man "who plays baseball politics night and day and stops at nothing to increase his standing in the realms of Czarism. Ban feels that he must be the front of every movement in baseball, but if he were out of office there would be less friction in the councils of the great national sport." He speaks also of Johnson's "mad career of composite Czar and Kaiser."[122] In a review article in 1921, Hugh Fullerton looked at the situation more dispassionately.

Two years ago complaints against the government of the game became so strong that the National League and three members of the American League were in open rebellion. The charge that Mr. Johnson and Mr. Herrmann ruled baseball without regard to the third member of the Commission led to the situation. The National objected to Herrmann, its own man.[123]

The National League chose to try to unseat Herrmann, since they could do nothing about Johnson, and to replace him with a man who would vote with Heydler against Johnson. The first part of this plan worked well. Late in 1919, Herrmann announced that he would resign as chairman of the National Commission. The New York *Times* noted that "the recent announcement of August Herrmann to retire from the Commission within thirty days probably means that Johnson's power on the Commission is at an end. For many years, club owners of both leagues have objected to the Johnson-Herrmann combination in the baseball court for, as in the American League, Johnson has held sway also on the Commission."[124] The *Times* was too optimistic, for Herrmann's successor was to be chosen by the two league Presidents and neither was about to choose a man who would vote against him. It is not surprising that no new chairman was ever named, though trial balloons were frequently flown, throughout the next year, in the press by both sides. It became clear to Johnson's enemies that to strip him of his power, the very nature of the Commission must be changed; there was no other way to get a man sympathetic to them into the chairmanship. During the next months there was frequent discussion in the press about the limitations of the National Commission and what kind of political structure might replace it.

It was apparent to everyone that the National Commission needed reorganization. The Johnson loyalists concentrated on the fact that the minor leagues were not included within the jurisdiction of the Commission. Thus they could call for "a new system of administration that will provide a central governing body."[125] This emphasis, which soft pedaled the fact that there was no head of the National Commission, in itself a problem, continued even after the Black Sox scandal broke in the fall of 1920. In August, another editorial in *The Sporting News* hoped for "a reorganization of baseball in which authority and powers of administration and personnel of administration may be more clearly defined."

Baseball generally has had a very prosperous year, but that does not mean it can thunder and blunder along without some more systematic and united organization. Problems come up in days of prosperity just as much as in days of adversity. Who are to handle those of the future and how are they to be handled?

The answer of the majors, so says Dame Rumor, is that they should be

> handled by a central reorganized authority with powers more far reaching than ever possessed by the old National Commission—National Board dual form of government. The same Rumor says a new plan of administration will be proposed and that those who subscribe to it will form the new Organized Baseball.[126]

Again, the lack of coordination of the Commission is its weak point. An October 1920 article was able to use one of the scandals as an example of how a centralized Commission could have prevented the scandals. Damon Runyan told the story, which originally appeared in the New York *American.* "Two ball players, suspected of gambling on ball games, were thrown out of the Pacific Coast League last season. They were immediately hired by a club owner in the Southern Association who was perfectly aware of the cause of their dismissal from the Pacific Coast, and the subsequent row threatened to disrupt the Southern Association." All this would certainly have been prevented, continued Runyan, if a central governing body with power over the major and minor leagues had been in existence.[127]

The anti-Johnsonites, strangely enough, since they had been complaining of his autocratic power, were calling for a "strong man" previously unconnected with baseball, to become head of the National Commission. In January of 1920, John Heydler issued a statement saying that "I think it most important that the new head of the Commission be a man big enough and firm enough to step forward immediately whenever there is anything suspicious along those lines," those lines being rumors of baseball gambling.[128] *The Sporting News* had him saying something somewhat stronger. "The head of the Commission must be a man powerful, fearless enough to reach out after any ball player, club owner or official of baseball who by his act or association or speech brings the national game into disrepute." *The Sporting News* continued,

> This certainly points out clearly enough what the President of the National League has in mind. It undoubtedly is his determination to have a man sit at the head of the Commission who has the courage of his convictions and who has the nerve and qualifications to see that baseball is kept free from scandals that wormed their way into the game within the last two years.[129]

The next September Heydler, before the world series scandal broke, spoke of the possible good effects of the grand jury hearings. "I feel certain that the lack of discipline in the present situation has been due in a large measure to the fact that the National Commission has been operating under a handicap. . . . If any good is to come from the proceedings it should result in the establishment of a third neutral member of the Commission which then will be empowered to officiate as a baseball court or tribunal as well as a board of arbitration, and the new body will be vested with authority to iron out all differences between club owners as well as dispose of the cases submitted by players."[130] Heydler here is still thinking in terms of the old Commission: he wants the new chairman to be neutral as well as strong.

Other voices joined Heydler's in calling for a strong man. James O'Leary, Boston correspondent for *The Sporting News,* noted the irony in this. "We hear a lot about the necessity of a 'strong man' at the head of the Commission—head, shoulders and everything else, a one-man Commission. Such a man may be found, but it is safe to say that some of those who are now screeching for a change will be the first to call him an 'autocrat' and cry for another shift when he begins to perform his duties 'without fear or favor.' "[131] On the occasion of the opening of the grand jury investigation, Barney Dreyfuss was quoted as saying, "I know we could have made more progress in the last year if we had a man of force heading the Commission, but Johnson apparently does not desire that kind of man at the head of the board. . . . I think a forceful character at the head of the Commission could do a great deal for baseball."[132] Even *The Sporting News* gave its grudging approval to this way of thinking, then added a qualification.

> One might suppose, to read the comments of some baseball writers, and some club owners that all the variety of troubles that beset the national game, ordinary and extraordinary, might have been avoided had there just been a chairman of the National Commission in the past couple of years. Particularly does the comment run along the line that the gambling menace, with its attendant crooked players, might not have raised its head had Ban Johnson and John Heydler been able to agree on the third member of the body of which they compose the majority. . . .
>
> Are we to understand that a "great" man from the outside of baseball, made chairman of the National Commission, would have his hands upheld any more than the club owners are willing to uphold the hands of the two Presidents of the major leagues? If so, then let us by all means have a chairman named instanter—that is, as soon as that oft-referred to "great" man can be discovered and identified, and prevailed upon to accept the job.

> If the failure to select such a chairman is to blame for it all, then certainly it is a situation so serious that for the good of baseball his selection should be unanimous and immediate.[133]

Clearly, *The Sporting News* feels that it is certain owners and not the lack of a chairman for the National Commission that is causing all the trouble, but it also seems willing to try a strong man.

The National Commission was unable to deal with the situation facing it. The crisis of the world's series scandal was seized on by Johnson's opponents as an opportunity to render him powerless by changing the structure of baseball government. They succeeded in doing this after a rhetorical battle that itself had a great effect on the future government of the game. The first gun of this battle sounded on October 2, 1920 when four major league clubs asked the others to consider what they called "the Lasker plan of reorganization."

In this plan the new three-man Commission was to be "representatives of the public" "with absolute power over both major and minor leagues." Besides noting that the two league Presidents were ill-equipped to serve on a Commission because of bias in favor of their leagues, the formal statement also noted that the National Commission "represented really the best interests of major league owners only, and failed to directly represent, because of the nature of its component parts, the interest of three factors, one of which had an interest away beyond that of major league owners, to wit, the minor league owners and the players." The statement further accounted for the scandal with "the lack of complete supervisory control of professional baseball" and insisted that the new tribunal "have unreviewable authority over Presidents of all leagues, club members, players and every other person, act and thing connected with the national game." The mere establishment of this tribunal, the statement continued, would result in the cleansing of the game.

> The practical operation of this agreement would be the selection of three men of such unquestionable reputation and standing in fields other than baseball that the mere knowledge of their control of baseball, in itself, would insure that the public interests would first be served, and that, therefore, as a natural sequence, all existing evils would disappear.[139]

Of course the Chicago papers carried the story too and the *Herald & Examiner*, a paper friendly to Comiskey's point of view, editorialized the same day in favor of the Lasker plan. The editorial announced that "the new Commission would be the supreme court of baseball. All troubles between players, managers and the public which supports the great game would be for its final settlement. And settlement by such a Commission would be final. There would be no chance of crookedness or complaint." If the Lasker plan was to be accepted, scandals such as the one the grand jury had uncovered could not happen again.[135] This editorial minimizes the dictatorial aspects of the Lasker plan by equating the role of the new tribunal with that of the supreme court, as, in fact, the old National Commission was equated with the supreme court.

A New York *Times* editorial following the announcement of the Lasker plan noted that the tribunal would have "virtually despotic authority over all professional baseball," but felt that the sport had "outgrown the whole system under which it has been operating for the last twenty years."[136] This metaphor of "growth" forestalls a number of questions which might have been asked about the "virtually despotic authority" the Commission would assume. *The Nation*, too, was happy about the shape of the new plan. It, of course, had responded to the idea that the new Commission was to represent the public.

> At least it is not without some lesson from public matters that a scheme has been proposed to take the conduct of the sport out of the hands of owners, players, and officials and put it at the service of the people as a whole, by placing the supreme jurisdiction in a group of men not financially interested in the game and so presumably better able to pass impartially upon the ways of the institution. This promises well.[137]

The Chicago *Herald & Examiner*, clearly partisan for the Lasker plan, contributed two more editorials in favor of it while the argument over how to reorganize baseball lasted. The first one accused baseball government of complicity in covering up the scandals.

> Last year not as much was known in detail about thrown ball games as is known now, but fully as much was publicly suspected. Yet nothing was done by the leaders of baseball. They hoped to get by without trouble. They did not. They may have been lazy, or it may only have been a case of bad judgment. Either way, they are discredited. The public has lost all faith in them.[138]

As a result the public "distrusts the management" and it is up to the owners to "provide a management above suspicion of carelessness and inefficiency." The second editorial offers the example of college football as a precedent (the setting up of football conferences with commissioners at their head had helped clean up college football at the turn of the century), and then concludes by accentuating the fact that the commissioners will represent the public. "There is no other way out for professional baseball. It is not a private business. The public is the principal partner. Therefore the representatives of the public, not the representatives of private financial interests, must guide it. And these representatives must be, in character, above the creeping of suspicion."[139]

This seemed to be the heart of the defense of the Lasker plan: that baseball government had previously been incompetent to deal with its problems, primarily because it was not sufficiently divorced from selfish interests, and that therefore it was necessary to replace the governors with men who could govern impartially. The defense of William Veeck, President of the Chicago National League club, in an article for *Baseball* Magazine, followed these lines. "The recent deplorable baseball scandal," he said, "was made possible solely through lack of a competent governing body." Veeck faced the question of despotism more squarely than most commentators on the plan.

> The fear of certain prominent baseball men that such a Commission would wield despotic power is perhaps a natural one. And yet the risk of such misused power is far less than the risk whereby the gambling evil emperils the very existence of the game. . . .[140]

Here we have the argument that dictatorship, though inadvisable under ordinary conditions, is sometimes a necessary evil. Perhaps, though, the attitude of most people is best summarized by a little poem George Phair printed in his column in the Chicago *Herald & Examiner.*

> I do not know the Lasker plan.
> Nor does the ordinary fan.
> But old-time methods need a can,
> So let us have the Lasker plan.[141]

The Lasker plan is most important because the owners who opposed Johnson did more than espouse it; they took steps to put it into operation. On October 19, the New York *Times* reported

> Representatives of every National League baseball club and three American League clubs went on record tonight as favoring abrogation of the national agreement between professional leagues. Resolutions proposed a complete reorganization of baseball with the National Commission abolished and a civilian tribunal of three men not financially interested in the game in complete control. . . .
>
> A statement issued after the meeting notified the clubs not represented that they have until Nov. 1 to signify their willingness to join in the reorganization. If they have not come in by that time, the statement says, a twelve club league will be formed without them.[142]

The clubs not represented were those friendly to Ban Johnson and this move was evidently calculated to persuade them to stop supporting him. A few weeks later the "reformers" went further, formally setting up a twelve club league and offering the job of Commissioner to Judge Kenesaw Mountain Landis.[143] Only a few days later, Johnson's supporters capitulated and agreed to what was essentially the Lasker plan for reorganizing the governmental structure of baseball.

They did not, however, give up without a fight, and we now should look briefly at some of the arguments they mounted against the Lasker plan. The most prevalent negative response to the plan was that it was premature. Almost every commentator stressed this. Ban Johnson himself led the way. His formal statement on the matter of reorganization said:

> The Grand Jury has accomplished already what no other agency has been able to do, and has done it with a celerity that astonished everybody. Its work is not finished. In fact, it is my information that clues are now in hand which may lead to the disclosure of more facts than have yet been dreamed of. I believe that all attempts to reform baseball by new tribunals should be deferred until we know 'who's who' in baseball. . . .

A metaphor used later in the statement made his position quite clear. "I believe in making a thorough housecleaning," he said, "before starting to remodel the house."[144] In an article for *Baseball* Magazine he reiterated his position and developed another dimension of the argument that plans for reorganization were premature. The expediency of establishing the Commission now was questionable, he argued, because, though strong central authority was necessary in baseball government, adopting one at this particular time would have an adverse effect on a case against professional baseball pending in the supreme court. Baseball ought to wait,

Johnson contended, until that case had been decided before making any plans for reorganization.[145]

This argument had two sides. Johnson had said that he believed that all attempts to reform the game should be put off until "we know 'who's who' in baseball." The other side of this argument stated plainly that among the reformers might be found the very people who were responsible for the scandal in the first place. *The Sporting News* suggested this in saying that Johnson's "idea is, it seems, that the 'reformers' should come into court with clean hands, so to speak."[146] The following, the opening of an editorial in *The Sporting News,* is representative:

> Every time there is a disturbance in baseball those who are responsible for the ruction through their violation of the principles of sportsmanship upon which the game rests declare themselves in favor of some man "big enough" taking hold to keep them straight. The people who were the anarchists in the Mays case proposed to enlist William Howard Taft to restore the order they had violated.[147]

The editorial goes on to list the backers of the Lasker plan and indicate the ways they have contributed to the situation. All this was rather negative, however, and Johnson's supporters had to come up with some sort of alternative to the Lasker plan.

This alternative was articulated almost immediately after the Lasker plan was announced. Robert Quinn, business manager of the St. Louis Browns, a team whose owner supported Johnson, responded to the Lasker plan by saying that "he was for a new National Commission—of practical baseball men, majors and minors, to take full and complete control of baseball, but that he wouldn't any more favor an outsider bossing the job than he would think of engaging a pastry cook as chauffeur of his Buick touring car."[148] Johnson himself advanced this alternative, of course. He was quoted in the New York *Times* as being of the opinion that "the management of baseball should remain in the hands of men who have given their lives to its development," and said that "they were better qualified to cleanse the sport of its crookedness."[149] There was an elaboration of this in his *Baseball* Magazine article. There he argues that "a Commission of prominent men unfamiliar with baseball might with the best intentions in the world be induced to take radical action, which would prove highly detrimental to the intricate mechanism of Organized

Baseball." He concluded by calling for the appointment of one man to complete the existing Commission, saying that there should be a physician called in, not an idealist, bent on "a wholly untried and Utopian project."[150] It remained to John B. Sheridan to devise the most baroque of metaphors for what the Laskerites wished to do and what really ought to be done. He wrote that

> Professional baseball cannot be purified by any but professional baseball men. You can't get religion from without in. Religion must come from within out. You can't squirt a soul into a man's body any more than you can squirt a set of brains into his head.
>
> So it is with the body of baseball. It cannot be purified with injections from without. It must get its purification by grace from within. And it must be purified by baseball men who have no smirch of scandal on their records; by men whose clubs have not been touched by the breath of gambling, of game-throwing or of indiscipline.[151]

In Sheridan's metaphor, baseball becomes an organic thing, a new kind of institution which will be purified, if it is ever to be, from within.

Johnson's supporters had to do more than talk, though, they had to come up with a concrete proposal to match the Lasker plan. This would be hard, since they evidently believed that no action should be taken at all at present. Their attack was on two fronts. First Johnson proposed, not an alternative to the Lasker plan, but an alternative way of arriving at a plan for reorganization. With an eye to wooing the minor leagues to his side, he suggested that "a committee of nine members—three each from the National League, the American League, and the National Association of Professional Baseball Leagues [minor leagues]—meet and work out a plan of reorganization. This committee, it was pointed out, will give due consideration, not only to the major leagues, but to the minor leagues as well. This plan of reorganization would be reported back to the two major leagues and the National Association for approval by each respective organization."[152] This suggestion was complemented by the report of the Cook County Grand Jury, which came out in early November, and which was plainly intended to support Johnson's position.[153] The New York *Times* reported the conclusions of the Grand Jury which concern us as follows:

> That part of the report which expresses faith in the leaders of the sport as

> being capable of keeping the game above suspicion may play an important part in the fight now looming up on the baseball horizon. One faction contends that the confidence of the public can be retained only by a change in government, while the other, which happens to be the minority, is fighting such a plan. The latter faction may now offer in support of its contention the opinion of the Grand Jury that no such unusual procedure is necessary. Following this lead the public, which apparently has seen fit to favor a reorganization, is likely to accept the view of the Grand Jury.[154]

Neither of these attempts to stall things was of any use, however, for Johnson's enemies went ahead with their plans, and the other club owners were forced to go along. It is significant, as Victor Luhrs points out, that at no time did Johnson object to the fact that the establishment of a tribunal meant that baseball would come under some sort of dictatorship.[155] He only cared what sort it would be: he wanted a "physician," not an "idealist." Nevertheless, when we hear of his plans, after baseball's government has been reorganized, we hear him saying that he would "like to see its [baseball's] government so arranged that the structure will stand as a model of organized sport and business combined, a true democracy within and in harmony with the greater democracy that is America's distinction and pride."[156]

After the reorganization had been completed, it was the tendency of commentators to minimize the conflict involved in arriving at the agreement. *Baseball* Magazine, in its editorial pages, borrowed a metaphor from Johnson to describe the situation. They changed it somewhat, saying that "two doctors may agree that a patient is suffering from pneumonia and that he should be cured. They may, however, entertain an honest difference of opinion as to the proper treatment whereby he is to be cured."[157] A *Sporting News* writer, just after the scandal broke, may have hit on the metaphor that describes the political changes that took place in this reorganization of baseball. He hoped that the scandal would bring the magnates and the players together "in informal, friendly meetings," so that they might become convinced that "they are, or should be, all working for the good of baseball—an old time family gathering where hearts would be opened and cards laid on the table."[158] Here two metaphors which describe the nature of the political community rather differently sit side by side. The first, the metaphor of the card game, suggests commercially based activity, equals maneuvering to outwit one another. The second, the image of the family, suggests quite a different basis for the community: instead of equals at war, there is a hierarchy present that demands order and security. In looking at the meeting that proposed the new National Agreement and at the meeting that ratified it, we shall be looking for a shift in the understanding of the nature of the political community of professional baseball from one of these images to the other.

Comment on the New National Agreement centered almost entirely on the role Judge Landis would play in the baseball world and the powers he would receive. The New National Agreement empowered the Commissioner both to investigate any action which he judged to be "detrimental to the best interests of the national game of baseball" and, further "to determine, after investigation, what preventive, remedial or punitive action is appropriate in the premises and to take such action either against major leagues, major league clubs or individuals, as the case may be."[159] Landis himself, particularly in explaining why he took the job, emphasized not the powers he would receive, but the public trust for which he would be responsible. In announcing his acceptance of the job, Landis said:

> The opportunities for real service to baseball are limitless. It is a matter to which I have devoted nearly forty years on the question of policy. All I have to say is this: The only thing in anybody's mind now, is to make baseball what the millions of fans throughout the United States want it to be.[160]

A story he told to elaborate his reasons for accepting the job was widely reprinted.

> After the meeting Judge Landis took Clark Griffith, a personal friend, over to a window.
>
> "Grif," he said, "I'm going to tell you just why I took this job. See those kids down there on the street? See that airplane propeller on the wall? Well, that explains my acceptance.
>
> "You see that propeller was on the plane in which my son, Major Reed Landis, flew while overseas. Reed and I went to one of the world's series games at Brooklyn. Outside the gate was a bunch of little kids playing around. Reed turned to me and said: 'Dad, wouldn't it be a shame to have the game of these kids broken up? Wouldn't it be awful to take baseball away from them?' Well, while you gentlemen were talking to me, I looked up at this propeller and thought of Reed. Then I thought of his remark at Brooklyn. Grif, we've got to keep baseball on a high standard for the sake of the youngsters—that's why I took the job, because I want to help."[161]

Quite clearly, from this story, Landis' real reason for accepting the job is that he will be performing a service for the "kids" of America. In order to protect these "kids," he said later, "we have got to have a higher standard of integrity and honesty in baseball than in any other walk of life—and we are going to have it."[162]

Nevertheless, an incident occurred at the ratification of the New National Agreement which made it clear that Landis had other motives in taking the job. He did not intend to be merely a figurehead, but wanted the sweeping powers of a dictator. The Chicago *Tribune* described the event with imagery that was to become popular at this time in describing Landis.

> A suggested change of one word in the new agreement almost caused organized baseball to drift from its ethical course yesterday and crash against destructive rocks. In the crisis Judge Kenesaw Mountain Landis mounted the platform and in plain, outspoken words delivered in his own impressive style, thwarted what appeared to be mutiny among the crew and directed the baseball ship back into the course.
>
> Instantly all members returned to their posts and accepted the Judge as master. The agreement as originally drawn up was adopted. Judge Landis now is the supreme ruler of the national game. Majors and minors are to operate under his rule and every one connected with the game, from league president to bat boy, must account for his acts to the judge alone.
>
> Proposed substitution of the word "recommend" for the word "take" caused the row. In the particular clause of the agreement where the substitution was proposed, the change would have meant the removal of most of the power granted to Judge Landis in the original agreement—the power the public had been led to believe he would have.[163]

Landis was almost universally praised for this move, and it made him absolute dictator of the baseball community. This, in fact, seemed to be the conscious object of most of the owners.[164] Only *The Sporting News*, loyal to the last to Ban Johnson, professed to be somewhat startled. Their editorial, essentially favorable to Landis' act, said also that "baseball men probably hadn't realized exactly the extent to which they had submitted their affairs in the keeping of the Judge—such absolutism, in fact, is a bit new to our natures."[165] *Baseball* Magazine probably best summarized the attitude of most people toward the nature of the political change which was taking place when it summarized it in the introductory paragraphs of an article on Judge Landis.

> The early Romans loved liberty more than most peoples. And yet in mo-

ments of great peril to the State, they chose a Dictator with absolute power. For reason taught them that however good was personal freedom, nothing but strong centralized authority would answer in a sudden crisis.

Organized baseball, long noted for its loose knit confederacy, its cumbersome government and inefficient laws, found itself in October confronted with a sudden crisis. The honesty of the game, the very foundation of its existence had been brought into question. Something heroic needed to be done to meet this peril. And following the example of the early Romans, the Major League magnates chose a Dictator.[166]

Here the change in government is seen as a move from democracy, a preferable form of government, but one inadequate to meet the demands of a crisis situation, to dictatorship, in order to meet the crisis. Landis becomes the man on the white horse, the heroic figure who will save baseball.

He is certainly referred to in terms of absolute power. All the terms used to villify Ban Johnson for what was considered his misuse of power are brought out again and used to praise Landis. F. C. Lane, in the *Baseball* Magazine article quoted from above, spoke of Landis as having "the extraordinary prerogatives of a Czar, a Kaiser and a Chinese Mandarin rolled into one."[167] The Chicago *Tribune* felt that Landis had received "authority and power over baseball greater than has been held by any one else since its organization" and called him "baseball's czar extraordinary."[168] A. D. Lasker, originator of the Lasker plan, the basis for the reorganization of baseball government, was quoted as saying of Landis that "there is no limit to his authority."[169] Metaphors of royalty also cropped up. The Kansas City *Star* spoke of "the coronation of Judge K. M. Landis, the new dictator of baseball."[170] Even *The Sporting News* captioned a picture of Landis and the club owners "The Royal Family of Professional Baseball."[171] Oscar Reichow, writing in *The Sporting News,* meditating on the powers Landis would assume, suggested an alternative metaphor to that of the ship of baseball with Landis as captain and pilot; one which, while retaining the hierarchical and dictatorial aspects of the ship metaphor, made the new political community seem more natural. "Baseball," he wrote, "ought to be one happy family, working under one central head located in Chicago. Judge Landis is capable of being that supreme head.[172]

According to J. G. Taylor Spink, his biographer, Landis was known as "a trust busting Judge" and it is because of this reputation that he first became known to the baseball world. Early in 1915, the Federal League, a league which had been operating on a major league basis outside of Organized Baseball and attempting to establish itself on a par with the National and American Leagues, instituted suit against Organized Baseball. The action was brought under the Sherman Anti-trust laws and the case was to be heard in Landis' court. In this case Landis did not behave like the trust busting judge he had the reputation of being. At one point in the hearing, Landis, according to Spink, "showed his love, faith and belief in baseball when he admonished both factions saying: 'Both sides must understand that any blows at the thing called baseball would be regarded by this court as a blow to a national institution.' " This statement might be taken as removing baseball from the ranks of trusts in Landis' mind, and in fact he never did make a ruling in the case at all, and the disputants finally settled the case out of court. This decision not to decide on the case, was, in retrospect, applauded by most baseball men. Spink has this to say about Landis' wisdom.

> Though making no public statement, Landis confided to intimates that he had put off rendering a decision, feeling that sooner or later the rival factions would come together. The general thought at the time was that Landis did not give a decision in the 11 months the case was before him because he did not wish to render an adverse verdict against Organized Baseball and its system of contracts.[173]

As a trust buster whose inclination was, in this case, not to bust them, Landis made friends with the people who ran baseball with his non-decision in the Federal League case in 1915.

Opinions on him, both as a Judge and as a baseball Commissioner, were sharply divided, though the majority in both instances approved of his actions. Both sides responded to essentially the same characteristics in him. In the days when Landis was first publicly mentioned for the job as chairman of the National Commission, Oscar C. Reichow in *The Sporting News* championed his candidacy from the very beginning, speaking of him in terms like these:

> Landis should be chosen, begged to take the job, because he is fearless, honest and knows the game of baseball from A. to Z. Baseball owes him that consideration. He saved the game from going to the wall when he failed to make a decision in the case between Organized Baseball and the Federal League.

That is why he ought to be named to replace Garry Herrmann. I have always been strong for Landis because I know his knowledge of the game, know his unlimited fondness for it, know his fairness and know that he will lend dignity to it as well as do everything within his power to keep it strictly on the level and leave no stones unturned to assist in its promotion.[174]

Landis' love of baseball, fairness and dignity are the characteristics Reichow considers significant for the job he wants Landis to have. Reichow adds another in a later column, written again to champion Landis for the Commission's job.

Landis is a power, he is fearless, has the courage of his own convictions and is the type of man who insists on the other fellow toeing the mark. He has the government behind him now and that is why he exercises his authority, baseball men say. Yes, and if placed at the head of the Commission I think he would exercise it there to the satisfaction of all and for the welfare of baseball.[175]

Here we learn that Landis is courageous and is interested in wielding authority. In this respect, he is, as another writer in *The Sporting News* put it, "as rare a bird as a dodo." This writer, Cullen Cain, went on to describe the peculiar courage which Judge Landis had.

He has the savage and invincible courage necessary to break through the nets and petty strings and red tape and mess of hampering debris sure to be encountered sooner or later. He will speak right out in meeting on any subject that comes up, and the country will hear him and back him up. He will lash out savagely against the insidious issues and events that will arise. He will not be afraid to hurt a magnate's feelings or a player's standing, if to hurt means the good of the game. And so it is upon this particular attribute of the new head of baseball that I bank to win for him, and not just because he is an eminent and successful and honest and able and widely known jurist who has been called by the assembled hosts to save baseball.[176]

Here Landis is presented as an autocrat, one who cuts through the complexity of legal issues to the simple justice of each case he is involved in. Landis is pictured as a man who is always willing to sacrifice individuals to ideas, and this is his appeal here.

He is portrayed in other places in a slightly different light. *Baseball* Magazine saw him as a man who gives the impression of "a man with whom no one would ever think of taking the slightest liberty. And yet when the asperity of that face is softened by a rare smile, the strong personality of Judge Landis immediately impresses you as a vital, kindly influence. Stern the Judge may be outwardly, but few men possess more warmth or friendliness of soul."[177] A stern dispenser of justice, the Judge, we are told here, is, at heart, a being guided by sentiment. Nevertheless, the summary statement of Landis as jurist asserts that "inflexible justice, which is absolutely no respector of persons, might well sum up Judge Landis' convictions as a jurist."[178] L. G. Edwardson, in a short sketch of the Judge, continues in this same vein.

> Judge Landis is the Calif Harun-al-Raschid and Chicago is his Bagdad. He is the friend of the opprest, the scourge of the oppressors; his court reflects every phase of the life of the city and is a field of wonderful adventure. His chief stock in trade is originality. . . . There are thousands who will bear testimony that Judge Landis is in a class by himself when it comes to getting to the bottom of things.[179]

Here the image of the eastern potentate is invoked to describe Landis. He rules according to his own personal conception of justice, and, we are assured, is expert in getting to the bottom of things. William Fleming French's article on Landis, published in March of 1922, takes pains to show that Landis is the same type of person that Teddy Roosevelt was. "America," he says, "had Theodore Roosevelt and today it has Judge Kenesaw Mountain Landis." He continues by saying that "Judge Landis is fearless—as fearless as the man he worshipped, the indomitable T. R." French finally offers Landis to his readers as Roosevelt's successor.

> When T. R. left us, the red blooded youth, especially the soldiers, needed a hero to worship, a man of understanding, an intense patriot, someone absolutely fearless and square.[180]

French saw these two qualities as making up the center of Landis' personality. "Two things only are known about Judge Landis: One, that he is absolutely fearless, and the other, that he is 100 per cent square. . . . 'Twould be far easier to predict an O. Henry ending or a Big Ten Conference winner than to forecast a Landis decision. . . . But when you get over your shock and analyze the case—the judge is always right."[181] Here we see that it is the sense of Landis' rightness that make his other qualities admirable. "He does not hold court" French tells us, "for the purpose of following tradition, but to deal out justice. And the way he does it is, to put it mildly, at times a little irregular."[182]

Landis' enemies would certainly agree with this. In fact, they were given to suggesting that Landis violated the spirit of every law in the books in reaching his "irregular" decisions. And Landis had enemies left and right. In a speech in Minneapolis at an anti-Nonpartisan League meeting, Landis asserted that "their program is destructive of government. They are guilty of treason. What we need is a new definition of treason. Then we could use the side of a barn for those who would destroy our government." Following this speech, Albert P. Prescott, a member of the Nonpartisan League, in a letter to the *NonPartisan Leader,* expressed his sense of the limitations of Landis' thinking.

> Let us speculate on what Judge Landis would do if given the opportunity of wielding his judicial club in the courts of North Dakota. By his own shameless confession he would deliberately set aside, ignore, repudiate, rape the Constitution of the United States; close his eyes to the principles of justice and democracy; forget that he is an American citizen; forget that the very foundation upon which this great republic was founded is liberty; would throttle the rights of American citizens; would trample justice in the dust; would murder the principles for which our forefathers gave their lives in the American revolution, in a shameless, ruthless effort to send the men and women of North Dakota behind prison bars because they believe in the right of self-determination, believe in the right of the use of the ballot, believe in the majority ruling, believe that the voters of a state have the right to make its own state laws as the honest principles and conscience of its citizens dictate.[183]

This passage gives us another perspective on Landis' personality and character. The meaning of the qualities praised becomes clearer when they are attacked as here. It is clear that it all depends on one's faith in the rightness of Landis' ideas, whether one thinks he is just, good or not. Other commentators had grave reservations about Landis, and, for the most part, his penchant for announcing that America ought to line one group of people or another, whom he considered unpatriotic, up against the wall, is what caused people to lose faith in his sense of justice. Frank Harris' *Pearson's Magazine*, for instance, which supported pacifists in their insistence in not fighting in the first world war, objected to Landis striking out at them in the same way. *Pearson's* quotes Landis as saying

> If this government had adopted this policy at the beginning of the war and stood every one of these offenders up against the barn as Lincoln undoubtedly

intended they should be set up against the barn, there would be many thousand fewer wooden crosses in France today.

Then he adds, attacking Landis' position,

Not a word of truth in the foul effusion: Lincoln pardoned many; was entirely incapable of malice even to his enemies; allowed wider freedom of speech and criticism than any other ruler, yet this is the way he is now traduced by a judge unfit to clean his boots.[184]

Even *The Sporting News* was worried by this tendency in Landis to want to have certain elements in American society done away with. They, too, picked up this same story, and wondered aloud whether a man who wanted to do these things was fit to serve as Commissioner of baseball.

Just now, the learned and much admired Judge is being put on the grill in certain quarters because he has been breathing the sentiments of a Dinedine against everything "radical," advocating the shooting at sunrise of men whose ideas may not agree with his opinions of what should be. He has been told by certain congressmen that such remarks as credited to him are improper for a Federal Judge to utter. A judge is supposed to view things from the standpoint of the law and not advocate what might be called official anarchy.[185]

"Official anarchy" is precisely what the Judge had a chance to institute when he became Commissioner of baseball, with absolute powers. It is no wonder he was interested in taking the job. Here was a group of people who were actually eager to have someone define and explain the moral law to the multitudes.

One incident sums up the public image of Judge Landis as Commissioner better than any other at this time, because in it he reveals so many of the dimensions of his public personality. This is his encounter with Babe Ruth after the 1921 World Series. Ruth had played in the series, as the Yankees had won the American League pennant for the first time that year, and now that it was over, he wanted to lead a troupe of players in a series of exhibition games, played in different parts of the country. One impediment stood in the way. There was a rule against players on the teams participating in the World Series going on barnstorming tours after the series had been completed. Ruth decided to go on the tour without the permission of Landis and as a consequence, Landis fined him the amount of his World Series bonus and suspended him for the first 39 days of the next season. Both

Ruth's action and Landis' decision received a great deal of comment in the press and from this comment we can see what qualities were admired in Landis' public personality.

Ruth and Landis defined the situation differently in presenting their positions to the public. Ruth, who had not played in the last World Series games because of a badly infected arm, announced that he hoped to take part in some exhibition games, once his arm had healed. When it was pointed out to him that there was a rule against playing exhibition games, he shrugged this off, and reporters were quick to point out that Ruth could pay off any fine that might be imposed and still make a tidy sum from any exhibition series in which he might participate.[186] When Landis learned that Ruth and two other players who had participated in the World Series might go ahead and play in an exhibition game, he announced that

> If Ruth breaks the rule against world's series players engaging in such contests, then it will resolve itself into an issue between the player and myself. I have no interest in the matter one way or the other, but as long as it is a rule I must enforce it or see that those violating it pay the penalty. Whether or not the rule is fair or unfair to the player is not the question. It was adopted for good reasons, I presume, and was in the code before I came into baseball. My duty concerns its enforcement or penalizing for violation.[187]

Here Landis takes a rather unusual stand, for him. Usually a man who seeks to transcend the legal aspects of a case to find the moral basis of it, here Landis takes a passive stance and construes his powers as Commissioner very narrowly. He can only enforce existing laws, regardless of the justness of the particular situation.

Ruth, after playing in his first exhibition game, made two points in his defense. He felt, first of all, that the rule was wrong. "I still think I am right and Judge Landis is wrong," he said, continuing "we think that our action was for the best interests of baseball."[188] It was for the best interests of baseball because "the rule prohibiting world's series players from going on exhibition tours is unfair and it ought to be changed."[189] "I have done my duty to the American League," Ruth also said. "If it is against organized baseball law that I can't play in the 'off season' I think it is unfair, unjust and unAmerican. We will continue our tour."[190] Baseball is being "unAmerican" because it is preventing Ruth from earning an honest dollar. This is clear from the following statement:

We are going to play exhibition baseball until Nov. 1 . . . and Judge Landis is not going to stop us. I am not in any fight to see who is the greatest man in baseball. Meusel, Piercy, and I think we are doing something in the interest of baseball. I do not see why we are singled out when other big players who participated in the World Series money are permitted to play post season games. I am out to earn an honest dollar and at the same time give baseball fans an opportunity to see the big league players in action.[191]

Ruth was insistent about making an honest dollar. He told newsmen that the Yankee owners "had offered him a sum equivalent to his earnings on an exhibition tour last year if he would abide by Judge Landis's order. 'I would not take it,' he said. 'Why should I receive a gratuity for doing nothing? I do not want money I do not work for. I want to earn money, but I will not take it to abandon a principle.' "[192] Thus Ruth presented himself as a working man trying to lift himself out of an oppressive condition.

Judge Landis had other ideas about what Ruth's action meant. He saw it simply as a violation of a rule which must be punished.

"I did not write the rule against barnstorming," declared Judge Landis yesterday, in discussing Ruth's plan to play, "but I am the enforcement officer of that rule and I am a stickler for obedience in such cases. To violate the rule is to challenge the authority of the Commissioner. Disregarding the personal side entirely, this case resolves itself into the question of who is the biggest man in baseball, the Commissioner or the player who makes the most home runs. It may have to be decided whether one man is bigger than baseball."[193]

Here, though Landis presents himself as simply a policeman, enforcing the existing laws, a personal element seems to enter into his attitude. Clearly he feels that baseball is threatened because of Babe Ruth's attempt to use his popularity to avoid punishment for breaking the laws. In another newspaper, he is quoted as saying that "no law abiding player need fear that the laws of baseball will not be enforced."[194] Later, he again injected a personal note into the conflict, saying that his decision, when it came, would show "what kind of a gentleman Ruth was."[195]

Approximately five days later, Ruth abandoned his tour and the newspapers reported that he was "ready to eat as big a slice of humble pie as Judge Landis, baseball Commissioner, thinks it advisable to dish up."[196] The tour was abandoned after Ruth conferred with Yankee owner Huston.

Colonel Huston said that for the present he would concentrate his efforts on Ruth's case and the possible discipline that might be meted out to him. "I intend to see Judge Landis myself and ask him to be as lenient as possible in his sentence," the Colonel stated. "Colonel Ruppert will also intervene with the Commissioner, and between us, perhaps we can help the affair to a satisfactory ending. Right now we are tickled that Ruth has decided to abandon his tour. He admitted to me that his so-called friends had given him some bad advice, and he was perfectly willing to call off the ill-fated expedition when the real facts were presented to him. We are breathing easier, now that Ruth, Meusel, and the other Yankee players have decided to come back of their own free will.[197]

Huston had gotten Ruth to abandon the tour and had presented it in as good a light as he possibly could. Now everyone waited for Landis' decision. Since it was six weeks in coming, everybody had plenty of time to speculate on what the punishment would be and what it ought to be and what the points at issue actually were.

Those who supported the actions of "the famous prodigal son,"[198] as the New York *Times* called him, did so on two grounds. Some felt that, as the underdog, the individual rebelling against the established order, Ruth would receive sympathy. Garry Herrmann remarked that "many fans are inclined to support a ball player in any action he may take as against the officials and magnates."[199] Harvey Woodruff in his column in the Chicago *Tribune* felt that "Ruth will receive that public sympathy which always is on the side of the ball player as against centralized authority."[200] Woodruff later printed a letter that showed that at least one fan felt this way. This reader wanted to know "who represents the ball players on the National Commission which pays the 'jedge' $42,500 per year?"[201] But even in this statement there is a concern for money which is more overt in other pro-Ruth responses. Many felt that he should not be denied a chance to earn the extra money. James Isaminger remarked that "the man in the street rather sympathizes with Ruth. He reasons that a ball player has a right to pick up some extra dollars after his contract has expired."[202] Robert Edgren, too, felt that "the public is with Ruth in his claims to life, liberty, and the pursuit of happiness and kale."[203] Letters from the fans themselves indicated that some of them did indeed feel this way. One letter printed on the editorial page of the Chicago *Tribune* stated that "each and every player is in the sport to earn a living and if his ability puts him so far ahead of others as to entitle him to additional money, why should this be prevented by some such rule?"[204] Another, printed in Harvey Woodruff's "In the Wake of the News" column, was less contentious.

> What will the "squire" do to Bambino? Nothing, of course. Why should he? Hasn't the King of Swat as much right to get himself an extra job as any one else, the Judge included? The Comish would do well to abolish such a rule or transfer ball parks south of the Rio Grande. Yours for sixty homers.[205]

The New York *Times* called this position an "ethical" one. They said that

> Babe Ruth can pick up as much money—yes, and more—in a week of exhibition games as the average player earns in a complete season. After he has performed his tremendous part in the scheduled activities faithfully and well, it seems hard to find an ethical argument that would hold even a drop of water against his converting some of the prestige which he had built up unaided into ducats.[206]

"Nevertheless," the *Times* continued, "the ethical must disappear before the legal, and Judge Landis is absolutely correct in his attitude. Baseball made Ruth, and not Ruth baseball, and the slugger is just as amenable to the code of rules as the veriest tyro just up from the bushes. He will not gain friends, either among fans or elsewhere, by an attitude of defiance toward the Commissioner, who has taken upon himself the great task of ridding baseball of abuses and keeping it free of them. Baseball needs a Landis much more than it needs a Ruth."[207] This quotation is representative of many statements which supported the idea that Judge Landis must punish Ruth, even though the rule involved be an unjust one. Landis' legalist position is supported, but the more important point made in the passage is that Ruth would be punished because he has grown too big for the sport and he must be taken down a peg. Many, many commentators made this point, which was covert both in this passage and in Landis' earlier announcement. As a correspondent of *Baseball* Magazine said of Ruth, "alas! He has succumbed to pride."[208]

The Sporting News quoted Frank G. Menke, who emphasized this aspect of the situation:

> Severe punishment for Babe Ruth by Judge Landis not only might prove quite beneficial for the bursting buster, but for baseball as a whole. . . .

The bulky slugger connected with the idea some time ago that he's the great "I am" of the athletic world. The glory and praise showered upon him has affected his mental equilibrium to such an extent that he has come to believe he is bigger than the national game itself.[209]

In short, Ruth was presented as a person under the impression that he is God. Walter Trumbull, writing in the New York *Herald,* was moved by the events to speculate on the kind of person Babe Ruth was. "He is a big, good natured, game fellow and one of the greatest baseball players who ever stepped on a diamond, but he frequently has shown himself less smart off the field than on it."[210] Ruth as described here seems to be possessed of a good heart, but not so good a head. Perhaps *Baseball* Magazine came up with the most grandiose metaphor to describe what Ruth had done and their response to it. To the editors of *Baseball* Magazine, Ruth was like an elephant in a small country circus. This elephant, of course, is a big attraction, "but let that well-fed elephant get the idea that he is too big for the show. Let him pull up a few tent pegs and smash a wagon or two and go lumbering off across lots seeking new diversions, and he ceases to be a star feature and becomes, all at once, a menace." The editors go on to suggest to Landis, that he "deal with Ruth not as a malefactor, but as a huge, overgrown, unwieldy attraction, who somehow loses proper perspective." They conclude by saying that "the public knows that their elephant is intractable and unruly; that he has faults and occasionally makes the life of the ringmaster something of a burden. But, after all, such is the nature of elephants."[211] Here Ruth again is pictured as a mindless animal who occasionally causes trouble.

Ruth's action meant to most people that more discipline was necessary in the baseball world. That Ruth could ignore the constituted authority indicated a breakdown of discipline. This tendency was what many people felt Judge Landis had been hired to combat. In the same editorial in which they developed their elephant metaphor, the editors of *Baseball* Magazine wrote

Judge Landis was chosen to govern baseball with a strong hand. That was for the security of discipline. But in a larger sense, if we understand the situation, he was chosen to preserve the needs of the community as the true National game.[212]

The Sporting News, in an editorial, was concerned with the injury done Landis' authority by Ruth's action. "It is not Landis personally, though the Judge deserves something more in the way of respect from a young upstart in baseball, but it is the authority he represents, the authority which exemplifies the organization which lifts an unknown young man off the lots and changes him from a twenty-dollar-a-week nobody to a near-hero in the public eye, that is insulted."[213] That the players should be more loyal to the game is the point of appeals like this. Their behavior should take the nature of the community more into consideration. Individual needs should be bent that the community may survive. It, after all, has made the individual what he is.

On December 5, 1921, Landis delivered his decision in the Ruth case. The newspapers the next day reported the event on page one. Most of them quoted Landis' statement in full.

> These players were members of the New York American League team, a contestant for the world's championship in 1921. Immediately after that series, willfully and defiantly, they violated the rule forbidding their participation in exhibition games during the year in which that world's championship was decided.
>
> This rule was enacted in 1911, only after repeated acts of disconduct by world's series participants made its adoption imperative for the protection of the good of the game. This rule was known to all players, and particularly to these men, upon one of whom a fine was imposed in 1916 for its violation.
>
> This situation involves not merely rule violation, but rather a mutinous defiance intended by the players to present the question: Which is bigger—baseball or any individual in baseball?
>
> There will be an order forfeiting their shares in the world's series funds and suspending them until May 20, 1922, on which date and within ten days thereafter they will be eligible to apply for reinstatement.
>
> Signed, Kenesaw M. Landis, Commissioner.[214]

Here the crucial paragraph is the third paragraph, in which Landis specifies the offense Ruth, Meusel and Piercy have committed. It is not that they have violated a rule, but that they have made their violation a "mutinous defiance": they have suggested by the violation that they are more important than baseball itself. Thus Landis finally levied the penalty, not for breaking the rules, but because the players' behavior insinuated the game could be manipulated. He had concurred with the writers who had found Ruth's conduct a menace to the national game.

Adverse reaction to Landis' decision was more substantial than the early support that Ruth had received, but it was still a distinct minority. The dominant concern in this reaction was still economic. For instance, when the inquiring reporter of the Chicago *Tribune* asked five people at random "what do you think of Judge Landis' decision in the Babe Ruth case?" only one of the five people asked felt it was "too severe." He said, "I am not in favor of the decision. Ruth earned his money during the world's series, and I don't think they have the right to take that from him."[215] Clark Griffith, President of the Washington Senators, made the most complete statement of the negative reaction to Landis' decision in an interview with Paul W. Eaton of *The Sporting News*. Griffith begins by saying that "the trouble with the Landis decision is that it punishes the New York Club, the other American League clubs and their patrons, the baseball public, more than it does Ruth. It will probably affect the American League race very materially, and anything that interferes with the result of the pennant race to punish an individual should be most carefully avoided."[216] Griffith then went into great detail on the financial cost to everyone that would result from Ruth's suspension. His assurances that the pennant race would be affected and that the fans would resent missing Ruth were not presented in such graphic detail. Clearly, those who resented the suspension were still thinking primarily of the money that would be lost.

Those who supported the decision were still thinking of discipline. The four people who told the inquiring reporter that they supported Landis' decision all cited discipline as something that could not be neglected. One said "the public now knows that just because a man is a wonderful star he cannot do anything he wants to do and get away with it." Another said, "he had the nerve to violate the rules of the game and try to bluff Judge Landis, but he was called."[217] Francis C. Richter put the case for Judge Landis' decision very forcefully in his column in *The Sporting News*.

> Jove has answered the lightning-defying Ajax. . . . Judge Landis announced the punishment meted out to Yankee players Ruth, Meusel and Piercy, for their needless, stubborn and defiant violation, for purely financial reasons, of the wholesome and necessary World's Series rule against participation of World's Series players in post-series exhibition games.[218]

This statement is radical only in the sense that it claims that the law Ruth violated was "wholesome and necessary." No one else suggested that it was anything but an unfair rule in Ruth's case. The interesting thing about Richter's statement is its attribution of commercial motives to Ruth and the others for breaking the rule. This is why the players are being punished. For financial reasons, they defy the rules of baseball. Another telling reaction was that of the editorial staff of the Chicago *Tribune.* They suggested

His retirement for the first eight weeks of the coming season is merely justice to the hundreds of his associates in the game. Without discipline the whole structure of organized baseball would collapse. It was a slackening of discipline with attendant disintegration of loyalty to employer, teammates, and fans which produced the Black Sox.[219]

Here we find discipline as the key to the new structure of the game. It will prevent a repetition of the Black Sox scandal, already a thing of the past. On the part of the player, the most important quality will be that of loyalty. Without loyalty, the game might become again what it was in the days of the Black Sox.

Through all this deliberation, writers were still trying to come to terms with the personality of Babe Ruth. *The Sporting News* described him in this way in an attempt to uncover the sources of his defiance of baseball authority.

But who sowed seeds of rebellion in the breast of Babe Ruth? Wasn't it done when the Yankees and the Red Sox magnates cooked up the deal to make him a member of the New York team? Wasn't it done when one of the Colonels at least encouraged the idea in Ruth's boyish noodle that he could do as he pleased, that the little shrimp of a manager didn't count for anything, and that maybe even Ruth himself would be manager some day?

Babe Ruth, as we know him, is a big spoiled boy, but the adulation of the fans has not spoiled him; he has taken that as simply and innocently as a child of six speaking a piece. The spoiling that has been done by the men who should have taught the Bambino that discipline is the first lesson of the ball player, but who on the contrary gave the Babe the idea he didn't have to obey any rules.[220]

Here again Ruth is pictured as a child, one who has been spoiled by the club owners but not the fans. To them he has responded "simply and innocently." *Baseball* Magazine, in considering the effect of the suspension on Ruth, pictured him as a child.

There is no face in baseball that is quicker to express all the human emotions than the face of Ruth. The Babe has often been described as a big boy who never grew up. That description is a little far-fetched, but the Babe can no more hide his feelings than the little boy caught stealing green apples.

> It is the face of a well-dressed kid, with a nice bow tie and clean collar, watching several of his intimate acquaintances on hands and knees shooting marbles . . . an irate Mamma has told him he must stay dressed up, sit on his own stoop and not play with those little ragamuffins.[221]

Ruth is pictured as a little child, but Landis is not his Mamma. He is, however occasionally pictured as Ruth's father, particularly after he announces Ruth's punishment.

> "It hurts me worse than it does you, my boy," has been the salve to the old man's conscience for generations whenever he felt it was necessary to apply the old razor strap to the erring offspring. . . . The thought that the old gentleman thus conveys is literally true in the case of "Dad" Landis and Babe Ruth.[222]

The sense of authority Landis wants to convey is well imaged in this old saw. The Chicago *Tribune* printed a letter which made the same identification. The letter said, "Judge Landis must feel like the father who after punishing his son said it hurt him more than the son." Even in articles that hoped for mercy from Landis and called on him to raise the suspension, sometimes embraced the idea of Landis as a father and the players as his children. The New York *Times* imagined Ruth and Meusel applying for pardon and the Judge saying, "Bless you, my children."[223]

Thus by the end of the Ruth case, the Judge was imaged as the father-leader of a hierarchical society based on discipline. The players in the society were expected to be loyal, hearty chaps, grateful to the game for allowing them to rise to the top of their profession. The commerical world was definitely left behind. Landis' decision went directly against the commercial interests of the game, he had created a society opposed to the commercial society in which it existed and dedicated to transcending the commercial interests it found in itself.

Part 3. The Style of Play

It is safe to say that no single baseball player, before or since, made such an impact on the game of baseball as Babe Ruth did during the years 1919, 1920, and 1921. During these three years offensive play in baseball was radically altered, with some effect on defensive styles as well, and Babe Ruth was a major force, though by no means the only one, in accomplishing this change. Our interest here will be to see how the public press understood the change that occurred, and to underline the shift in values that accompanied it. This may be easiest accomplished by focusing on the representatives of the two styles of play: Ty Cobb, as we have seen, regarded by Ring Lardner in 1915 as the greatest of offensive players, and, of course, Ruth himself.

We can turn to the sporting journals, *The Sporting News* and *Baseball* Magazine, for some initial impressions as to what the significant differences in style are. Ernest Lanigan offers the following opinion in *The Sporting News*:

> It is saying nothing new to say that all the world loves a hitter and that Ruth has a legion of admirers. So has Cobb. It doesn't seem to me that the Babe has taken any constituents away from the Peach and I don't think he is likely to for some time to come.
>
> Tyrus Raymond may not be as speedy as he once was, undoubtedly isn't, but there is one thing in which he hasn't slipped, and that is in his brain play. He can still outthink any past-timer in the profession and the dear public prefers brain to brawn.[224]

Here the contrast is simply drawn: brains vs. brawn. *Baseball* Magazine was more analytic about the situation, and more interested in viewing it as a part of the evolution of baseball. Consequently, they focused on the change that was occurring. In the July issue of 1921, F. C. Lane considered the phenomenon of "The Home Run Epidemic" as follows:

> Baseball, year by year, had grown more scientific, more a thing of accepted rules, of set routine. This slow evolution of the sport displayed itself in batting, in the form of the bunt, the place hit and various other manifestations of skill. . . . Ty Cobb, perhaps, had as much to do with this batting evolution as any one man. Ty taught the world the supreme value of place hitting. . . . Under his magnetic leadership, batters tried for safe hits rather than long hits. . . . And because Ty was supreme among batsmen, no one even dared to question the merit of the system he employed.
>
> We do not intend to question it even now. To our mind, Ty is the greatest batter who ever lived. He was the supreme exponent of scientific hitting and science has a surpassing value in baseball just as in everything else. But every so often some superman appears who follows no set rule, who flouts accepted theories, who throws science itself to the winds and hews out a rough path for himself by the sheer weight of his own unequalled talents. Such a man is Babe Ruth in the batting world and his influence on the whole

system of batting employed in the Major Leagues is clear as crystal.[225]

The metaphor of evolution controls *Baseball* Magazine's understanding of the situation. Cobb represents the ordinary course of baseball evolution; Ruth represents those cataclysmic events that occasionally occur in the course of geological time. "Science" takes its place beside brains on the one hand: Ruth's activity is pictured as anti-scientific, he "throws science itself to the winds and hews out a rough path for himself by the sheer weight of his own unequalled talents." It is natural talent rather than scientifically acquired skill that enables him to accomplish what he has.

The following quotation from a 1908 edition of *Baseball* Magazine will serve to give us a sense of how baseball, Cobb's game, was regarded previous to 1920:

> Baseball is not merely an interesting and scientific game. It is the game which calls into play the dominant traits of Americans in its demand for agility, quick thinking, and a tremendous exertion and excitement. It is peculiarly popular and fascinating to us because it means a contest, a personal hand-to-hand encounter. Baseball has all the elements of the personal battle which makes every red-blooded American itch to see a glove contest.[226]

Baseball here is scientific and it is a contest, with "quick thinking" as a necessity. Ty Cobb's autobiography provides a passage that seconds and deepens this view of what baseball is.

> When I played ball, I didn't play for fun. To me it wasn't parchesi played under parchesi rules. Baseball is a red-blooded sport for red-blooded men. It's no pink tea, and mollycoddles had better stay out. It's a contest and everything that implies, a struggle for supremacy, a survival of the fittest. Every man in the game, from the minors on up, is not only fighting against the other side, but he's trying to hold his own job against those on his own bench who'd love to take it away.[227]

Baseball for Cobb is a mirror of the commercial world, a competitive jungle in which each has an equal chance to survive. This is the system which results in the best coming to the top.

We are concerned immediately with the scientific aspect of the old game, and the most necessary quality to have in order to be successful at it was thought to be "brains." As the Chicago White Sox approached the 1919 World Series, one thing that was celebrated about them was their braininess. Charles Comiskey was quoted, just before the series started, as saying:

I have merely spoken of the physical aspects of baseball, the trade ability of the men to perform. I have always believed that brains count as much as base hits—sometimes even more. I think I have a fast-thinking team, and the Lord knows I don't like a slow thinker. If we can't outthink and out-play Cincinnati we will lose, and I'll have no kick coming if it happens. But it won't.[228]

Tris Speaker was of the same opinion. He saw the White Sox as a "brainy lot of players who will make few, if any, mistakes."[229] The brainiest player of them all was apparently Eddie Cicotte. A poem by Grantland Rice appeared in *The Sporting News* in September of 1919, in celebration of Cicotte, in which he was praised for "A noodle that was packed with brains."[230] Later commentators considered Cicotte's case with some confusion. Billy Evans, commenting on Cicotte's banning for taking a bribe, considered some of the things he had contributed to baseball.

In the passing of Eddie Cicotte, baseball loses one of the craftiest pitchers that ever stepped on the rubber. Not only was Cicotte a master workman, who carefully studied his batters, but to him goes the credit or discredit of originating a lot of the new fangled deliveries that, for a time, had baseball agog.[231]

F. C. Lane, in an article on the men who had turned crooked, was also rather taken aback that Cicotte had sold out. He had always considered Cicotte an honest and intelligent man. Cicotte had, according to Lane, "a keen business mind."[232] Others began to wonder about the crafty workmen with keen business minds who had taken bribes to lose games. George Phair's "Breakfast Food" column in the Chicago *Herald & Examiner* began to contain sayings like "clever ball playing is much desired in a world's series, but it has been demonstrated that a ball player can be too clever."[233] Clearly, other qualities might be more important than braininess in baseball.

What was the offensive style of these brainy ball players? How did they approach the task of making runs? The various techniques they used are for the most part described in articles which bemoan the disappearance of various lost arts; bunting, base stealing, and so forth. We can get an idea of how the game was played from these articles. In his 1961 autobiography, Ty Cobb described the old game as the "game of hit-and-run, the steal and double steal, the bunt in all its wonderful varieties, the squeeze, the ball hit to the opposite field and the ball punched through openings in the defense for a single." These are all techniques of offense as "an act of skill rather than simple power," which, according to Cobb, contained "fine, scientific nuances."[234]

These "fine, scientific nuances," according to many writers, were becoming fewer and fewer. James Isaminger reported the following in *The Sporting News* in June of 1921:

> In the slam-bang style of ball played at Shibe park during the series with the Western teams only in the games with Cleveland has any real baseball cropped out. The champions of the world won a game from the Macks Wednesday through a display of inside stuff that reminded one of baseball of previous years. In this game Tris Speaker opened the eleventh inning with a single and stole second. A land sacrifice put him on third and then a sacrifice fly let him tab the winning run home. With whole series being played here without a sacrifice hit, two such hits in a row startled the fans. . . .
>
> Baseball used to be a contest of wit, skill and courage, but this season it has degenerated into a mere tug of brute force.[235]

"Force" has replaced "real baseball" according to Isaminger, and real baseball involves skills of more subtlety and value than simple brute force. *Baseball* Magazine ran an article in July of 1920, with the peculiar title "Gladstone J. Graney, a Player Who Bats With His Brains" in which it made this statement about batting.

> The fan's idea of batting is primitive. In his mind batting consists of hitting the ball. . . . There are other ways of showing batting ability besides the crude and obvious one of leaning on the ball. And he comes to the conclusion, in time, that these finer, more subtle methods are even more effective than lambasting the horsehide to the far corners of the lot.[236]

John B. Sheridan is a great deal more specific in describing what goes into this more scientific offensive play when he describes Ty Cobb and what he likes about him as an offensive player.

> Like most lovers of baseball I like to see long hitting, but I got more than enough of it in 1920 and 1921. Much as I like to see hitting I find, upon examination, that I love base running better than I love slugging. I know this: Cobb's work on base always intrigued me more than not only his actual hitting but more than his really wonderful work at the bat, more than the amazing manner in which he worked pitchers and out-guessed them, outgeneralled them, made them do what he wanted them to do, or did what they tried to keep him from doing. It always has been a delight to watch Cobb hit, more of a delight to watch him work the pitchers, but greatest delight of all to watch him run bases.[237]

These were the things at which the scientific batter was accomplished, but there now seemed no reason for them. They were taken up, one by one, by *Baseball* Magazine, and analyzed to see why they were dying out. A May 1921 article described "the Bunt as 'Scientific' Batting." The article began by quoting Rogers Hornsby to the effect that "a good batter is a slugger, for slugging is natural batting."[238] The article went on to point out that while Hornsby's statement might be perfectly true, there were not many batters around who had the batting skills to afford to be natural. For them, brains were more important than brawn. "Bunting is skill and practice and self control all in one and where did you ever find a slugger with self-control?" The article concludes that "Bunting is the last word in batting skill because it marks the furthest departure from slugging, which is natural batting. Bunting is scientific batting because it is science which takes us from the beaten path of the merely natural."[239] Two articles in *The Sporting News* announced that the bunt was now out of fashion as an offensive weapon. The first, published somewhat before the *Baseball* Magazine article, told of the lack of good bunters active in the major leagues, then spoke of the excellent bunters of the past.

> The bat became an instrument rather than a bludgeon in the hands of such men as Keeler and Browne, an instrument of which they, more than others, realized the possibilities. I don't suppose any other two batters harassed a pitcher more than did Thomas and Huggins. You couldn't play in on these men because they'd shift and hit them past you.

Ty Cobb is the chief of the modern players mentioned, but with the comment that "he is such a hard, versatile batter that we do not think of him particularly as a bunter."[240] The second article in *The Sporting News* simply announced that "the sacrifice bunt" is "no longer . . . considered an important part of the training of a ball club."[241] It is no longer, the writer concludes, considered an effective play.

Baseball Magazine next considered the fate of the stolen base in the new era. In two articles, "Is Base Stealing Dead?" in the June 1921 issue, and "The Sensational Decline of the Stolen Base" in the May 1922 issue, F. C. Lane argued that "As Major League baseball develops, base stealing declines. Increased efficiency in pitching and fielding automatically crowds out the stolen base."

In spite of this evolutionary trend, Lane felt that base stealing "should be encouraged so far as possible for it offers greater scope for individual initiative and varied attack than batting."[242] The gradual extinction of the stolen base was, to Lane, a product of the gradual evolution of baseball. The play is to be "sacrificed on the altar of mechanical perfection." "In this painstaking effort, to make of baseball an exact science, the managers, however, have overlooked one very important point. . . . Beyond and above all rules and regulations must be placed human daring and ingenuity."[243] John B. Sheridan suggested another reason for the decline of the stolen base in his column.

> Yet is seems to be a pity that play at many of the fine points of the game, notably at base running, must be permitted, for the present at least, to decay while the slugger is making his brief strut upon the stage. With slugging at its apogee base running, naturally, declines. There cannot be any sort of sense in breaking a leg to steal a base when the giant at the bat is liable to make a four-base hit and chase the runner home ahead of him.[244]

Sheridan here suggests that it is the fad for slugging that has caused the decline in the stolen base. He also suggests that the slugging style is a fad, and that it will not last long, which, as we will see momentarily, is an opinion shared by many.

F. C. Lane joins John B. Sheridan in both these opinions in a 1922 essay, "What's Wrong With the Three Base Hit?" This offensive weapon is also not as much used as in the past. Lane calls the three base hit "about the nicest hit of all, a line drive of terrific force, well placed between the outfielders, combined with nice judgment and speed of foot in base running." He is quite clear as to why this kind of hit is no longer in use.

> When Babe Ruth ceases to be the dominant influence in modern day batting and the bubble of home run popularity is exploded, then the three bagger along with other suppressed baseball features will come into its own. And the return of the triple to its normal position will probably mark a saner, less feverish, better balanced contest than has been possible under the brilliant but irrational domination of the home run.[245]

For all these men who espoused "scientific baseball," the popularity of the home run seemed an "irrational domination." Before Ruth, apparently, no one thought of actually swinging the bat with the purpose of hitting the ball out of the park. The only home run of the 1919 World Series was shrugged off by the pitcher whose pitch was hit as "an accident that is likely to happen to any pitcher."[246] Babe Ruth is thought of as "a freak, an unknown quantity."[247] Thomas Rice, in speaking in defense of other aspects of baseball than the home run, said in *The Sporting News* that "there is a thrill in the home run, but there is an equal, and more protracted, thrill in the steady fielding behind a good pitcher that is saving him hits. A home run is a spectacular incident."[248] W. A. Phelon summarizes the view of the situation held by these men in the following manner:

> The Home Run has been set up and established as the idol of baseball. The brilliant, snappy game of old; the intricate methods of defense; the fast subtleties of the attack; the stories of magnificent pitching—all these have been subordinated to the God of Slug. . . .[249]

Thus we find that Ring Lardner's estimate of the condition of professional baseball concurs with that of other experts in the field.

The man these men all idolized for his ability on the field was Ty Cobb. A great deal of verse was composed to celebrate his offensive capabilities, one of the better stanzas of which came from the pen of one Howard T. Walden, II (with apologies to Kipling).

> He is Cobb! Cobb! Cobb!
> When they want a run he's always on the job;
> Either hits or sacrifices,
> When the game is at its crisis
> There's one man you can count on—Tyrus Cobb![250]

Cobb is a money ball player, and he treats his profession seriously. One sports writer lectured major league players by holding Cobb up as an example to them.

> Ty Cobb is a living example of the value of brains and courage in baseball, but more than half the big league players fail to realize why he is so great a star. It is because he outgames and outthinks the average player. With Cobb, baseball is a serious business in which he has earned a large salary for many years and he considers it worthy of his attention.[251]

The chief value of brains is in the learning of new things, day after day, and this is what Ty Cobb was popularly believed to be able to do. Grantland Rice describes him early in his career.

> . . . Ty Cobb . . . the greatest offensive player of the game . . . Cobb saw that he was only a fair base-runner, so he went forth alone, to slide and practice by himself, hours at a time. He kept plugging at this art until he knew that he could handle himself around the bases.
>
> Shortly afterward he began to find that he was weak against left-handers. . . . At morning practice he got all the left-handers he could find to pitch to him. And if there were none available from the team he would pick up corner lotters or camp followers, and set them to work, blazing away at his weakness.[252]

The man who complied the highest batting average of all time was admired by his contemporaries not for his talent but for the hard work he put in acquiring the various skills of scientific play.

Cobb himself had this advice to give to others who wanted to follow in his footsteps: "Scheme, scheme and keep scheming."[253] This seems definitive. Cobb is the representative of the kind of crafty braininess that Lardner liked to see in ball players. Cobb himself seemed to worry about the lack of this characteristic in other players. He was quoted as saying in 1919,

> Although the game has grown faster and more scientific in my mind, there has not been the individual improvement you might look for. The boys of today play scientific baseball because it has been taught them, not because they dope it out themselves. They don't study the game like young doctors or young lawyers or engineers study their professions. After a game these kids are through with baseball until the next day. They don't take their chosen profession seriously enough. My success was due entirely to self-application and study.[254]

There is no role for a community to play here; the statement seems totally individualistic.

Part of the reason for the change from this point of view lies in the public figure of Babe Ruth. The public response to Ruth was overwhelming. Paul Gallico insists that it was unique. "In times past," he reflects, "we had been interested in and excited by prize fighters and baseball players, but we had never been so individually involved or joined in such a mass out pouring of affection as we did for Ruth."[255] It is hard now to imagine what it must have been like to watch Ruth perform. Gallico says that "the home runs amassed by Babe Ruth, and in particular his great record of 60 in 154 games, was the sheerest pioneering and exploration into the uncharted wildernesses of sport. There was something almost of the supernatural and the miraculous connected with him too."[256] Ruth in 1920, hit 54 home runs which record, as the *Times* noted in awed tones, was "a greater number than any entire team in either major league compiled."[257] Then in 1921, Ruth broke his own record again, hitting 59 home runs. Feats of this sort prompted players to make remarks like the following by Chet Thomas, a Cleveland catcher:

> I am not so certain now that Ruth is human. At least he does things you couldn't expect a mere batter with two arms and legs to do. I can't explain him. Nobody can explain him. He just exists.[258]

Clearly Ruth's impact on the game was awesome.

His home run hitting was thought to inaugurate a new style of play, but opinions on the importance and permanence of this style of play varied immensely, beginning with the attitude that he was a freak, held by many exponents of scientific baseball. John McGraw exemplifies this point of view in his explanation of how he had his pitchers pitch to him during the World Series. The central fact to remember was that "Ruth . . . is a ball player of the freak type that is likely to bust up a game at any moment."[259] Sam Hall of the Chicago *Herald & Examiner*, in an article on Ruth during the 1920 season, spoke of Ruth's desire to raise his batting average in the following terms:

> Yes, the Babe longs for a big batting average now more than he wished home runs. Not that he won't sock them if he gets a chance. But he's going to quit swinging with all his might at every pull, cease hitting with two and three balls and no strikes on him and bat like a regular hitter and not a freak—for a high average, and the good of the team.[260]

This essentially friendly paragraph contains many assumptions that are not friendly to Ruth's style of hitting.

Slugging as a batting style was generally looked down upon and those hitters who were merely sluggers were ordinarily depreciated. John B. Sheridan's remarks on Frank "Home Run" Baker show how a slugger was looked down upon. In speaking of the New York Yankee team in general, he dismissed Baker with the following words: "What has Frank Baker ever been? A slugger. That's all. Never could field or run bases. Could hit."[261] There was also considerable resentment of the fact that sluggers always got all the glory, though they weren't always the best players. The following verse by George Phair, called "Science," speaks of the same sort of man as Sheridan's version of Frank Baker:

> His feet were like a pair of scows,
> But he could hit.
> There was a void behind his brows,
> But he could hit.
> He fielded like a four-wheel hack—
> He never seemed to get the knack—
> And yet he always got the jack,
> For he could hit.[262]

Like Baker, this player can do nothing but slug. He can't run, he can't think, he can't field. In short, he can't play scientific ball.

Some people felt that Babe Ruth fell into this mold. Jack Doyle, Pacific coast scout for Chicago Cubs, voiced their attitude clearly in a statement for *The Sporting News* in which he criticized "bum ball players like Babe Ruth." He maintained that "baseball is an athletic science that requires nine men working in harmony to produce teams of championship caliber" and that Ruth disturbed that harmony. He went on to assess Ruth's talents.

> Ruth is a third-rate outfielder. As a base runner, he is in a class by himself. I'm not complimenting him, either.
>
> As a batter, Ruth is an accident. He never plays inside baseball at the plate. He goes up trying to take a swing on every strike, a style that would cause any other player to be benched. He either knocks home runs or strikes out. Any man who strikes out as many times as Ruth did last year can never be classed as a great hitter. . . .[263]

These are the classic criticisms of an old style baseball man. One of the ways Ruth was defended was to argue that he had, really, all the talents of the old ball players in addition to his special talent for hitting home runs. William B. Hanna's reply to Jack Doyle was structured in this way. He argued that Doyle was all wrong in his assessment of Ruth's talent, that Ruth "is a good base runner and a smart and bold one. Match him against such wide-awake citizens as Cobb and Speaker, and he holds his own."[264] *The Independent,* in a feature article on Ruth, denied the "freak" theory to the extent that they attributed to him the same background of study and preparation for his calling as was usual in reviewing the case of Ty Cobb. In speaking of his home runs, the article reads, "he does not do this by any accident or by reason alone of some special gift of nature. He does it very largely by art, the result of long and careful study and practice."[265]

The revolution in baseball styles Ruth brought on led to the domination of sheer strength and speed over brain power on the baseball diamond. Baseball had become largely a "simple, primal game"—as John B. Sheridan called it—"hit it a mile and run until you are put out."[266] F. C. Lane sums up the shape of the revolution in an interview with Ruth.

> It may be a triumph of brawn over brain. It may even suggest the dominance of mere brute strength over intelligence. It may show a preference for the cave men over the finished artist . . . rest assured it's a fact. Babe Ruth is the uncrowned king of the diamond, the master figure of the baseball season, the big noise in the biggest game on earth.[267]

To most writers, it might be true that Ruth could be a brainy ball player, but it wasn't relevant to the situation at hand.

Lane and *Baseball* Magazine could never make up their minds as to precisely how Babe Ruth fit into their scheme of the evolution of baseball style. The title of Lane's July 1921 article, "The Home Run Epidemic" suggests that they might see it, as many saw the baseball scandals, as a momentary illness of which baseball could eventually be cured. The substance of this article, though, suggests something else. In it Lane calls Babe Ruth a "superman."

> Now and then a superman arises in the domain of politics or finance or science and plays havoc with kingdoms or fortunes or established theories. Such a superman in a narrow, but none the less obvious field, is Babe Ruth. The big bat wielder might not make much impression in the fine arts or classical literature. . . . Nevertheless, in his own particular field, Babe is a true superman.[268]

The article goes on to present Ty Cobb as the prototype of hitting style followed by most players before Ruth came on the scene and then concludes that "the home run was a victim on the altar of improved methods and general development just as we saw last month that the stolen base was a victim. Batting flourished as never before. But the home run became more and more of a rarity."[269] Lane refers then to the statistics of the last two years, which show a 156% increase in the number of home runs hit. He declines to accept two possible causes for this: a restriction on the use of certain popular pitching deliveries such as the spit ball, and the introduction of a "livelier" ball into the game. The rise of home runs is due rather to a change in batting styles. Ruth, according to Lane, "has taken the place-hit [Cobb's specialty] from its pedestal as the batter's universal model and has set up in its place the home run."[270]

. . . can there be any doubt that Babe Ruth was the man who showed the world the value of the circuit clout? . . .

A leader in any field speedily obtains a following. . . . We do not mean to contend that the chop hitter who chokes up on his bat and punches out an occasional feeble single is hitting any more home runs than he ever did. But we do say and the records bear us out, that almost every batter who has it in him to wallop the ball, is swinging from the handle of the bat with every ounce of strength that nature placed in his wrists and shoulders.

. . . Babe has not only smashed all records, he has smashed the long-accepted system of things in the batting world and on the ruins of that system he has erected another system or rather lack of system whose dominant quality is brute force. . . .

Does Babe's advent into baseball herald a new era of development? We cannot say. For a time, at least, the old order of things is in complete eclipse. . . . We are in for a true carnival of true home run hitting which evidently has not yet reached its peak.[271]

Here, certainly, Lane is prevented from understanding Ruth's batting style as a new model for players only by his understanding that baseball is to evolve in scientific ways. He cannot understand Ruth's style as a scientific improvement on that of Cobb. Consequently, when he speaks of Ruth's system, he qualifies this, saying, "or rather lack of system whose dominant quality is brute force." Later Lane pulled back even from the position he had taken in this article. A year later he spoke of the "home run epidemic" again, and this time he was a little truer to the implications of the word "epidemic."

Just how long the epidemic of home runs will endure is not clear. That it is a permanent trend in baseball is hardly probable. More than likely it is a transient demonstration of brute force *a la* Babe Ruth, which will pass with the passing of the great hitter who invoked it.[272]

There are some indications that others saw Ruth's hitting as the basis of a new offensive style. *The Sporting News* suggested

That many batsmen are following Ruth's system is an open fact, and it will be only a short time when big league teams will encourage one or more in the line-up who possess the ability, which means giant strength and a keen eye, to try for homers every time. . . . There is no reason why George Ruth should have a monopoly or divine right to absorb all the glory and home runs derived from this style of hitting. If club owners and managers come to the conclusion that this mode of attack is effective and really a valuable asset in winning games, then there will be a general training in that direction and in a few seasons the woods will be full of more or less Babe Ruth style of swatters.[273]

Of course the crucial point here is the question of whether this style, if pursued, would contribute more to winning games than the style presently followed. In 1919 and 1920, this was a real question. In 1919, when Ruth had begun to hit home runs, the Boston Red Sox, on which team he played, had changed from a championship team to a second division team and, in fact, the owner of the Red Sox announced that he had traded Ruth to the Yankees because he was a disruptive force on the team.[274] In 1920, despite the fact that Ruth hit 54 home runs and drew monstrous crowds everywhere the Yankees played, the team still finished third in the pennant race. Since the Yankees won pennants in 1921, 1922, and 1923, the argument might be said to have completed its first phase by then.

Numerous short statements that spotted the Chicago newspapers tended to indicate that Ruth's home runs were magnificent, but that other than that they seemed quite meaningless. George Phair, for instance, printed the statement that "Babe Ruth's forty-seventh home run was a noble achievement, but it didn't mean anything." Presumably he meant that it had no effect on the outcome of the game, and therefore had no significance. In the same column appears a poem on the relation of home runs to winning.

A home run hit may cause a grin
  Upon the rooter's face,
But four-base wallops do not win
  A pennant race.[275]

The problem of the relation of slugging to winning was discussed by Christy Mathewson in his New York *Times* column. Mathewson wrote

There seems to be a great demand these days for star sluggers. There is no doubt of their value to a team, and the man who can rap out a home run frequently furnishes the fans with the most spectacular play in the game.

> But from the point of view of winning contests, my experience has taught me to prefer an aggregation of good base runners to a batting order of hard hitters. I believe the former can do more to help a pitcher win games. . . .
>
> When a man is pitching for a team of base runners he knows that every time a player with a reputation for stealing bases gets on the bags, with half a chance, he is pretty sure to score a run. Then, too, when a club has a name for possessing base runners it helps to get the opposing pitcher's goat. He has to devote a lot of his energy to watching the men on the circuit and has less to devote to his pitching.
>
> On the other hand, a hard hitter who is slow on the bases is only a hindrance.[276]

This puts the case against the slugger well. A little more than a year later, Hugh Fullerton spoke of a heated argument among ball players and managers "concerning the value of long distance hitting and its effect upon baseball teams and baseball leagues." Fullerton feels that whether or not one argues for or against slugging depends entirely on whether or not one is on the same team with a slugger or not. He points out that the fans love slugging but suggest that "there may be a sharp reaction of sentiment when the fans discover that long distance hitting is not winning baseball, but even that is doubtful." He concludes that "the real baseball is the middle ground, the judicious mixture of real baseball and slugging, with the manager deciding when and how the batters shall hit."[277] This essay suggests that things are beginning to change. Fullerton has moved the "reality" of baseball more toward the position of the slugger, even though his language ("the judicious mixture of real baseball and slugging" is a phrase that still refuses to admit slugging to the realm of "real" baseball) is inadequate for this task. Slugging is becoming a legitimate tactic, even in the minds of the defenders of the old style.

We should speak finally of some of the personal qualities of Babe Ruth as a public person. They too suggest a shift in values from a commercially oriented individualistic community to one hierarchically structured. Where Cobb had a rural, protestant background, Ruth was a Catholic from Baltimore. Though in his public image, Ruth was first presented in the same way Cobb had been, soon it was found that his personality was vastly different and a new way of presenting him had to be found. One thing Cobb and Ruth had in common and that Ruth was proud of all through his life was the fact that he had risen to the top of his profession from lowly origins. He made this point very early in his autobiography.

Too many youngsters today believe that the age of opportunity has passed. They think it ended about the time people stopped reading Horatio Alger.

There are more opportunities today than when I was a boy. And all these opportunities are open to every type of American. The greatest thing about this country is the wonderful fact that it doesn't matter which side of the tracks you were born on, or whether you're homeless or homely or friendless. The chance is still there. I know.[278]

Ruth's is the story of the American boy, but, we shall see, even though his story fits the American success story mold in this respect, that, like the story of his successor as Yankee, Joe DiMaggio, his image reveals a different set of values than those usually found in the American success story in all other respects.

Early articles worried rather ineffectually about Ruth as a capitalist. *Current Opinion* remarked that "in winter he manages his cigar factory in Boston and is possessed of shrewd business sense as well as a sense of humor."[279] The article fails to give any examples of his "shrewd business sense" other than the existence of the cigar factory and goes on to describe his sense of humor. Much the same thing happens in an article in *The Independent*:

His outlook on life is kindly but shrewd. He has various sources of income in addition to his salary and he is not spending all he makes. When baseball finishes with him Ruth will have money. Being a likeable young man he will also have friends who are willing to do real services for him. He will probably have his choice of a dozen good business offers.

And he may turn them all down and decide to go it alone in some field of big business. If he does, his admirers will expect him to make good. They say he has business sense.[280]

Again, his business sense is not documented. It seems only a pious hope in the minds of his interviewers.

Instead of a burgeoning capitalist, Ruth was pictured in various images that relate the natural, the instinctual, and the childlike. He was pictured as a natural force, as a man who plays the game for love, not money, as a kind of foolish or simple person, and finally as a child. "Brute force" is a familiar term with which to describe Ruth by now, but it seemingly applies to his character as well as his physical strength. The following quotation appeared in the New York *Times* on the occasion of Ruth's fiftieth home run of the 1920 season:

> Baseball has never before developed a figure of such tremendously picturesque proportions as this home-run king of the Yankees. With no weapon but a primitive club, he has manipulated it in a manner which would make the famed clubbers of the Stone Age look like experts in battledore and shuttlecock. Ruth has hit almost as many home runs as Heinz has pickles. In fact, he is a greater pickler than the world has before known.[281]

Here Ruth stands for the primitive, the brutish and the natural. His bat is a club, not an instrument. Furthermore, as we learn from the following quotation, his knowledge of baseball is instinctive rather than learned. The occasion is speculation on whether Ruth will be asked to manage the Yankees.

> Unquestionably Cobb is a great player and in his day better than either Speaker or Sisler, but as an attraction, Ruth has him beaten. And the Babe knows baseball. Knows it and plays it instinctively. He may make errors—they all do—but you'll rarely, if ever, hear of him pulling a bad play.[282]

That a player of this sort should be the largest gate attraction in the game was something new. The greatest players before had always had great talent, of course, but always they had worked and worked to improve and perfect their talent. This Ruth was not doing.

One of the things that saves Ruth from himself is, according to writers, his love for baseball. Hugh Fullerton writes of this quality in him in an article in *American* Magazine.

> In the past two years the baseball public of New York has fallen into the same habit. The fans flocked by millions to see the Yankees play ball, apparently caring little whether the team won or lost, so long as Babe Ruth made a home run.
>
> Yet "Bambino" himself is exactly the opposite. With him the game *is* the thing. He loves baseball; loves just to play it. I remember one day in Boston, when he was with the Red Sox, fighting for a game which meant perhaps the winning or the losing of a championship. He started in the game as an outfielder, stepped into the breach as a pitcher, and finally won the game with a smashing hit.
>
> It was almost dark when some of us emerged from the park and started downtown. Two blocks away, a bunch of kids was assembled in a vacant lot, playing ball. And there was Babe, hitting the ball, just for the fun of it; just because he loved it; not to win something, or to keep from losing something, but just for the sake of doing it. . . .[283]

Here we find that Ruth is interested in playing baseball, not merely working at it. This is what his "love" of the game seems to mean. It is hard to imagine Ty Cobb in a sandlot game, with his "scheme, scheme and keep scheming" motto for human action. Ruth himself explained his behavior with reference to a love of baseball. On the occasion of being suspended for five days for arguing with an umpire, Ruth made this statement to the press:

> I do not regret being out of the game because of the money it costs me. I really don't need the money, but I do love to play baseball. For that reason it hurts when I can't get into the game.
>
> Another thing that hurts is the criticisms. Some persons are saying that I welcome the suspensions because it gives me an alibi for not equalling my home run record of last year. That is ridiculous, as I realize that that is impossible. Others claim that I have a "swelled head." My friends know different. I want to be in there every minute because I love to play baseball.[284]

Here Ruth uses his love of the game to remove himself from the suspicion of having commercial motives for his actions. These kinds of images center eventually on the image of Ruth as a child. In defense of Ruth, when he was being criticized by Harry Frazee just after Frazee had traded him to the Yankees, *The Sporting News* attacked Frazee and told its readers that Ruth was "pretty well spoiled, but a good boy at heart."[285] Again, W. J. Macbeth in the New York *Tribune* defends Ruth against detractors by describing him as a child at play.

> Ruth is nothing if not a big grown up kid. Nobody in camp is working harder than he. He runs out every hit as if sprinting for a base knock in the real show and already runs them out past second base. Afield in fly chasing Ruth has shown a judgment and speed that matched the best efforts of Sammy Vick. Samuel was one of the speediest of Huggins' 1919 aggregation.
>
> Babe is working to improve his speed and range as instance a sample of his days' work. After his hitting practice he indulged in about an hours' "shagging" of fungoes while the infielders practiced fielding. Then Ruth came in to third base for a half hour more. He finished up the day with a few clownish antics for the benefit of the grand stand managers.[286]

Without the first and last sentences, this could be a paragraph about Ty Cobb. But the two sentences give the activity an entirely different context. Billy Evans has the final word on Ruth as a child. This particular passage concerns the size of his head and the effect that being a celebrity has had on him.

> What kind of a fellow is Babe Ruth? That is a question I have been asked hundreds of times since Babe hogged the sporting spotlight. Ruth's remarkable ability to hit home runs has made him the most discussed individual in the history of the game. Thousands of fans wonder what kind of a fellow he really is, when not engaged in busting them over the fence.
>
> No doubt a great many people have the impression that Ruth feels his greatness. Nothing could be further from the truth. Ruth is a big, likeable kid. He has been well named, Babe. Ruth has never grown up and probably never will. Success on the ball field has in no way changed him. Everybody likes him. You just can't help it.[287]

Ruth the child is the perfect representative citizen of Judge Landis' kingdom. With this picture of Ruth the change of the community of professional baseball from a community identified with a democratic capitalistic world to a community which sees itself as authoritarian and above commercial concerns is complete. Far from being a capitalist engaged in competition, Ruth is a child exercising his talents out of love for the game. Professional baseball has become a big, happy family.

To summarize, as a result of the scandal, which uncovered deep areas of corruption in the democracy that could not be handled by a democratic government, baseball chose the option of calling in a dictator to purify itself. Coincidentally, a style of play which emphasized the virtues of a paternalistic, hierrarchical society arose. Thus by 1922, professional baseball was able to view the American community at large from a position of superior purity, a position it would hold until the 1960's, when the public discovered, for reasons we shall presently consider, that professional football made a better representation of the alternatives to the confusions of a democratic society.

V

VINCE LOMBARDI'S WORLD

THIS FINAL CHAPTER WILL FOCUS ON PROFESSIONAL FOOTBALL, A SPORT which has passed professional baseball in popularity in the years since World War II and is thought to have established itself as a successor to baseball as America's national game. Baseball is now a sport which represents to many the "good old days," while professional football reveals the various stresses of contemporary society. We might turn to Marshall McLuhan for an expression of this attitude. In *Understanding Media* he argues that

> . . . baseball is a game of one-thing-at-a-time, fixed positions and visibly delegated specialist jobs such as belonged to the now passing mechanical age, with its fragmented tasks and its staff and line in management organization. TV, as the very image of the new corporate and participant ways of electric living, fosters habits of unified awareness and social interdependence that alienate us from the peculiar style of baseball, with its specialist and positional stress. When cultures change, so do games. Baseball, that had become the elegant abstract image of an industrial society living by split-second timing, has in the new TV decade lost its psychic and social relevance for our new way of life. The ball game has been dislodged from the social center and has been conveyed to the periphery of American life.
>
> In contrast, American football is nonpositional, and any or all of the players can switch to any role during play. It is, therefore, a game that at

present is supplanting baseball in general acceptance. It agrees very well with the new needs of decentralized team play in the electric age.[1]

Here baseball embodies all values now obsolete: football embodies the values of the new, electric age. It will be the purpose of this chapter to discover why football, at least in the minds of many people, is replacing baseball as America's national game. Though part of the reason for this may, as McLuhan maintains, be found in the new kind of role technology plays in it, my purpose is to show the extent to which values formerly associated with professional baseball are now associated with professional football. One important reason professional football is now thought to be our national game is that, like professional baseball, it has become associated with the anti-democratic, anti-individualistic, heart-and-will oriented ideals toward which we are trained to look in order to give our urban, industrial activities meaning.

The chapter has two parts. In the first, the transition of the aforementioned values from baseball to football is traced through the writings of Eliot Asinof, a former minor league baseball player whose books include a baseball novel (*Man on Spikes,* 1955) and a work of non-fiction about the New York Giants football team (*Seven Days to Sunday*, 1968). In these two books, we see Asinof reject professional baseball as a profession in which virtue and talent triumph and an individual is able to find happiness and accept professional football as a profession in which this remains true. The second section returns first to Carlyle's *Past and Present* for analysis of the kind of society Abbot Samson creates at his medieval monastery. This society should show the same essential characteristics the world of professional baseball under Judge Landis and the world of professional football in Asinof's *Seven Days to Sunday* do. Secondly, the section will deal briefly with Herman Melville's *Moby Dick*, considered both as a fictional "trying out" of the kind of community instituted by Abbot Samson, and as a study of the type of leader the community demands. Finally, the actual contemporary world of professional football will be considered, as seen in various writings, both fictional and non-fictional. The emphasis in this section will be on the public image of Vince Lombardi during his tenure as coach of the Green Bay Packers football team. In considering Lombardi's public image we should find that the present world of professional sports, as embodied in football, embodies values very much like those of the great nineteenth century critics of industrial democracy, and that in both cases these values are those which Huizinga associates with *play*, but not with sports.

I

Eliot Asinof grew up during the twenties and thirties in New York City and learned how to play baseball in the streets of that city. In spite of his teachers' encouragement to become a writer, his greatest ambition as a boy was to become a baseball player. He spent several years playing in the minor leagues in the farm system of the Philadelphia Phillies before entering the Air Corps during World War II. It wasn't until after the war, apparently, that he began to write professionally. He says of his experiences in the minor leagues, that the world of professional baseball "proved interesting and considerably informative to work with in spite of the limitations of the form."[2]

The form of *Man on Spikes* is particularly important to its theme. A look at its table of contents suggests that we will get a panoramic view of the whole structure of organized baseball. Each chapter is titled after the particular type depicted within it. Thus we have chapters on "The Scout," "The Old Ball Player," "The Manager," "The Negro," etc. By this means we get a picture of the whole political and social structure of professional baseball. This, however, only provides the background for the events of the book, actually the story of one ball player's rise through the minor leagues to the big leagues, the typical American journey from lowly origins up the ladder to success. We follow our protagonist from the day of his discovery by a big-league scout ("The Scout") to the day he first breaks into the major leagues ("The Rookie"). That the latter event occurs eighteen years after the former is the central fact of the book and underlines its theme: that the Ben Franklin version of the American dream is a destructive illusion, even in professional baseball.

Mike Kutner, the central character of the novel, is a first generation American. His father had fled Germany and come to America. Having grown up in a German coal mining community and having seen his father shot down by soldiers during a strike, Mike's father "fled that insane chaos" and came to the home of the only relatives he had left, in a mining community in Kentucky. There he got a job in the mines. The narrator comments that "it had not surprised him to find them as poor as his own family, burdened by the same uncertainties, struggling over the same dried bread and beans. He went down into the mines to earn his keep, the only thing he could do in a mining town. It never occurred to him that there was anything ironic about leaving the old country to come clear across the ocean only to bury himself in the mines again."[3] Joe Kutner, the father, is a man unresponsive to the supposed promises of American life. Talking to the scout who has discovered and wishes to sign his son, he tells the story of the discovery of Lana Turner by a movie scout in a soda fountain. Fame and fortune, he argues, are the result of chance rather than virtues and talents. Americans, with all their talk of success, "make kids dream too much." The scout accepts his version of Lana Turner's success but argues that baseball is different. "But this is baseball!" he argues. "A game of skill. You were talking about Hollywood!" (p. 33) For the scout, baseball is an aspect of life where the road to the top is still open to men of talent.

And Mike Kutner is a talented baseball player. We see him, at the beginning of his career, through the eyes of a veteran ball player.

> This was a ball player, up there only to hit. Look at him; no jerky movements, no wild waving of the bat, almost no preliminary swing. He stood simply, his feet spread wide and his bat cocked high over his shoulder. Herman thought, Kutner probably looked the same playing stick ball behind his grammar school. A natural. (p. 76)

In addition to being talented, Mike Kutner has an "undaunted, naive drive to the top," as another character puts it. (p. 195) But talent and ambition are no guarantee of success, as other characters in the book keep warning him. At the beginning of the book, the scout thinks to himself that "talent alone was no guarantee, for there were too many dumbheads along the way hunting for lousy reasons to smother it." (p. 11) Mike speaks his creed as follows: "I've always thought you had to sweat for what you want, and if you're good enough, and you sweat hard enough, you get it!" (p. 109) That this is not true, even in professional baseball, is the theme of the book. As Kutner's wife at one point tells him, "Lots of guys are good and don't make out. They don't ever make out. Not only in baseball, Mike . . . in everything." (p. 222) By the end of the book it is clear that this assumption, "the assumption of his inevitable final triumph," is what has most imprisoned him during the course of his baseball career. (p. 273) When he exclaims, having failed major league game, that "I'm free of it!" he speaks as much of this assumption that he now is forced to give up, as of the environment of professional baseball, which, it is clear, he will also be forced to leave. (p. 276)

Asinof's picture of the *environment* of professional baseball is also important to us. Mike Kutner's fate is bound up in more than his own understanding of himself. It is also bound up in the relation of his particular talents to the style of play honored in baseball and also in the political and social structure of the community of baseball. We should look at each of these in turn.

When Mike exclaims "I'm free of it!" he is also free of a community which is incapable of appreciating the style of baseball he plays. We see him perform for his high school team through the eyes of Durkin Fain, scout for the Chicago Lions, in the first chapter of the book. Fain's first impression is one of speed, in the way Mike runs out an inside-the-park home run. "For a moment, he even forgot the strong wrists that had clobbered that shot against the wall like a cannon ball. It was the running that amazed him." In Fain's judgment, Mike is a smart ball player, one who plays baseball the right way, and finally one who in his playing demonstrates a love for baseball. (p. 2) He is just the kind of ball player that Fain has been good at discovering. "They were smart, reliable, aggressive. They had the plus factor that made them invaluable to the club, playing furiously for the win, always ready with some extra piece of business on the diamond that helped the team." (p. 6) These are the kinds of players Ring Lardner admired, who found themselves largely undervalued after the coming of Babe Ruth. "The kid was young, say nineteen or so" Fain concludes, "but he looked like he'd been playing scientific baseball all his life." (p. 7)

Fain's ideas of what constitutes a good ball player are, however, in the minority even in his own organization. Actually he has been sent to this small town in Kentucky to scout a player of another kind.

Then he looked at the giant, lumbering third baseman they had sent him down from Chicago to sign, and the thought disgusted him. He wrenched the sloppy cigar from his mouth and threw it away. The dumb punks . . . goddam Jim Mellon and the dumb punks that kiss his butt. They hear about some oversized palooka who swings from the heels and can drive a ball 500 feet against the patsy pitchers, and they itch all over to corner him. For three

> games Durkin Fain had watched him, a big country clown who didn't know three strikes were out. This giant would sit sprawling on the bench, mute and patronizing, while the kids half his size yelled and scrambled and played their hearts out for a few runs. When it was time for him to hit, he'd strut pompously to the plate, swinging four bats with one hand, just to tickle his giggling fans. Then for a brief moment, he'd be alive, digging in with his big feet, shaking the fat bat at the timid pitcher who'd heard of his mighty wallops. (pp. 2, 3)

All the scorn that Ring Lardner felt for the new kind of baseball is visible in this passage. The big man is an idiot and a clown: he has strength but no intelligence. He is "the epitome of the new game." (p. 6) Fain's boss, Jim Mellon, owner of the Chicago Lions, has instructed him as to the kind of player he is to look for. "Look, Fain," Fain remembers him as saying, "Baseball has changed since you played it. It's the goddam long ball they want now. If a man can belt 'em that far, he goes up. The clever boys can only wave at the damn apple as it disappears over the wall. That's baseball today. It just ain't a little man's game!" (p. 4) Naturally, supporters of the new philosophy evoke the name of Babe Ruth. Fain mediates.

> Sure, they blamed it all on the public. The public wants the long ball! It recently had its taste of the great Babe Ruth and his sixty home runs in a season. It seemed so easy to win games that way. There was a dramatic finality to it that any child-mind could understand. There it goes, up and out, sailing over the outfielders, miles out of reach, into the bleacher bedlam and that hysterical adulation! It doesn't matter that Babe Ruth could have won more games with a timely, well-placed bunt or a tap through that crazy, unbalanced infield. Fain often argued that the great Babe would execute such a simple maneuver only to show how clever he actually was. Baseball had become less a question of winning games than the way you won them. (p. 5)

Mike's talent, it is clear from this, is clearly not one Jim Mellon will want to use. Still, as we learn in the course of the narrative, there are other teams in the major leagues that could use his services, and it is natural to assume that he would eventually be transferred to one of them. This, however, does not happen. It does not happen because of the peculiar political structure of the community of professional baseball.

The key chapter which shows this structure and what Asinof thinks is wrong with it is the one entitled "The Commissioner," and the key figure is, of course, the Commissioner himself.

Asinof's Commissioner places himself in the tradition of Kenesaw Mountain Landis. He is most concerned with "the power and, what was more important, the dignity of his office." (p. 190)

> When he took office, the Commissioner had wanted to believe his job would be an ennobling one. He had seen himself as the czar for the protection of baseball, the purifier of the almost pure. He would keep the game honest and clean, free of the corrupting touch of gamblers and racketeers. He would be the final arbitrator of disputes within the baseball world. For baseball must remain a game and the baseball world a big family, whose house he would keep in order. (pp. 205-206)

The harmony of the Commissioner's world is disrupted by Mike Kutner's complaint that he is sure that he is being returned to the minor leagues through a gentleman's agreement among the owners and not because none of the other clubs in the league can use his services. He asks the Commissioner to speak to Jim Mellon and see if he cannot get him sold to another major league club instead. Kutner tells the Commissioner that "the talk is you're a good man . . . and *for* the ball players. . . ." (p. 195) With this statement the Commissioner senses the possibility of conflict within his "big family." "The Commissioner had never really looked at professional baseball that way, as a possible conflict of interests." (p. 196) Later, when he confronts Jim Mellon with Kutner's statement, he is torn to shreds by the club owner. Here is part of their talk:

> "Talking that way won't get you anywhere, Commissioner. You should've learned that by now. When you get interested in the players you gotta learn just how far to go. I can tell you, Commissioner, the owners might not like it."
>
> "At the moment I happen to be mostly concerned for the players."
>
> "Well, that's too damn bad, Commissioner . . . you've been forgetting another rule that comes closer to home. The rule that the Commissioner is elected by twelve of the sixteen owners—and none of the players. I'll tell you, Commissioner, you get paid your fat sixty-five thousand dollars a year to keep peace in this business, and I got strong feelings that twelve of the boys ain't gonna see it your way." (pp. 204-205)

What is happening here is that the "family" as a metaphor for political order is not operating well at all. The Commissioner finds Jim Mellon's voice "too damn paternal." He refers sarcastically to his farm system, which serves to keep many deserving ball players like Kutner out of the majors, where their talent and desire ought to have brought them, as "Old Jim Mellon's happy family. . . ." (p. 200) The Commissioner is upset at himself because baseball has not remained "a game and the baseball world a big family, whose house he would keep in order." (p. 206)

Though it is ambiguous as to whether the Commissioner imagines himself in the role of the father or that of housekeeper here, Asinof clearly imagines that if the baseball community functioned as a family, it would work better; that is, the people with talent would have a better chance to rise to the top. The fault is in the functioning of the baseball community, not in its ideal structure. This implicit acceptance of a benign authoritarian political structure as a prerequisite for insuring that the most talented people will get to the top is made explicit in Asinof's 1968 book on the New York Giants football team, *Seven Days to Sunday.* The world of professional football will prove to have what the world of professional baseball has lost.

Eliot Asinof lived with the New York Giants for two years gathering material for his book. When he asked the owner of the Giants, Wellington Mara, for permission to do this, he was not sure whether Mara would be able to find his request acceptable, even if he wanted to. He must have found Mara's responses gratifying, for he reports that Mara indicated his acceptance of the idea by saying, "Welcome to the family."[4] The book is dedicated, in part, to "the entire family of Giants."

As Asinof presents them, and as they think of themselves, the Giants are a family. "The Giants," he tells us, "are like a family that sustains the loyalty of its members over the years. Players and coaches who have served them well become part of that family and are inevitably included in the organization staff." (p. 134) The coaches' ideal is to get the whole team feeling like "blood brothers" on the playing field. (p. 23) One offensive lineman describes the relationship of all offensive linemen as one of feeling like "brothers all together, sharing the same problems." (p. 126) The team itself forms a kind of fraternity into which newcomers find themselves feeling intruders. (p. 65) At the end of the book, Asinof quotes Wellington Mara speaking of an injured halfback, Tucker Frederickson. He characterizes Mara's speech as follows: "When he spoke about Tucker's courage, he sounded like a father talking about his own son." (p. 305)

Though the idea of the family forms the basis for understanding the structure of the Giant community, it does not explain it completely. A related set of images likens the structure of the community to that of a military operation. The long training camp which precedes each season particularly fits that characterization. The following quotation, containing this metaphor, suggests many of the stresses on the players during the training camp:

> Training camp is in no sense a picnic. The daily drills are more tortuous than satisfying, regardless of a player's love of football. It is eight weeks of physical battering far more agonizing than the fourteen weeks of the regular season. It is an army camp of rigid discipline and restrictions, of little time off, of abstinence and continence, of endless meetings and chalk-talks and eye-wearying returns of tired football film played over and over until every required move is drummed into each player, then repeated a dozen times more. Above all, it is a time of great emotional stress, when grown men clash violently over trivia, when rookies desperate to make another weekly cut, walk the floors like frightened children in the middle of the night, when any man may crack up and some do. To all of them, football is more than a game, it is a livelihood that will take them out of a dreary nondescript life, and to some, free them from the squalor of their backgrounds. It is their shot at the glamour world of the big city, with money and prestige and a return home in winter with a flashy car and fine clothes and a celebrated status that makes them feel like a man. (p. 150)

Here is a life that transcends the squalid activities of ordinary existence and removes one from them. We learn also that, when the camp begins, "Sherman would turn that lovely rolling campus at Fairfield University into a military enclave." Allie Sherman, then coach of the Giants, is also described at training camp as "a general preparing his troops for the war that would begin on opening day in September." (pp. 157, 159)

This image of Sherman holds throughout the book. Later, we are told, in explanation of something Sherman has said, that "like most generals during a campaign, he was a relatively lonely man. In the tension of a night before the battle, he needed to say these things just to bathe in the sound of them, a declaration of the record as it stands in the face of tomorrow's threat." (p. 234) And if a general has his problems of the night before a battle, so do the troops. Theirs are somewhat different.

> It was only a game, but to these forty men, it was at the essence of their lives. It was pure drama, for no one had the slightest notion of how it would come

out. . . . They were not actors playing parts, titillating an audience with their roles in a predesigned script. They went way beyond that. They were putting themselves on the block, their bodies as well as their talents, not only to win or lose, but to whip their opponents in dozens of bone-jarring collisions that could break them apart. Like soldiers into battle, they speculated on survival as well as victory. The magic word was fear . . . each of them had suffered the worst kind of pain at some time in his career, had tasted the fear of flinching, of saving his body at the expense of his teammates, and each of them had seen men carried off the field, never to play again. (p. 263)

With this kind of fear comes its opposite, a sense of brotherly love. This too, is connected with the military image. "Like soldiers in a combat mission," Asinof tells us, "their lives seemed dependent upon their love for one another." (p. 160)

To many people, it is this kind of love that keeps the whole world of professional football spinning. The players themselves say this. As a character in *The Name of the Game is Murder* says, "you wanna play winning football, you gotta have love out there." (p. 92) Asinof quotes Pete Case, then guard on the Giants:

"there's a closeness between us guards and tackles. It would have to be that way with interior linemen. We care about each other. You might say it's stronger than that. It's like love in a way. Brothers, all together, sharing the same problems. I really feel for Greg and Bookie and Willie and all, I couldn't play this game right unless I did. I would have to know it was that way all around. To be a lineman, a man just couldn't take all that punishment unless the man next to him was his brother." (p. 126)

Just as necessary as this fraternal feeling for success in professional football is a love of playing the game itself, and an appreciation of its beauty. Asinof quotes Aaron Thomas, an offensive end, on this subject:

"I love this game. I'm not talking about the money and the glamour and all the other benefits, I'm talking about the game itself. I love the way the pro game is laid out, the beauty of the passing techniques. I tell you, I leave a huddle when my pass play has been called and I'm so full of that great feeling of anticipation that I can hardly keep it all to myself. As the years go by, the more I know, the more I love it. I can handle myself so much better now. I think of the difference it makes, the passes I catch now that I would end up steps away from years ago. It makes me cry when.I think of what I wasted in those last years with Y. A. [Tittle]. I mean, knowing what I know now, I could have caught a million. Maybe it will all work out with Junior [Tarkenton]. He's another QB who can make football a beautiful game." (p. 257)

One might imagine the object of these sentiments about love and beauty, the team itself, might command a metaphor from the world of the arts to describe it. This, however, is not the case. Thomas, in the preceding quotation, clearly thinks of himself as a technician rather than as artist. The coaches, too, tend to think of the team as a machine which must be well oiled to run smoothly. (see pp. 50, 187) In an earlier newspaper article, Asinof had described the condition of a football team on the Friday before a game in the following manner: "At Friday's work-outs, you can sense the perfection of the machine, like a clean and powerful engine with all pistons beautifully timed."[5] Professional football, Asinof concludes in the same article

> has become a science to its new brain men, a carefully worked-out system of basic strategems designed to take advantage of size, weight, speed and skills of the best young men available. The game has become so specialized that there is little room for diversity, no room for rebellion. . . . As a result, we see 14 NFL teams using the same basic system, to date the most effective system ever devised. . . .
>
> The outcome is a remarkably better football game. And if there is a sameness to the style of play, there is also a magnificent difference: the execution. Here, the subtleties and variables are limitless. And here, the quality of coaching becomes paramount. And that is why the Giants reportedly pay their head coach $35,000 a year plus fringe benefits.[6]

Here we must note the difference in Asinof's attitude toward the style of play in professional football from his attitude toward that of professional baseball. Football is achieving the best it is capable of, while in baseball, concepts of what constitutes good play keep out many players.

In *Man on Spikes,* Mike Kutner's manager sometimes had a hand in keeping him back. But in professional *football,* the coach is the difference between a successful team and a poor one. By studying Asinof's characterization of Allie Sherman, a man he obviously admires, we can discover what qualities a good coach ought to have.

Sherman is characterized in a series of somewhat disparate metaphors. That he is a general, first preparing his troops for, then directing them in, battle, we have already noted. Though this position is necessarily an authoritarian one, Asinof will not say that Sherman fits it. Here he describes Sherman's role during training camp.

Sherman played this authoritarian role as strongly and severely as his non-dictatorial personality would permit, resisting all tendencies toward leniency as though it were a sickness. He was, in fact, extremely proud of this stern posture. (p. 160)

Here both Sherman and Asinof look past the actual Sherman to an ideal figure, perhaps better described by Asinof in his novel *The Name of the Game is Murder*. Here Barton Fain is described.

He was an authoritarian leader of almost absolute proportions, structuring his organization into a quasi-military unit. Discipline was rigid. His control was not to be questioned. He dominated every aspect of his practices with the severity of a general leading his men into battle. During the games, he made all substitutions, called every play from the bench. (p. 48)

This military image is reinforced by the first description of Fain in the book. In the images involved in this description, we are taken away from the democratic capitalist modern society in which Fain operates and returned to the middle ages.

He was a giant of a football coach with the passion and purity of a knight in armor, driving his warriors in the image of his ferocity, shaking his fist at them, bellowing at officials in protest, never stopping for a moment of joy when a game was going well, never once quitting even under the most humiliating defeat. He was a lion roaring in fury at the world around him, and no one ever dared to cross him. (p. 7)

The coach is an heroic figure, his world is medieval, and Sherman appears to see and to regret his distance from the stereotype.

Asinof uses two other metaphors besides that of the general to describe Sherman. He imagines him as a kind of artist, comparing his labors in preparation for each Sunday's game with those of "a playwright creating the structure of a new dramatic work."[7] Asinof is inclined to describe sporting figures by comparing their activity with that of artists. For instance, he once described the extensive putting practice of Billy Casper, a professional golfer, by saying that it was "like a great violinist working over a difficult cadenza until it became a part of him."[8] Sherman, however, disagreed with his use of the metaphor.

I used to tell him, "You keep using this phrase 'in this business.' I don't see you as a man in business, Al; you're more like a symphony conductor or a movie director, welding all these many parts together into one cohesive unit. That's an art, not a business." And he'd reply, "Yes, you're right. I see that

> now." But, as it turned out, it wasn't right. The job doesn't call for beautiful music, it calls for victory. The paying public demands it. There was no peace without victory, for there would be no prestige, no stature, and in the end, no money. (p. 194)

Just as his players' love results in a flawless machine, so does Sherman's artistic talent serve, finally, a business. He sees himself as a businessman and, in the end Asinof comes to see him that way too.

> That was Alexander Sherman at his very essence, this clarion call to success. It was all there, all the driving intensity of a man with a purpose, all the old-fashioned credos of the Protestant ethic. Talent, dedication, ambition, and influence, equals success, money, power, and prestige. His belief in himself was pure and thorough, and his faith in the system matched it. He was, perhaps, a living symbol of all these classic American virtues. (pp. 236-237)

And here Asinof discovers a world where the American dream is still intact. The setting is still professional sports, but professional football now seems the symbol of values that were deliberately fathered around professional baseball after the Black Sox scandal. But the "Protestant ethic" is at work in a medieval, warlike community. This mix of medieval and urban-industrial values we have met before and shall meet again, now, in Thomas Carlyle.

II

Asinof's mention of Barton Fain as a "knight in armor" may recall to us Carlyle's presentation of the ideal life against which he juxtaposed that of "The Modern Worker" in *Past and Present.* He does this in section two of the book, "The Ancient Monk," concerned with his understanding of life in medieval England. Here we encounter Carlyle's ideal leader, Abbot Samson, and discover the qualities he needs to effectively govern a monastery in the days when "the country was still dark with wood . . . ; and Scotland itself still rustled shaggy and leafy, like a damp black American Forest, with cleared spots and spaces here and there."[9] These qualities, as we shall see, will be those which both Allie Sherman and Vince Lombardi embraced, within a more businesslike context.

First we must consider the people Abbot Samson has to deal with. Carlyle describes Jocelin, the author of the old manuscript, early in the book as "an ingenious and ingenuous, a cheery-hearted, innocent, yet withal shrewd, noticing, quick-witted man . . ." (p. 40) Here Jocelin sounds a bit like a Yankee pedlar. Perhaps we can compare his characteristics in relation to Abbot Samson to those of the thrall of Cedric the Saxon, Gurth.

. . . Gurth, with the sky above him, with the free air and tinted boscage and umbrage round him, and in him, and in him at least the certainty of supper and social lodging when he came home; Gurth to me seems happy, in comparison with many a Lancashire and Buckinghamshire man of these days, not born thrall of anybody! Gurth's brass collar did not gall him: Cedric *deserved* to be his master. The pigs are Cedric's, but Gurth too would get his parings of them. Gurth had the inexpressible satisfaction of feeling himself related indissolubly, though in a rude brass-collar way, to his fellow mortals in this Earth. He had superiors, inferiors, equals. (p. 204)

The best way to learn to govern these kinds of people, was the way Abbot Samson had learned. He had served "a right good apprenticeship to governing; namely, the harshest slave-apprenticeship to obeying." He serves as a model in justification of the statement that "to learn obeying is the fundamental art of governing." (p. 86)

This paradox is worked out by Carlyle in the following manner. First, he tells the reader that Samson is a natural governor:

There is in him what far transcends all apprenticeships; in the man himself there exists a model of governing, something to govern by! There exists in him a heart-abhorrence of whatever is incoherent, pusillanimous, unveracious, —that is to say, chaotic, ungoverned; of the Devil, not of God. A man of this kind cannot help governing! He has the living ideal of a governor in him; and the incessant necessity of struggling to unfold the same out of him. (p. 85)

Here he governs by obeying his innermost instincts. These instincts, as we discover later, are the implanted laws of God. In this passage Carlyle resolves his problem of the relation of freedom and order.

And yet observe there too: Freedom, not nomad's or ape's Freedom, but man's Freedom; this is indispensable. We must have it, and will have it! To reconcile Despotism with Freedom:—well, is that such a mystery? Do you not already know the way? It is to make your Despotism *just*. Rigorous as Destiny; but just too, as Destiny and its Laws. The Laws of God: all men obey these, and have no 'Freedom' at all in obeying them. The way is already known, part of the way;—and courage and some qualities are needed for walking on it. (p. 271)

Samson, as a natural leader, is able to correlate the hatred within him of chaos with the order given to the universe outside himself by the laws of God. This enables him to make his despotism just.

And a just man is Abbot Samson. Carlyle speaks frequently and in varying circumstances about Abbot Samson's sense and frequent uses of justice. He says at one time that "indeed, except it were for *idonei*, 'fit men,' in all kinds, it was hard to say for whom Abbot Samson had much favour." (p. 91) It was best for those who failed to fit this description to give him a wide berth. "Let all sluggards and cowards, remiss, false-spoken, unjust, and otherwise diabolic persons have a care: this is a dangerous man for them." (p. 89) Dangerous for two reasons: first, because he has a sense of justice, he recognizes fitness when it exists in a man and rewards that and nothing else; secondly, because he is an emotional man. He is quick to anger. Carlyle later describes an example of this "terrible flash of anger in him" which could singe those who were not fit. (p. 109) Finally, as Carlyle praises the quality of justice in Abbot Samson, so he praises the world that produced him because it is a just world. In it

> a most 'practical' Hero-worship went on, unconsciously or half-consciously, everywhere. A Monk Samson, with a maximum of two shillings in his pocket, could, without ballot-box, be made a Viceking of, being seen to be worthy. The difference between a good man and a bad man was as yet felt to be, what it forever is, an immeasurable one. (p. 237)

A final characteristic of Abbot Samson does not seem to blend with the others. In addition to being a natural leader, an emotional man, and a just man, he is also a practical man who knows when to compromise. We are told that "he tempers his medicine to the malady" in making his judgments, "now hot, now cool; prudent though fiery, an eminently practical man." (p. 108) The example with which Carlyle follows this judgment suggests that the Abbot will willingly indulge in commercial trickery. Carlyle eventually labels this "worldly wisdom."

> No one will accuse our Lord Abbot of wanting worldly wisdom, due interest in worldly things. A skillful man; full of cunning insight, lively interests; always discerning the road to his object, be it circuit, be it short-cut, and victoriously travelling forward thereon. Nay rather it might seem, from Jocelin's Narrative, as if he had his eye all but exclusively directed on terrestrial matters, and was much too secular for a devout man. But this too, if

we examine it, was right. For it is *in* the world that a man, devout or other, has his life to lead, his work waiting to be done. (p. 111)

But this worldiness is not quite so surprising if we remember that, in the modern world, these true leaders of men are now the industrial giants, the Captains of Industry. And the imagery Carlyle uses in the following passage connects them at many points with Abbot Samson.

Captains of Industry are the true Fighters, henceforth recognizable as the only true ones: Fighters against Chaos, Necessity and the Devils and Jotuns; and lead on Mankind in that great, and alone true, and universal warfare; the stars in their courses fighting for them, and all Heaven and all Earth saying audibly, Well Done! (p. 261)

It is appropriate then that Captain Ahab, Melville's anti-Carlylian hero, is a kind of Captain of Industry. His task is to take the ordinary whaling voyage and turn it into a kind of wrestling match, to transform a commercial venture into a contest, thereby making it meaningful.

The problem of how to make the industrial world meaningful to all individuals who were involved in it seemed a real one to Herman Melville as well as to Thomas Carlyle, and Melville's novel, *Moby Dick*, may serve as an ironic commentary on the ideal society Carlyle set up in the medieval monastery of Abbot Samson. Instead of outlining an ideal society, Melville gives us a specific instance of the operation of a world like that of Abbot Samson; the microcosm of the whaling voyage gives him opportunity to consider the strengths and limitations of Carlyle's ideal world.

If Ishmael as narrator can be said to have invested the profession of whaling with a kind of tragic dignity, it must also be admitted that he insists on calling it "this business of whaling" and in giving his tragic vision a solid foundation of commercial fact.[10] Thus it may be possible to regard Ahab's tragic voyage as a problem of the management of men. In doing this, we ought to consider first, the character of Ahab himself in his role of Captain of the *Pequod* and secondly, the ways he is able to motivate the crew to do his wishes.

It is Captain Ahab who defines the meaning of the whaling voyage in the book. And Ahab transforms the commercial voyage into a quest, a crusade, a contest. Like Abbot Samson, he makes ordinary commercial activity a wrestling with reality. He describes his purpose in the following passage:

> The prophecy was that I should be dismembered; and—Aye! I lost this leg. I now prophesy that I will dismember my dismemberer. Now, then, be the prophet and the fulfiller one. That's more than ye, ye great gods, ever were. I laugh and hoot at ye, ye cricket players, ye pugilists, ye deaf Durkes and blinded Bendigoes! I will not say as school-boys do to bullies—Take some one of your own size; don't pommel *me*! No, ye've knocked me down, and I'm up again; but *ye* have run and hidden. Come forth from behind your cotton bags! I have no long gun to reach ye. (p. 166)

The association of sports here with Ahab's purpose works both ways. Like the boxers and cricket players, Ahab is engaged in something best understood as a contest. Compared to his contest, though, theirs fade into insignificance.

When Ishmael gets his first look at Ahab, he thinks: "There was an infinity of firmest fortitude, a determinate, unsurrenderable willfulness, in the fixed and fearless, forward dedication of that glance." (pp. 121, 122) Here Ahab's central characteristic is identified as his great will to complete his task, to win the contest. At the end of the chapter "The Quarter Deck," Ishmael describes Ahab's attempt to unite the crew behind him in search of the white whale. "It seemed as though, by some nameless, interior volition, he would fain have shocked into them the same fiery emotion accumulated within the Leyden jar of his own magnetic life." (p. 164) The force of Ahab's will enables him to exact the homage of "implicit, instantaneous obedience." (p. 144)

A willful man, Ahab is incapable of taking the final responsibility for the actions his will leads him to take. "The path to my fixed purpose," he meditates, "is laid with iron rails, whereon my soul is grooved to run." (p. 166) He regards himself here as the agent of fate, not as a man in control of his own destiny. He is sometimes upset by this situation, as when he talks with Starbuck the day before the chase begins.

> "What is it, what nameless, inscrutable, unearthly thing is it; what cozzening, hidden lord and master, and cruel, remorseless emperor commands me; that against all natural lovings and longings, I so keep pushing, and crowding, and jamming myself on all the time; recklessly making me ready to do what in my own proper, natural heart I durst not so much as dare? Is Ahab, Ahab? Is it I, God, or who, that lifts this arm? But if the great sun move not of himself; but is as an errand-boy in heaven; nor one single star can revolve, but by some invisible power; how then can this one small heart beat;

this one small brain think thoughts; unless God does that beating, does that thinking, does that living, and not I. By heaven, man, we are turned round and round in this world, like yonder windlass, and Fate is the handspike. (p. 536)

Here his relation to Fate renders him helpless, and the way he images it is appropriate. Later, during the chase, the image changes from one involving the technology of the sea to a military one and Ahab becomes "the Fate's lieutenant." "This whole act's immutably decreed," he cries. "'Twas rehearsed by thee and me a billion years before this ocean rolled. Fool! I am the Fate's lieutenant; I act under orders. Look thou, underling, that thou obeyest mine." (p. 554) As he is far from the helldogs of contemplation, his relation to the Fates becomes a source of strength.

Finally it is interesting to note how Ahab manages men, what kind of leader he is. As Melville has pointed out, the whaling captain is, because of the nature of the whaling voyage itself, a dictator. We must understand how Ahab transforms this into "an irresistable dictatorship." Ahab's dictatorship is made irresistable through sheer force of personality. Ishmael speaks of Ahab's dominance over the crew as essentially a mysterious thing: "All this to explain," he says, "would be to dive deeper than Ishmael can go." (p. 184) In fact he seems to ascribe Ahab's dominance to Fate rather than to Ahab's captaincy.

From such a crew, so officered, seemed specially picked and packed by some infernal fatality to help him to his monomanic revenge. How it was that they so aboundingly responded to the old man's ire—by what evil magic their souls were possessed, that at times his hate seemed almost theirs; the White Whale as much their insufferable foe as his; how all this came to be—what the White Whale was to them, or how to their unconscious understanding, also, in some dim, unsuspected way, he might have seemed the gliding great demon of the seas of life. . . . The subterranean miner that works in us all, how can one tell whither leads his shaft by the ever shifting, muffled sound of his pick? Who does not feel the irresistable arm drag? What skiff in tow of a seventy-four can stand still? For one, I gave myself up to the abandonment of the time and the place; but while yet all a-rush to encounter the whale, could see naught in that brute but the deadliest ill. (pp. 184-185)

It is first of all important that in this passage Ishmael announces that he is under Ahab's sway, and this in itself affects his understanding. After this confession, *Moby Dick* proceeds as an objective narrative, the narrator no longer being involved in the whaling voyage, until the chapter "The Try-Works," during which Ishmael emerges from under Ahab's spell. Thus Ishmael suggests that at the time of the voyage he did not understand the source of Ahab's power. In other places in the book, however, he comments on it, and in addition, the events of the narrative themselves are a comment on it.

The fact of Ishmael's submission speaks of Ahab's success as a manager of men. What Ahab is doing is spelled out in the chapter "Surmises." Here Ishmael reconstructs what he imagines to have been Ahab's thinking on how to handle a crew on a voyage such as he contemplated.

> Nor was Ahab unmindful of another thing. In times of strong emotion mankind disdain all base considerations; but such times are evanescent. The permanent constitutional condition of the manufactured man, thought Ahab, is sordidness. Granting that the White Whale fully incites the hearts of this savage crew, the playing round their savageness even breeds a certain generous knight-errantism in them, still, while for the love of it they give chase to Moby Dick, they must also have food for their more common, daily appetites. For even the high lifted and chivalric Crusaders of old times were not content to traverse two thousand miles of land to fight for their holy sepulchre, without committing burglaries, picking pockets, and gaining other pious perquisites by the way. Had they been strictly held to their one final and romantic object—that final and romantic object, too many would have turned from in disgust. I will not strip these men, thought Ahab, of all hopes of cash—aye, cash. They may scorn cash now; but let some months go by, and no perspective promise of it to them, and then this same quiescent cash all at once mutinying in them, this same cash would soon cashier Ahab. (p. 211)

Here Ahab sees that, once he has established a transcendent purpose for the commercial voyage, he must continue to hold out the possibility of cash reward. The crew must chase whales for love *and* money. Neither alone is enough to motivate them. Accordingly, Ahab does not change the purpose of the voyage. His goal simply enhances it, gives it an additional dimension. Like the goals of the Crusaders, the goals of love and money cannot be considered apart. Earlier, the scene on the quarter deck has provided the action that symbolizes this in the book. As Ahab addresses them, the crew changes character.

> More and more strangely and fiercely glad and approving, grew the countenance of the old man at every shout; while the mariners began to gaze curiously at each other, as if marveling how it was that they themselves became so excited at such seemingly purposeless questions. (p. 159)

Following this Ahab produces a gold Spanish coin which, he announces, shall belong to the man who first sights the White Whale. Thus he unites his own purpose for the voyage with the ordinary commercial one. Whenever one of his men thinks of the White Whale, he will think of the twenty-dollar gold coin, not of his captain's madness.

As is mentioned in the same chapter "Surmises," Ahab needs his crew to accomplish his purpose. Under his spell, the men become his "tools; and of all tools used in the shadow of the moon, men are most apt to get out of order." (p. 210) He must be continually alert particularly of Starbuck, whose personality will not stand the bringing together of his spiritual and commercial worlds. For Starbuck, particularly, and for the crew as a whole, "Ahab plainly saw that he must still in a good degree continue true to the natural, nominal purpose of the *Pequod*'s voyage; observe all the customary usages; and not only that, but force himself to evince all his well known passionate interest in the general pursuit of his profession." (p. 212) Stubb, though not as dangerous as Starbuck, seems the opposite of Ahab among the Knights and Squires. He is practically without a spiritual dimension. He is pictured as constantly smoking a pipe, as constantly possessing a sereneness alien to Ahab. He is first described as "a happy-go-lucky; neither craven nor valiant; taking perils as they came with an indifferent air; and while engaged in the most imminent crisis of the chase, toiling away, calm and collected as a journeyman joiner engaged for the year. Good-humored, easy, and careless, he presided over his whale-boat as if the most deadly encounter were but a dinner, and his crew all invited guests." (p. 115) Stubb's indifference and serenity make him the least likely person to come under the sway of Captain Ahab, though these same qualities make him comparatively harmless to Ahab.

Because of this Melville underlines the success of Ahab in dominating his crew when, on the second day of the chase, when the cry is raised again for Moby Dick, he has Stubb exclaim, "I knew it—ye can't escape—blow on and split your spout, O Whale! the mad fiend himself is after ye! blow your trump-blister your lungs!—Ahab will dam off your blood, as a miller shuts his water-gate upon the stream!" (p. 548) This surprising committedness to Ahab's goal on Stubb's part sets the stage for a description of the crew at work under Ahab's spell.

> They were one man, not thirty. For as the one ship that held them all; though it was put together of all contrasting things—oak, and maple, and pine wood; iron, and pitch, and hemp—yet all these ran into each other in the one concrete hull, which shot on its way, both balanced and directed by the long central keel; even so, all the individualities of the crew, this man's valor, that man's fear; guilt and guiltiness, all varieties were welded into oneness, and were all directed to that fatal goal which Ahab their one lord and keel did point to. (p. 548)

Here they are Ahab's tool, an instrument by which he achieves his purposes or, perhaps we ought to say, attempts to achieve them. They are also, we might note, a perfect team, capable of a unity that expresses the purpose of their leader. It is Ahab's purpose, rather than their own failures, that leads to destruction. Let us now turn to another leader of men, Vince Lombardi.

Vince Lombardi's world is descended from those of Abbot Samson and Ahab. Basically, there are four areas in which the similarities are meaningful. Initially, the general image of professional football provides an alternative society to the democratic commercial society within which it exists, as do both Abbot Samson's monastery and Ahab's *Pequod.* The nature of the community of professional football as it understands itself also demonstrates that it is an alternative, although, as in Carlyle's and Melville's, it will seem in some respects strikingly similar to the American community at large. The social structure of professional football adds to this sense that professional football is an alternative, and a better, society in, first, the portrait of the players it shows and, second, in the portrait of the coach. We will consider each of these areas in turn, keeping in mind the possible relations of the ideals derived from these public images to the ideas of work and play and the role of sport in embodying them with which we have been concerned.

Generally, professional football is now thought of as our national game. Its supporters argue that it involves more people more directly than professional baseball now does. Its image begins to take on a distinctive shape in the early sixties as writers begin to contrast professional football with professional baseball. We have already seen the development of this contrast in the works of Eliot Asinof. Many writers would agree with the judgment of Herbert Warren Wind, delivered in a 1962 *New Yorker,* that since the Second World War, pro football has become "a game so precise, tactically fascinating, and deeply enthralling that today, in the judgment of many observers, it has supplanted major league baseball as America's favorite spectator sport."[11] Since 1962, many others have taken the same position and have attempted to develop a rationale for doing so. The pace of football, they suggest, corresponds psychologically to the pace of the contemporary world. William Phillips, for instance, in *Commentary* Magazine, suggests that

> All sports serve as some kind of release but the rhythm of football is geared particularly to the violence and the peculiar combination of order and disorder of modern life. Baseball is too slow, too dependable, too much like a regional drawl. Basketball is too nervous and too tight; hockey too frenzied; boxing too chaotic, too folksy. Only football provides a genuine catharsis.[12]

Although the meaning of this passage is not altogether clear, it is clear that Phillips feels that football reflects the stresses of the modern world in some unique way that none of the other professional sports do.

In a more extensive essay published in the same magazine earlier in 1969, Richard Schickel tries to spell out some of the differences between professional football and professional baseball. He begins his essay by announcing football as the successor to baseball as America's national game. "By common consent, the most striking sports phenomenon in the 1950's has been the displacement of baseball by professional football as the Great American Game.[13] Football," he continues, "is quite a different game from baseball . . . in the requirements it makes of its coaches and players."[14] The coach, according to Schickel, dominates in football more than in any other sport. This is for two reasons: first, "the complexity of the game"; second, because there are so few actual contests in a football season, "he truly must be an inspirational leader."[15] Football here may be seen both to embody the old "scientific" style of play of baseball and the political structure which evolved after Judge Landis was appointed Commissioner.

When Schickel talks of "the requirements . . . of its . . . players" he returns us straight to the world of play Huizinga described. The coach "by taking so much on himself," he says,

> made it possible for his players to find a clear well-defined place in the middle of confusion. Indeed, I believe that the heart of football's enormous appeal

> to all of us at the moment lies in witnessing this process: We see men making order for themsleves out of chaos, and, although violence is implicit in that effort it is not, to my mind the thing that we really care about. What we really like about football is its clearcut resolution, its release from the tensions of ambiguity.[16]

If Schickel is right, football, unlike all other modern sports, has the quality of a game. This leads us to Schickel's statement of "the real secret of the force this game has come to exert on the national imagination." He finds this force in the kind of community these coaches and players make up together. The "inspirational leader" controls finally the "complexity" of the game. Schickel only implies, never divulges, the nature of this community. He quotes Jerry Kramer of the Green Bay Packers as saying, "There's a great deal of love for one another on this club," . . . "Perhaps, we're living in Camelot." These words, he says, reveal "the real secret of the force this game has come to exert on the national imagination."[17]

One of the connotations of the word Camelot concerns war, not love, for the knights of Arthur were concerned with combat above all. This moves us to a consideration of the images of the nature of the professional football community with which we are presented. War, indeed, is a metaphor that pervades writing about professional football and if Jerry Kramer can dream of (or actually be in) Camelot, another Green Bay Packer can say, tersely, in describing the relation of the team to Vince Lombardi, the coach, that "he's the general and we're the privates."[18] Kramer himself nods in this direction when he describes a scene in the Green Bay locker room just before a game.

> I looked around the locker room, and I saw Bart taking his codeine, and I saw Herb Adderley, who had a torn muscle in his right bicep, getting a shot of novacaine, and I saw Ray Nitschke getting his leg taped from his ankle to his hip. We looked like a lost army getting ready for battle.[19]

In addition the sections of his book, *Instant Replay,* are titled in a military manner; such as "Basic Training," "Mock Warfare," and "Armed Combat." We see this same impulse in Gary Cartwright's novel, subtitled "A Novel of Professional Football" and titled *The Hundred Yard War.* Dave Meggysey, too, speaks of "the whole militaristic aura surrounding pro football."[20] Finally, in the autobiography of Mike Holovak, a former coach of the Boston

Patriots, *Violence Every Sunday,* war becomes a paradigm for all meaningful human activity. Holovak's opening chapter describes his war experiences and sets the tone for the whole book. In its second paragraph he says, "I was a combat man now and never again would I be anything less."[21] War and sport both thrust Holovak into and sustain him in a more real state of existence than the normal.

War perhaps best describes the foreign relations of the community of the football team. We should consider the various relationships within the community, its domestic relations. In a book entitled *Packer Dynasty,* Vince Lombardi's successor as coach at Green Bay, Phil Bengston, speaks of the social functions of a football team. "In recent years," he says, "the social scientists have been examining the game of football with an eye to explaining its function as that of (1) a paramilitary function in a militaristic society, (2) a manifestation of the "family" approach to a societal grouping, and (3) a tribal folk religion."[22] It may be that Bengston's own position as coach prevents him from seeing the validity of all three of these functions. As a coach, he sees the functions of football as primarily paramilitary. In the rest, he is uninterested. Like most other communities, however, the community of professional football is three dimensional, and the two functions Bengston rejects correspond rather well to the other two dimensions. Bengston is primarily concerned with the foreign relations of a football team; thus he responds to the military image. Those who look on football as primarily a "tribal folk religion" are primarily concerned with its effect on the spectator. That the team is also seen as a "family" reveals the metaphorical content of the political term "domestic policy." It is with this that we shall be concerned here.

Internal relations on a football team have been described variously. Vince Lombardi's term as coach and general manager at Green Bay prompted people to speak of that situation as a "fiefdom" or an "autocracy."[23] Lombardi himself had difficulty distinguishing what he wanted to accomplish from the purpose of a concentration camp. Here he describes the first letter he wrote to his players after he was appointed coach.

I tried to plant that seed of single purpose in the first squad letter I wrote before training camp that first year. I must have rewritten it ten or twelve times, trying to tell them what I hoped to do without making it sound like I was setting up a slave-labor camp.[24]

Images of technology are also used to describe the football team. Though he sees football as primarily a paramilitary activity, Phil Bengston is fond of technological situations as metaphors in describing the football team in action. He describes the practice situation as follows: "Some people come to our practices expecting to watch a football game. What they see instead is a laboratory, a kind of football diagnostic center in action."[25] The player sees himself as a kind of technician. Like the sailors on the *Pequod*, professional football players are technicians and specialists, and this is an important part of their image. It is this that accounts, according to Vince Lombardi, for the superiority of professional football over the college game. Lombardi says, "In fact, it is specifically the number of superior receivers and the specialization permitted by Two Platoon, more than any other factors, that make the pro game more skilled."[26] Many players see themselves primarily in this way. Nick Pietrosante, formerly of the Detroit Lions, makes this point to George Plimpton. He speaks of the college game "where there just isn't the talent to mount a pro attack, which is spread out wide to split and disperse the defense, and consequently needs experts and technicians to make it work."[27] Dan Currie, formerly of the Green Bay Packers, prides himself on his professional accomplishments. "I like the scientific, the artistic side. I mean I like the feeling you get when you make the good, clean, perfect tackle. With me it's the tackle instead of just belting the other guy."[28] Jerry Kramer puts things very simply when he says, in analyzing why he likes playing professional football, "I suppose I enjoy doing something well."[29] Thus the community of pro football is a community of professionals; those who have enough technical knowledge to do something well.

Yet the major metaphor covering the internal relations of a professional football team is the metaphor of the family. This image turns up everywhere in the literature of professional football. In a book on racial problems in sports, Jack Olson has great praise for Lombardi. "Whenever racial questions are discussed by NFL players," he says, "the Packers are mentioned."

In a league beset with racial confrontations, the Packer players get along. Success has something to do with this; a winner always finds life more pleasant than a loser. But more to the point is the attitude of the Packers' remarkable Vince Lombardi.

Aided by the fact that Green Bay is an isolated community with no significant Negro population of its own, Lombardi has insisted that his Packers be a family. "If you're black or white, you're part of the family," he says.[30]

It is important to understand the limitations of this concept of the family, as it is limited to players who have made the team. A sort of sacred society is formed, and attachments which are personal at their base rather than professional are vigorously excluded. Phil Bengston is moved to attack the image of the family when it threatens to operate against the enforcement of rigorous professional standards. Speaking of Lombardi's relationship with Paul Hornung, he says, "Vince had a special affection for Paul, almost as father to son. But the Packers were not a family; a forty-man roster did not leave room for sentimental positions of halfback emeritus."[31] Yet he can also use the metaphor approvingly, as in this statement on the nature of human relations within the team.

. . . It's the brotherly affection that comes from living, working, and literally growing up together. As Jerry Kramer put it in our 1967 season highlights film, "Brothers can criticize each other and fight among themselves, but just let somebody outside the family say it and he's in trouble."[32]

The family image is rigidly enclosed within the image of football as a ruthless business. In *Instant Replay* we first meet Vince Lombardi just after he has learned that Hornung has been drafted by the expansion team, the New Orleans Saints.

He looked up at me and he started to speak and his jaws moved, but no words came out. He hung his head. . . . I just stood there and Lombardi started to speak again and again he opened his mouth and still he didn't say anything. I could see he was upset, really shaken. . . .

Finally, he managed to say, "I had to put Paul—" He was almost stuttering. "I had to put Paul on that list," he said, "and they took him."

I stood there, not saying anything, and Lombardi looked at me again and lowered his head and started to walk away. He took about four steps and then he turned around and said, "This is a helluva business sometimes, isn't it?[33]

Thus the world of the family is a kind of oasis surrounded by the sands of the business world. As we shall see, however, it is very real to the player who has made the team and joined the family.

A metaphor closely connected with that of the family is one

that involves the school. In this metaphor the coach is primarily a teacher and the players are students, or just "kids." After his initial success at Green Bay, Vince Lombardi was presented this way in the popular press. *Look* Magazine described him as "brilliant and tough-minded, a driving perfectionist, natural leader and born teacher," and went on to say that "Lombardi is above all a teacher. He has graduated *cum laude*, studied philosophy and law, and has taught physics, chemistry and Latin."[34] In *Run to Daylight!* we discover that he is aware that he runs his team somewhat in the manner of a boarding school. He speaks of "grading our players for what you might call our Honors Assembly after practice on Friday." His discussion of this grading makes him sound very much like a schoolmaster.

> The key to grading players is the recognition of the fact that some positions are more difficult to play than others. On pass plays, for example, your center and your guards and tackles should make 85 percent for a passing grade, while your ends have no blocking responsibility. On running plays 55 percent is a passing grade for your split end, 60 percent qualifies your center, guards, and tight end, while your tackles should make 65 percent. The percentages for backs are 60 percent on runs and 85 percent on passes, and anyone who hits his percentages on both running and passing wins acclaim. You grade your defensive backs on a plus-and-minus point system, and an interception helps the score the most. On a good day a defensive back will break even, and a plus score means he played an unusually fine game.[35]

The probable psychological results of treating adults this way are suggested in a passage from Robert Daley's novel of professional football, *Only A Game.* In it, the protagonist of the novel, Duke Craig, reflects on the possibilities of talking over his personal problem with other men on the team.

> Pro football is a cruel and ruthless way of life. Although all the players have been to college, and some intellectually are very bright, nonetheless the mental level of the team as a whole—its attitudes—is on the level of schoolboys. The humor is schoolboy humor, and the cruelty is schoolboy cruelty. The players have the schoolboy's lack of interest in any form of sophistication—except the sophisticated brand of football they play. Conversation invariably is shop talk—very, very technical. Craig has found that he cannot speak to his teammates of that part of life that troubles him, because this is serious stuff and they always react to serious stuff by mocking it. Craig no more wants to be mocked than the next man, but he might have risked mockery. What he cannot risk is the chance that his teammates will find out who he really is, will decide he does not fit in, and will slowly, inexorably close him out.[36]

Here again, we have the sense that professional football is a play world. Duke Craig knows that no one else wants to hear about his personal helldogs. The passage also suggests the presence of a sort of enforced adolescence, in which the player is trapped, a sort of dark underside of the family, schoolboy society which is proposed. Many players, though, are very enthusiastic about this kind of society. Jerry Kramer, in fact, seems to regard it as 'the best experience of his life.' In his second book, *Jerry Kramer's Farewell to Football,* he looks back on his experiences as a player.

> The worst part, I think, is giving up the way of life. It is a beautiful way of life, sharing setbacks and triumphs with a group of guys whose interests, if not the same as your own, are at least similar. I've said before that what I like best about pro football is the camaraderie, and I mean it. Basically, I like all kinds of people, and I like meeting new people, but no matter what I do from now on, no matter where I go, I doubt I'll ever be so close again to a group of people as I was to my teammates on the Green Bay Packers. We laughed together. We swore together. We struggled together. Sure, we laughed at stupid things, and we struggled to play a silly game. We were big kids in many ways. But, damn, it was fun.[37]

It may be that what is happening to Jerry Kramer is similar to what Nick Carraway saw happening to Tom Buchanan in *The Great Gatsby.* He described Tom as "one of those men who reach such an acute limited excellence at twenty-one that everything afterward savors of anticlimax. . . . I felt that Tom would drift on forever seeking, a little wistfully, for the dramatic turbulence of some irrecoverable football game."[38] Certainly both men, though quite different, have to deal with the same problem. Let us consider now in greater detail what Kramer here calls "the camaraderie."

This too is linked to the image of the family. What Kramer the player calls "the feeling of eleven men working together, trying to do everything in harmony," Mike Holovak, the coach, calls "a teamwork concept" and says he learned it in the army.[39] In *The Hundred Yard War,* when one character tries to arrive at a definition of what comprises a successful team, he concludes that it "consists of four or five great athletes, and thirty-five good friends."[40] Kramer makes clear what all this means in *Instant Replay.*

In *Instant Replay*, Kramer explains what he meant when he said "we're living in Camelot." He says first that "I was referring to the idea of one for all and all for one, the ideal of King Arthur's Round Table, and I meant it."[41] Despite the fact that this allusion is mixed, its meaning is clear. He is speaking of "camaraderie"; the feeling of adventurers bound together, the attitude which Ulysses embraces in Tennyson's poem. Kramer makes these remarks over national television, and later, when he is asked again about their meaning, we find they have changed somewhat and now have a political-utopian dimension. Kramer tells us that "a sports writer from Philadelphia phoned and wanted to know what I meant by my remark on television that perhaps we're living in Camelot. I told him I felt that Camelot was the ideal situation, the perfect place, the epitome of everything good."[42] Here we are asked to regard the Packers as an alternative to American society, who have succeeded in building the perfectly successful community where the society as a whole has failed. This camaraderie has a definite religious dimension. A character in *Only A Game,* speaking of the pre-game prayer, says, "Sometimes it makes me choke up. I know it helps us play better. The team spirit, the love we have for one another, is very intense during the prayer. It's the most religious experience that I've ever had."[43] A Catholic newspaper in Milwaukee, in its enthusiasm, in 1967, proclaimed Lombardi had established a Christian society on earth. " 'What a world it would be if all of us respected and loved one another with the same ferocious loyalty displayed by the Packers,' said the paper. . . ." The editorial continued, "What better practical theology could there be?" than a society based on man's respect and love for each other.[44]

The area of race relations is one in which, we are told, this society succeeds where society at large has failed. As we have seen, even books which seek to expose the shoddy treatment of the black man in athletics hold up teams like the Green Bay Packers as examples of the possibility of equal treatment of the races.[45] Both Kramer, in *Instant Replay,* and George Plimpton, in *Paper Lion,* discuss the problem of race relations in professional football. Of the two, Plimpton, who trained with the Detroit Lions to find out what professional football was like, is the more skeptical about pro football's solution. He also articulates the feelings of most players best.

Discussing the subject [racial problems], they often said that in professional football it was performance that counted, that was all, that football was a business in which a player was rated by his ability to help the team. The concept of the team and team play was essential. Nothing else made any difference. All players knew that. If their prejudices got in the way, that was the end of them. You could be prejudiced against a rookie trying for your position—that was a clash of one man's ability against another's—but prejudice in respect to race or color were violations of an unspoken code.[46]

Kramer, as a player, seems to substantiate this attitude, particularly for the Packers. He says, "There's no friction on the field, not even a hint of prejudice. You've got to give Lombardi the credit. . . . We rarely think in terms of race. The way we look at it, guys like Wood and Herb Adderley and Lionel Aldridge aren't Negroes—they're Packers."[47]

It is the limitations of this attitude that make it interesting. It is only in Camelot, or, as Kramer now puts it, "on the field" that racial prejudices cease to exist. Apparently it is the game itself that lifts the players above prejudice. In Lombardi's case the intense pressure to win, to identify oneself in terms of the team rather than anything else, accomplishes this. As Plimpton records players' attitudes, they seem to indicate another version of this: that professional football is one area of American life where the American ideal of being judged solely on the basis of one's virtue and talents still holds. But no one, it appears, feels that this attitude must continue off the field. Kramer reports a conversation between Willie Davis (black) and Henry Jordan (white southerner).

"Henry, do you believe in that segregation stuff?"

"No, Willie," said Henry, "I don't."

Willie brightened. "You don't believe in segregation? Then you must believe in integration."

"Nope," said Henry.

"You don't believe in segregation," said Willie, "and you don't believe in integration. Henry, what do you believe in?"

Henry smiled, "Willie," he said, "I believe in slavery."[48]

Kramer's final comment on the exchange, that "Henry was only kidding, I think," sums up all the uncertainties involved in such a relationship. Blacks and whites have learned in professional football, as they presumably have at any other job requiring teamwork, to get along while on the job. John Gordy, formerly of the Detroit Lions, sums up the attitude of many whites in conversation with George Plimpton. Plimpton has been considering the possibility that the kind of comradeship on a football team might remove the prejudices of its members, and has concluded that this would not happen. Gordy agrees with him.

> "Sure," Gordy said. "Why not? You come to the leagues with your prejudices already set for you—from your home, your school—and not much happens to change them. What is increased is understanding. After all, you're living together, playing together, and you learn it's easy enough. Perhaps that undermines the prejudice. But not too much. We get along."[49]

It seems, then, that in professional football, like other areas of work, the nature of the work acts to throw the races together. If it is unusual in any way, it is unusual because of the fact that, football being so divorced from ordinary life, prejudices ordinarily continue intact outside the football field. In spite of this, we continue to regard the football field itself as an area where prejudices do not exist, and to admire the sport because of this.

Prejudice may be obliterated in the action of the game, but Jerry Karmer suggests more than this when he says the black players on the Green Bay Packers "aren't Negroes—they're Packers." The Packer family provides an insulation from the world's problems at large. Within this world they regard themselves, as we have seen, as individual technicians. The power of the image of the family is seen in the fact that it is not ability that is finally admired, but the quality of brotherly love the players are able to effect. Both the players and the coaches realize that something more than technical proficiency is necessary in order to be successful in professional football. Kramer, in fact, seems to brush technical proficiency off as being finally unimportant. In speaking of a comparatively meaningless regular season game, played after the conference championship has been decided, he says

> I didn't play much of a game. I tried to make all my blocks crisp and low, perfect them for the playoffs, but the emotion wasn't there. Without the emotion, you can't play this game.[50]

This denial of the value of talent in the absence of emotion results occasionally in the kind of argument Ring Lardner gave for the excellence of the 1914 Braves. When Lombardi speaks to his team as they prepare for the game which will make them world champions for the third straight year, he stresses the emotional element in their characters.

"Lots of better ball players than you guys have gone through here," he said. "But you're the type of ball players I want. You've got character. You've got heart. You've got guts."[51]

He gives us a glimpse of his ideal player in *Run To Daylight!* in the following description of John Symank, a defensive back:

> There is no actor in Symank. He is serious and intense, and in a game he'd just as soon break your leg as not. He has made it in this league because he gets a great deal more out of himself than his ability and size justify, and I wish I could say this about all the rest of them. Many of them will rise for one game or two, but John gets the maximum out of himself in every game, and if I had thirty-five others like him I'd have a far better team than I have.[52]

Thus we have the contradiction of the flawless technicians whose most admirable quality is one that makes this technical ability irrelevant.

Lombardi himself has been aware of this contradiction and has tried to explain it by suggesting that all professional teams are of equal talent, and that consequently the team with the most spirit will win a given game. The following is a representative expression of his point of view:

> Pro football is more than anything else a game of mental reactions. When Team A loses to Team B on a given day, it is usually because Team A is less mentally alert. To be mentally alert, you must not only have experience, but desire.

Where is this desire to come from? Lombardi refers to the old amateur ethic.

> The pros have more experience and no less desire than collegians. To argue otherwise would be to argue that college spirit, which I would be the last to devaluate, can motivate a man more strongly than the desire to do well at his job for the sake of his future and his family. I can't buy this.[53]

What Lombardi is wrestling with, a refashioning of the notion of the professional ethic in the same mold as what he calls "college spirit," becomes a central theme in Mike Holovak's autobiography, *Violence Every Sunday.* Holovak succeeds in redefining the notion of the professional ethic by the simple method of distinguishing between those who are "professionals" and those who are "mercenaries." He begins making this distinction in the introduction to his book, when he rehearses his reasons for writing it. "I hope that in reading it, you will discover why some of us stay in this sport for life; why, even though we are professionals, the sport is more a disease and a joy than a method of making money."[54] Here Holovak is conscious of the commercial connotations of the word "professional" and is careful to distinguish his meaning from them. Later, when he describes his relationship to the team, he finds words for the distinction.

> All coaches are different. As I take you into the locker room in succeeding chapters, I'll demonstrate that I don't work very emotionally. At least on the outside. Other coaches give the big spiels. Who knows which system is the best? We just adjust, I guess, to the team. If I ever gave an impassioned speech, my players would think I had gone nuts. I expect one thing from them. They are professionals, not mercenaries. Professionals. I will support them. They must support me.[55]

Later in the book he elaborates on what he means by this distinction in describing the kinds of people who play professional football.

> I have to respect them. All of them. Some are just grown men with the pure souls of ten-year-old boys recently escaped from reform school. Others are men who could be brilliant in any field. To their credit, they chose football.
>
> In between come those who are just passing through—big enough to do it, cowardly enough to fake it against smaller men or bigger, dumber men, willing to participate, but never daring to really take a chance. These are the half percenters. To the crowd in the stands they look like giants. To the team and the coaches they are pygmies headed for the garbage can. A coach keeps his mouth shut about them. He sees them for what they are, uses them accordingly and then dumps them off on somebody else who needs a warm body to fill a big hole for a season or two. We never rap them because this is pro football and some are only mercenaries. Some of us play it for sport. Some of us play for reasons of ego. Some of us play it because it is a way of life—these are the professionals.[56]

Professionalism has here become a kind of religion. Those who are "the professionals" are possessed of a certain spirit which the others are not. This, and not their talent, technical equipment, is the mark of their sanctity.

Even though he is thought of as a kind of modern day saint, the professional athlete is not considered an adult. Holovak above refers to some as possessing "the pure souls of ten-year-old boys recently escaped from reform school," and this is a representative estimate. Dave Meggysey's *Out of Their League* is written in opposition to what he calls the "enforced infantilization" of players.[58] Vince Lombardi has commented, in this regard, about "an almost adolescent impulsiveness in many of them." He goes on to explain what this means to him.

> This is something that the abandon with which football must be played encourages. Beyond that, and for as long as most of them can remember, which would be back to their first days in grade school, they have been subject to regulation. As their athletic ability turned them into privileged high school and college celebrities, many of them became masters of the art of circumvention.[58]

He also quotes Lou Little to the effect that "When I see them on the field they look like gladiators . . . but when I see them off the field, they're just kids."[59]

The problem of discipline in a community of children is seen as a central one. The players themselves tend to regard themselves as essentially undisciplined and ask that discipline be imposed on them. Here Jerry Kramer describes a day off, accounting for its necessity on the grounds that he can't stand the discipline for any length of time.

> I let go today. I enjoyed myself completely. I drank a few beers and played a little cards, a lovely day off. I'd put a great deal of time and mental effort into the Detroit game, so I felt I'd earned a day of relaxation. I'm not a very well disciplined person anyway, and for me to regiment myself for any length of time is difficult.[60]

One of the problems Rylie Silver, protagonist of Gary Carwright's *The Hundred Yard War,* has is with ordering his life during the off season. Here he is sitting in a bar with friends.

> The bar is pleasant and almost empty. Arrested and convicted by their thoughts, they drink in silence. Rylie Silver is thinking: What I really miss is the discipline, the challenge of hard routine, the season. What day is this? What day are any of them? The winter is a vacuum of sterile days and long silent calls to tedium.[61]

Here discipline is equated with meaning. The season will give special meaning to each day in the week again. There is some evidence to indicate that the coaches are responsible for instilling this attitude in players when it does not already exist. Dave

Meggysey states that this is the case, but it can also be seen in statements the coaches themselves have made. Witness the following quotation from Lombardi's book, which suggests that he regards anything that even remotely questions his authority as evidence of lack of discipline on the part of the players.

> Somebody behind me kicks over an empty pop bottle and it rattles on the concrete floor. We've told them time and time again to put those bottles in the wooden boxes, and one of these days one of them, walking around barefoot or in just those white woolen socks, is going to get cut. They're like children.[62]

Though Lombardi presents Johnny Symank as his ideal in terms of what he would like a professional player to be, he also speaks in this vein about Jerry Kramer. Kramer, he says, "has the perfect devil-may-care attitude it takes to play this game. He not only ignores the small hurts, but the large ones, too. . . ."[63] Kramer, sure enough, is portrayed later in the book as a naughty child.

> I start through the door to the coaches' room to get into my sweatclothes and rain jacket. Jerry Kramer is coming out and he has that small-boy half-grin on his face again. He has been at the coffeemaker and is smuggling a doughnut out between the pages of his playbook.
>
> "Good morning, coach," he says.[64]

Kramer himself has published two books: the first of which is concerned centrally, the second in part, with the question of why he plays professional football. "Perhaps, by setting down my daily thoughts and observations," he says in the introduction to the first book, "I'll be able to understand precisely what it is that draws me back to professional football."[65] This seems to be a real question for him, for later in the book, he says that "I often wonder where my life is heading, and what's my purpose here on earth besides playing the silly games I play every Sunday. I feel there's got to be more to life than that. There's got to be some reason to it."[66]

He finds his meaning in "the silly games I play every Sunday." It is a two-fold meaning, and in both of its dimensions it may be said to be child-like. The first dimension emerges when Kramer meditates over his selection to the All-Pro team.

> My selection gave me a great deal of satisfaction. I've been All-Pro five times during the last eight seasons; the other three years I was sick and hurt and

forgotten. Being chosen again is a strange feeling, sort of like having a fickle lover come back, I guess. I'm tempted to say that the selection doesn't mean anything, but it does. It really does. It means recognition—which may be part of the reason I keep playing this silly game.[67]

Kramer is speaking of his role as a heroic figure here. He clarifies his meaning in the opening pages of *Farewell to Football.* Here he says that giving up football is "giving up the hero's role." He continues:

I worry about that. I wonder how much I'll miss being recognized, being congratulated, being idolized. For years, as an offensive lineman, I worked in relative obscurity, but with the block against Jethro Pugh and with the success of *Instant Replay*, I became as well known as a running back. I was recognized in restaurants, on the golf course, in the streets, and I loved the strange, sweet taste of recognition.[68]

The second dimension is one of which we have spoken before, and it is one that looms larger in Kramer's imagination than the first. At the end of *Instant Replay,* he makes this statement:

I know now that for me the main lure of football is the guys, my teammates, the friendship, the fun, the excitement, the incredibly exhilarating feeling of a shared achievement. When I look back upon the 1967 season . . . I remember a very special spirit, a rare camaraderie, something I can't quite define, but something I've tried to capture in this diary.[69]

Kramer here looks to the time when he was "living in Camelot" to explain "the main lure of football" for him.

Unique among players, and set off from them, somewhat like Fedallah from the crew of the *Pequod,* is the figure of the quarterback. He is best described in the books by the coaches, Vince Lombardi and Mike Holovak. Holovak says the quarterback is "the coach on the field. This is the quarterback. There is the coach on the sidelines. The man on the sidelines is powerless. He has planned. Only the coach on the field will execute."[70] Later in the book he becomes quite mystical about the qualities quarterbacks possess. He says

They have all the chill faced courage of those Rangers in black face climbing into the rubber raft off New Georgia.

They are thieves. They are commandos. They are hunters. They are the hunted. They are the kind who go into the bush after a wounded tiger and count it a loss of the moment if the tiger doesn't charge them from ten feet.

> Good quarterbacks can't be bought for money. They are already in on the steal. They and they alone know the moments.[71]

The ultimate professional, Holovak's quarterback is both identified with himself in the war imagery and with the players who play for joy rather than money. Vince Lombardi, though, is perhaps the best interpreter of Holovak's statement. He says of the relationship of coach and quarter back that

> Of all the people on your ball club—and you are involved with all of them—there is no other with whom you spend as much time as you do with your quarterback. If this is a game through which you find self expression—and if it isn't, you don't belong in it—then that quarterback is the primary extension of yourself and he is your greatest challenge.[72]

It is not surprising that Lombardi himself thinks of the quarterback's function as that of "the authoritarian leader that your quarterback must be."[73]

Which brings us to our final consideration, the image of the coach himself. There are probably two major types of coach in professional football, representing two sides of the same coin. Mike Holovak and Vince Lombardi are undoubtedly representative of these two types. George Plimpton, though, best describes the two types and gives us a most thorough portrait of one of them in George Wilson, coach (then) of the Detroit Lions. Vince Lombardi will serve as the prototype of the other kind of coach.

Plimpton's contact with Wilson came through his desire to participate in a professional football game, however briefly, so that he might report what it was like. He found it difficult to get any professional football team to agree to his playing because of its possible disruptive aspects, until he met an official of the Detroit Lions.

> He said he'd put in a word for me with the club officials, and he recommended that I write George Wilson, the head coach of the Lions, to see what he might say. He was encouraging. He said that there were two types of teams in the league—each reflecting the head coach's disposition. Some were primarily no-nonsense, tight, stiff organizations, which would be adverse to any such idea of mine, and others, relatively few, were disposed toward something that might catch their fancy—"loose" was the word.[74]

Plimpton describes Wilson thoroughly during the rest of the book: showing his behavior on the practice field, during games, before games and when he is relaxing.[75] At all times he retains what appears to be the essential quality of a leader. Plimpton observes him playing cards.

> It was difficult to learn much from George Wilson's play. He had the most fun with the game, full of comment, and his play was haphazard and difficult to categorize, as if the occasion was what he took pleasure in—to sit in that cool bar, after the heat of those August afternoons, with his confederates and relax in that camaraderie. His was the strong character at the table. For all the piques of play, it was obvious the staff got along well; a strongly knit group with Wilson surely its leader—though it was never deference that was indicated, but respect, subtle but evident.[76]

Wilson thinks of his system of coaching as a "relaxed operation" as opposed to the "hard martinetcy" of other coaches, Lombardi presumably being one. We want to consider Lombardi's way. In the novel *The Hundred Yard War*, the action of the novel includes a coaching change from the Wilson type of coach to the Lombardi type. At one time in the novel one of the players describes the Lombardi type as a kind of Ahab figure.

> "Oh, baby, you think Dandridge is a son of a bitch," Temple was telling them, "Curly Sandusky at Washington thinks he's Captain Ahab. You ought to see him up in front of the squad. He gets this crazy glint in his eye and thump-thumps around the speaker's platform—you'd swear he has a wooden leg—'Aarr, lads 'n' buckos, he's a White Whale! A White Whale, I tell ye! You know what he does? He keeps you on two-a-days right up till about ten days before the season. He's a beaut. . . ."[77]

Certainly the element in Ahab that moves the character to make this comparison is not the possibility that the coach is a taskmaster, nor that he is a frenzied orator, but the willfullness that infuses all his action. This quality is certainly evident in Lombardi, who said in a speech to the American Management Association in 1967, that "I think it is obvious that the difference between the group and the leader is not so much lack of strength, not so much in lack of knowledge, but rather in lack of will. . . . Unless you maintain discipline, unless you enforce it in a perfect manner, I think you're a potential failure at your job."[78] Before we consider Lombardi's public qualities, it may be best to look at the situation in Green Bay before he arrived and to consider some of the historical aspects of his career as a coach.

The situation in Green Bay with respect to the local football team before Lombardi was hired was a chaotic one and resembled in important respects the situation in professional baseball before Judge Landis became Commissioner. The team was actually being managed by a committee of businessmen from the local community. This committee, according to an article in *Fortune* Magazine, "even went to the extent of criticizing plays and negotiating with players. But such Monday morning quarterbacking inevitably led to confusion and dissension, both within the club and in the community."[79] This "confusion and dissension" reached such a height after the 1958 season that the board of directors began to feel that the system had to be reformed. Jerry Atkinson, one of the directors, recalled that the board "felt that no group, even a group of successful businessmen, can run anything. Somebody has to be in charge." Out of that judgment, according to an article in *Fortune* Magazine, grew the "autocratic" regime of Vince Lombardi.[80] Thus Lombardi, like Judge Landis, was asked to give order to a situation the owners of which despaired of controlling in a democratic manner.

In *Packer Dynasty,* Phil Bengston sees nothing startling in the shape of these events.

> There was nothing really revolutionary about what they called the Miracle of Green Bay. It was mostly a matter of setting up an orderly administration, starting with the front office. Lombardi had convinced the Packer directors that a winning team could not be put together by a committee of Monday morning quarterbacks. Power and leadership had to be vested in one man, and that man had to be Vince Lombardi, coach, general manager, and spiritual leader—not necessarily in that order.
>
> He demanded and was guaranteed absolute authority to hire, fire, budget, and deal with the press. . . . If it smacked of dictatorship, that was what was needed.[81]

Bengston's rather pragmatic mind accepts the necessary thing in any situation without questions. That this operation worked is a matter of history; Green Bay was the most successful and accomplished team in professional football for ten years. But Lombardi, in 1968, decided to get out of coaching. He did this for one year, then returned to coaching, forsaking Green Bay to accept a job as coach and general manager and vice president of the Washington Redskins.

This shocked the people of Green Bay who, according to Lombardi's successor as coach at Green Bay, Phil Bengston "weren't like a typical sports crowd, just out for a good time. They were more like the people of a small nation, gathered for a coronation: all of them personally involved and intensely interested. . . ."[82] Thus Lombardi, by leaving Green Bay, qualified as a traitor (even to himself), and his explanations for leaving and for taking the Washington job had to be elaborate and convincing. First of all, the Washington job afforded him the same kind of authority he had exercised in Green Bay. *Newsweek* quoted him as saying, upon accepting the job, "I will be executive vice president, I will coach, I will have a substantial equity. Mr. Williams will be president, but he will go back to his law practice, I guess. I will have control. I will have everything."[83] These words might as well come from a Napoleon as a football coach.

But Lombardi presents himself and is presented as a man of the spirit rather than as a politician. In fact, this is how the transition from Green Bay to Washington is handled by *Sports Illustrated.* They speak of him as the former "Emperor of the Green Bay Packers" who has "transcended the offices" of that team for those of the Washington team where he "has been treated as if he were some kind of home-rule Moses." This transition has occurred through inner need rather than as the result of material inducements. Says Lombardi, "I don't need the money. Money, I've got. I need to *coach*!"[84] In the end, however, the decision was not his to make. It was of such importance that he could act only as "the fate's lieutenant." Lombardi describes this to William Johnson, *Sports Illustrated* writer.

> Given Lombardi's own Happy Ending version to the Green Bay episode of the saga, how does he feel about his new beginning in Washington? Absolutely transcendental. "Before I went to Green Bay, I'd had other offers in the '50's," he said. "I didn't take them, and I still don't know why. But when Green Bay came along–I knew–it was right! Now this time I've had other offers. . . . But I didn't take any of them. NO, I took Washington." He sat for a moment, musing with a distant look in his eyes. Then swiftly he clapped himself on a shoulder, and his eyes blazed behind the glasses. "That's the way it was with Green Bay. And that's the way it was with Washington–as if the Lord's hand were on my shoulder and I *knew* which was the right thing to do."[85]

Thus Lombardi identifies himself as an agent of God rather than as a shrewd businessman. In what kind of world does he live?

Lombardi's world has the same shape as that of Eliot Asinof's

Allie Sherman: Lombardi is a leader of men, a molder of men, and a commercially successful man. His world thus has political, artistic, and business dimensions. We can consider each in turn.

Lombardi has presented himself as his players' servant, dedicated to seeing that they fulfill themselves to the greatest possible extent. He says that

> For six months of each year, you must deal daily with 40 individuals, and your effort must be to motivate each of them equally toward the same ideal. Their flaws as football players are obvious; hidden are the reasons why they are not overcoming these flaws and fulfilling their potentials.
>
> "I will try," I promise the new men when I talk to them as a group for the first time, "to make each of you the best football player he can possibly be. I will try with every fiber in me, and I will try and try and try."[86]

Here he is both a leader and a molder.

As a leader he had what can be called a political philosophy and it was rumored, after he had quit coaching early in 1968, that he might enter the political arena. His statement in August of 1968 that "they'd eat me alive in politics . . . I'm too much of an idealist for politics," only seemed to certify what had before seemed a possibility.[87] He had indicated that he would have to be called (as he was afterward called to Washington though only to coach the Redskins), and his obvious electability in the state of Wisconsin probably would have persuaded one of the political parties eventually to call him. His political philosophy was formed on the football field and he wisely decided to remain there, though he continually insisted that his principles had a wider application than the football field. At the press conference at which he was announced as the new coach of the Washington Redskins, he told newsmen that "I will demand a commitment to excellence and to victory," not unusual words for a football coach to speak, then added, "and that is what life is all about, too."[88]

Lombardi's philosophy is based on the idea that there are two kinds of people in the world; leaders and followers. Put simply and in football terms, there are coaches and players. He described it this way to Leonard Shecter.

> Everywhere you look, there is a call for freedom, independence, or whatever you wish to call it. But as much as these people want to be independent, they still want to be told what to do. And so few people who are capable of leading are ready and willing to lead. So few are ready. . . . We must gain

respect for authority—no, let's say we must *regain* respect for authority. . . . We must learn again to respect authority because to disavow it is contrary to our individual natures.[89]

In Gary Cartwright's *The Hundred Yard War* a richer version of this philosophy is put into the mouth of Ward Dandridge, the Lombardi-figure of the novel. Dandridge speaks of the younger generation:

"They're a bunch of crybabies. Hippies! Ban the bomb! Independence! Freedom! They wouldn't know what to do if you told 'em!" . . . "It's a fuckin' crime! Listen, my old man told me one thing: People are goats! Independence, my hind foot! I'll give you independence and they'll walk around all day with their foot in a bucket. . . ."

"Yeah, well they're talking about *their* rights! What about what's right? The rights of the individual has got to be put above everything else? Bull shit! People are goats! Ninety-nine point nine per cent of the people have to be told, otherwise they'll stand around and piss in their boot."[90]

It is clear from these quotations that both Lombardi and Ward Dandridge are anti-democratic in their politics and that the basis for this is their opinion of human nature. Lombardi saw very few people capable of what he called leadership, Dandridge lives in a world where people have to be told what to do. Both apparently feel that the world would be a better place, for leaders and followers both, if people obeyed their leaders, and both decry lack of leadership in contemporary society, at least off the football field. If people did obey their natural leaders, according to Lombardi and Dandridge, the chaos occasioned by the search for freedom would disappear, and life would be much more orderly and understandable. People could then concentrate on "what's right."

In this world, freedom is in total opposition to authority and must be done away with before any kind of self-fulfillment is possible. "We need followers," Lombardi has said, "who will accept authority. . . . In our search for individual freedom, in struggling to liberate ourselves from ancient creeds, we sometimes have idealized freedom against order. It has been the new against the old and, by reducing authority, we have lost discipline. Thus the freedom—too much freedom—has had an adverse effect."[91] Lombardi offers, as the heroic follower, " 'the company man' because he is dedicated to a principle he believes in. . . ."[92] The reestablishment of authority will bring fulfillment for the individual and progress for the organization. This is true within the community of the professional football team. Lombardi thought it ought to be true in the community at large. Shecter quotes him as saying:

> I think the rights of the individual have been put above everything else . . . which I don't think is right. The individual has to have respect for authority regardless of what that authority is. I think the individual has gone too far. I think ninety-five per cent of the people, as much as they shout, would rather be led than lead.[93]

In addition to thinking that an authoritarian state is a more productive one than a free state, Lombardi had another main point to make about the relation of the community of the football team to society at large. This one has a religious basis and has led Leonard Shecter to speak of "Vince Lombardi process of natural selection."[94] This has to do basically with the question of talent. Lombardi believed that for an individual to do anything but his best would be cheating both himself and his team. "We have God-given talents and are expected to use them to our fullest ability whenever we play."[95] He could think of no excuse for not doing this, and consequently, when he looked out at contemporary society at large, he did not care particularly for the welfare programs, because they tended to equalize conditions between underprivileged and privileged, whom he equated with untalented and talented. He has said that

> It is hard to have patience with a society which has sympathy only for the underprivileged. . . . The talented are no more responsible for their birthright than the underprivileged. We must have sympathy for the doer, too. . . . We must help the underprivileged, certainly. But let us also have respect for success.[96]

Lombardi apparently wanted to restore a "natural" order. Talented people must have the opportunity to succeed, to rise to the top of their profession, as they do in professional football.

The dominant image of the social and political order that Lombardi had created on his football teams and wanted for America was that of the family. He preferred to see himself as the leader of this family, as a father. That this authoritarian image has less than charitable implications is clear from these derogatory images, used by some writers, that are associated with it. Gary Cartwright's

The Hundred Yard War has reference to the Lombardi figure as a "South American dictator" and Leonard Shecter suggests that some of Lombardi's political statements may be "out of the memoirs of some South American general."[97] Shecter characterizes Lombardi's situation at Green Bay in this way:

> It's as coach and general manager of the Packers that Lombardi exerts his real power. He runs a sort of fiefdom in Green Bay, complete with automobile dealers who thrust free cars on him just so he will be seen driving them. The Packers are, theoretically, municipally owned. In fact they are an autocracy, run by Vince Lombardi.[98]

Lombardi preferred at first to think of himself as a teacher rather than a coach. In *Run to Daylight!* he says, "they call it coaching, but it is teaching. You do not just tell them it is so, but you show them the reasons why it is so and you repeat and repeat until they are convinced, until they know. It was the way, back in Brooklyn, the good teachers I had and admired did it. . . ."[99] The authoritarianism is here, but it is blunted by the image of the teacher showing the students why what is so is so. This same relationship operates in the parent-children image.

This image comes through strongest in two places, in Jerry Kramer's *Instant Replay* and in Lombardi's own comments about what he missed after giving up coaching. At one point in *Instant Replay* Kramer remarks that Lombardi is "more than anything else . . . a psychologist. Maybe a child psychologist."[100] Here Kramer acknowledges his own role as a child. He tells us early in the book that Lombardi "thinks of himself as the patriarch of a large family, and he loves all his children, and he worries about all of them. . . ."[101] Later in discussing his own history of injuries, he remembers Lombardi's attitude toward him then as that of a father.

> . . . in 1964 when I almost died with all my intestinal ailments, Lombardi visited me in the hospital and he told me not to worry, that the Packers would pay my salary in 1964 and 1965 even if I couldn't play and that the club would pay all my hospital bills. He does things like that. His players are his children, and he nurses them when they're sick and scolds them when they're bad and rewards them when they're good.[102]

Dave Meggysey offers confirmation of this point of view in his *Out of Their League* when he refers to the football coach as "a sort of substitute father," suggests that "the father-son relationship" is "football's cornerstone," and speaks of Kramer's need to build Lombardi "into an epic father-figure."[103] Lombardi himself, so far as I know, did not directly acknowledge this role, or give any indication of his attitude toward it until after he retired from coaching after the 1967 season. Then he was asked what he missed in the coaching profession, if anything. *Life* reported that

"Right now," he said, "I miss it fiercely. First of all I miss the rapport with the players. I was close to them and they to me. Today I feel as if I'm nothing to them. When I meet one of them, he says: 'Hello, Mister Lombardi,' and that's it."[104]

Lombardi didn't indicate the nature of this rapport until after he had signed a contract to coach the Washington Redskins. Then he said

"What I missed most was—well, it wasn't the tension and the crowds and the game on Sunday. And it certainly *wasn't* the winning. And it *wasn't* the spotlight and all that. The fame. No, it wasn't. There's a great—a great *closeness* on a football team, you know—a rapport between the men and the coach that's like no other sport. It's a binding together, a knitting together. For me, it's like father and sons, and that's what I missed. I missed players coming up to me and saying, 'Coach, I need some help because my baby's sick,' or 'Mr. Lombardi, I want to talk to you about the trouble I'm having with my wife.' That's what I missed most. The closeness."

William Johnson suggests that "in Lombardi's own terms this role of being more parent than employer, more father confessor than professional coach, is the essence of his career."[105] Certainly we see that what Lombardi missed is the kind of community created within the system of professional football.

Actually, it may be that we have to seek elsewhere for "the essence of his career." It may, I think, be found in this paragraph from Jerry Kramer's second book. Here Kramer is trying to imagine how the 1968 season (a disaster for the Green Bay team) would have been if Lombardi had still been coach.

I don't know if we would have won if Lombardi had still been coaching. I tend to think that Vince, too, would have had a hard time making us into champions in 1968. But I really missed him for those Chicago and Minnesota games. He was the genius of the locker-room speech; he always knew exactly how to treat us. In 1967, for instance, before the Bears game that clinched the division title, he didn't say anything but a silly little joke to break the tension; a few weeks later, before the game for the Western Conference title, he quoted passionately from one of St. Paul's Epistles and really fired us up. He played us like a virtuoso.[106]

Kramer here regards Lombardi as a maker of champions, and he calls him a virtuoso artist. It may be that it is this artistic dimension, Lombardi's ability to make champions, rather than the social situation, that is the essence of his career.

Kramer seems to have this dimension of his personality in mind when he speaks of Lombardi as a perfectionist. "I guess," he says, "more than anything else, he's a perfectionist, an absolute perfectionist."

He pays such meticulous attention to detail. He makes us execute the same plays over and over, a hundred times, two hundred times, until we do every little thing right automatically. He works to make the kickoff-return team perfect, the punt-return team perfect, the field-goal team perfect. He ignores nothing. Technique, technique, technique, over and over and over, until we feel like we're going crazy. But we win.[107]

Kramer sometimes thinks that Lombardi values perfection over winning. He reports this team meeting in which Lombardi expresses dissatisfaction with the team's play.

Coach Lombardi seemed more disturbed than angry during our meeting this morning. He said there's a general lack of enthusiasm on the club, a lack of desire, something he can't quite put his finger on. He said that sometimes he would rather lose and have everybody play a perfect game than win and have everybody look sloppy. My immediate reaction is to say that's crazy, that's ridiculous, he couldn't really mean that, but, somehow, I suspect he does, at least in theory. His desire for perfection is immense, and he's been very unhappy with our habit of doing only as much as we have to do to win.[108]

This may be regarded, as Kramer does regard it, as sacrilege, but it does seem to be, as Kramer also points out, Lombardi's theoretical position. In his second book, Kramer imagines what Lombardi would dream, given the opportunity to choose.

Vince Lombardi never told me whether he had any dream or not, but I can imagine what his ideal dream would be. First, because he always takes the long-range view, his dream wouldn't cover one play or one game. His dream would cover, at the minimum, a full season, from the start of training camp to the end of the Super Bowl. In his dream, his team would win every exhibition, every regular-season game, every post-season game. . . . But the

> scores in his dreams would be secondary to the style. . . . Beyond any spectacular runs or spectacular passes, Lombardi would dream of a season without a single mental or physical error. He would dream of perfection, because Vince Thomas Lombardi, above all else is a perfectionist. Which is why, over the past decade, he has the finest record of any coach in professional football.[109]

Vince Lombardi, then, is an artist, and his materials are those of the professional football coach: the schedule, the game, the men.

Lombardi himself would seem to agree with this point of view, though he too never explicitly characterized himself as an artist. Rather he saw himself as a maker of men, helping athletes to achieve for themselves the best they have in them. Here he considers the problems of coaching.

> It is amazing how on that first day one or two impress you with the grace with which they move. Even before some of them put on a uniform you get that feeling from them. And then there's another one and you'll wonder why you ever brought him into camp. You have two reactions. First you feel an urge to work just on that good one, to see how perfect you can make him. But then you realize you must work on the others, too, in order to make a team, and so you spend most of the time you can give—and it's never enough—with the ones who lack natural ability, but whom you need.[110]

This is the dilemma of a man who regarded himself fundamentally as an artist, a man primarily involved in perfecting athletes. He has said that "every coach's team is an extension of himself, and so the personality of the coach becomes the personality of his team."[111] Out of himself and his players, he makes something. "You cannot be successful in football—or in any organization—unless you have people who bend to your personality."[112] Lombardi's great success was an artistic one: politically (and since his materials are men both spheres are relevant) he cannot be said to have succeeded. It is probably because his endeavors crossed the line between art and politics that so many stories about him as a god-like figure have arisen.[113]

It is, however, unfair to conclude this chapter on the public image of Vince Lombardi, without ever noticing the actuality. Though (or, perhaps, because) he was in many stories made a god figure, he was, actually, a shrewd businessman and this, it seems to me, is the quality most responsible for his success. It is hard to tell whether or not Lombardi fooled himself in this respect for he tells us that he is fundamentally an emotional man. "I've got all the emotions in excess and a hair-trigger controls them. I anger and I laugh and I cry quickly, and so I couldn't have told you five minutes later what else I said or just what I did," he says in *Run to Daylight!*[114] In his political statements he professed to believe that "heart power is the strength of the Green Bay Packers. . . . Heart power is the strength of America."[115] But, as Herbert Warren Wind has pointed out, "Lombardi considers himself an emotional person, which he is, but his chief characteristics are a really formidable intelligence, thoroughness, pride, and a quiet but relentless drive."[116] What seemed most to impress people about Lombardi was his intensity. William Johnson describes him in person:

> But even when he is physically still, Lombardi's intensity is a phenomenon to behold. In leisurely conversation he seems constantly to be willfully exerting the force of his personality—on himself, on anyone near him, on the humming flow of traffic outside the window on Connecticut Avenue, maybe on the universe. It is almost like a religious act of Zen discipline. He exerts his personality not so much to control things as to keep himself taut, conditioned, perfectly disciplined. It is a kind of isometric exercise of the will—or perhaps of the soul. But the awareness of Lombardi's will, of the nearly physical intensity of his ego, never quite disappears when one is in his presence.[117]

Even Jerry Kramer, who is most insistent on Lombardi's image as a father figure, as one who cared intensely for his players, ends by saying that "his personal feelings, I suspect, end up running second to his professional feelings, which are summed up in another one of his favorite sayings. 'Winning isn't everything,' he tells us. 'It's the only thing.' "[118] Lombardi's successor as coach at Green Bay, Phil Bengston, probably has his priorities right when he describes Vince Lombardi as "a hard-working, practical, religious, dedicated, fair-and-square businessman who happens also to be a football genius and a leader of men. Most people are disappointed," Bengston adds, "that the explanation isn't more complicated."[119]

NOTES

INTRODUCTION

[1]Harold Dean Cater, ed., *Henry Adams and His Friends: A Collection of Unpublished Letters* (Boston: The Riverside Press, 1947), p. 682.

[2]David Quentin Voigt, *American Baseball: From Gentleman's Sport to the Commissioner System* (Norman: University of Oklahoma Press, 1966), p. 80.

[3]Voigt, *American Baseball*, pp. 81-84. See also Harold Seymour, *Baseball: The Early Years* (New York: Oxford University Press, 1960), pp. 330-336. Seymour offers evidence for the idea that, in spite of this image, "taken as a whole, ballplayers were not much different from any other men of comparable background and education." p. 332.

[4]Quoted in Lawrence S. Ritter, *The Glory of Their Times: The Story of the Early Days of Baseball Told by The Men Who Played It* (New York: The Macmillan Company, 1966), p. 164.

[5]Quoted in R. W. Stallman, *Stephen Crane: A Biography* (New York: George Braziller, 1968), pp. 10, 14.

[6]Quoted by Seymour, p. 345.

[7]Mark Twain, *A Connecticut Yankee in King Arthur's Court* (New York: Pocket Books, Inc., 1948), p. 323.

[8]David Quentin Voigt argues that "baseball is a pioneer sports form which came to be widely imitated. In time other American team sports like football, hockey, and basketball imitated baseball's structural pattern in order to compete as commercialized spectacles." *American Baseball*, p. xvi.

[9]James Reston, "Bouquet is Tossed at Sports," Minneapolis *Tribune*, October 8, 1966.

[10]Frederick Exley, *A Fan's Notes: A Fictional Memoir* (New York: Harper and Row, 1968), p. 8.

[11]Gregory Stone, "Appearance and the Self," in Arnold Rose, ed., *Human Behavior and Social Processes* (Boston: Houghton Mifflin Company, 1962), p. 116. See also Daniel J. Boorstin, *The Image: A Guide To Psuedo-Events in America* (New York and Evanston: Harper Colophon Books, 1964), p. 254, and Douglas Wallop, *So This Is What Happened to Charlie Moe* (New York: W. W. Norton, 1965), p. 135. Academic studies include John Von Neumann and Oskar Morgenstern, *Theory of Games and Economic Behavior* (Princeton: Princeton University Press, 1944), and Erving Goffman, *The Presentation of Self in Everyday Life* (Garden City: Doubleday Anchor Books, 1959). Play theory is used in other fields than those mentioned here. In the field of journalism see William Stephenson, *The Play Theory of Mass Communication* (Chicago and London: University of Chicago Press, 1967). Theological and philosophical analyses of life in terms of play and sport are also available. See Hugo Rahner, S. J., *Man at Play* (New York: Herder and Herder, 1967), Howard S. Slusher, *Man, Sport and Existence: A Critical*

Analysis (Philadelphia: Lea & Febinger, 1967), and Paul Weiss, *Sport: A Philosophical Inquiry* (Carbondale and Edwardsville: Southern Illinois University Press, 1969).

[12]Johan Huizinga, "The Task of Cultural History," *Men and Ideas: History, The Middle Ages, The Renaissance* (New York: Meridian Books, 1959), pp. 38-39.

[13]Gertrude Jaeger and Philip Sleznick, "A Normative Theory of Culture," in Robert Merideth, ed., *American Studies: Essays on Theory and Method* (Columbus: Charles E. Merrill Publishing Co., 1968), pp. 114-115.

[14]See Lionel Trilling, "Reality in America," *The Liberal Imagination* (Garden City: Doubleday Anchor Books, 1950), pp. 1-19, and R. W. B. Lewis, *The American Adam: Innocence, Tragedy and Tradition in the Nineteenth Century* (Chicago and London: University of Chicago Press, 1955).

[15]I depart here from the argument of Jaeger and Selznick, who go on to speak of the differences between "cultural" and "aesthetic" objects. "A Normative Theory of Culture," pp. 115-116.

[16]In John W. Ward's *Andrew Jackson–Symbol for an Age* (New York: Oxford University Press, 1962), the opposite is attempted. Melville's *Moby Dick* is used to confirm the construction of ideas and images Ward finds in the popular culture.

[17]Lawrence S. Ritter, *The Glory of Their Times,* p. 242. The player speaking is Bob O'Farrell.

CHAPTER 1

[1]The source of this and other biographical information contained in this essay is R. L. Colie, "Johan Huizinga and the Task of Cultural History," *American Historical Review,* LXIX, 3, pp. 607-630.

[2]Pieter Geyl, "Huizinga as Accuser of His Age," *History and Theory,* II (No. 3, 1963), p. 232.

[3]*Ibid.*

[4]Cowlie, p. 616.

[5]Johan Huizinga, *In the Shadow of Tomorrow: A Diagnosis of the Spiritual Ills of Our Time* (New York: W. W. Norton and Co., Inc., 1936), p. 217.

[6]*Ibid.*, p. 170.

[7]Colie, p. 620.

[8]Geyl, p. 246. In 1927 Huizinga published another book dealing with American culture, *American Living and Thinking.*

[9]Huizinga, *In the Shadow of Tomorrow,* p. 173.

[10]*Ibid.,* pp. 174-175.

[11]Geyl, pp. 262, 261.

[12]*Ibid.,* p. 239.

[13]Colie, p. 614.

[14]Johan Huizinga, *Homo Ludens: A Study of the Play Element in Culture* (Boston: The Beacon Press, 1962), p. 7. Future references to this book will be included within parenthesis in the text.

[15]Huizinga, *In the Shadow of Tomorrow,* pp. 177-178.

[16]Ralph Barton Perry, *Puritanism and Democracy* (New York & Evans-

ton: Harper Torchbooks, 1964), p. 255.

[17]*Ibid.*, p. 257.

[18]Michael Walzer, *The Revolution of the Saints* (New York: Atheneum Books, 1968), p. 303. I would like to thank the Harvard University Press for permission to quote from this book.

[19]*Ibid.*, p. 19.

[20]*Ibid.*, p. 300.

[21]*Ibid.*, p. 110.

[22]*Ibid.*, p. 209.

[23]*Ibid.*, p. 211. Walzer argues in a footnote on this page that "the stress of the preachers is most often on the social and moral effects of hard work and not on its spiritual significance. The new ethic is at least as much a response to the overriding problem of social order as it is to the individual's anxiety with regard to his fate in the life to come."

[24]Harvey Wish, "Introduction" to William Bradford, *Of Plymouth Plantation* (New York: Capricorn Books, 1962), p. 11.

[25]Thomas Morton, *New English Canaan* (Amsterdam: Jacob Frederick Stam, 1637), p 132.

[26]*Ibid.*, pp. 134-135.

[27]William Bradford, *Of Plymouth Plantation,* p. 140.

[28]*Ibid.*, p. 141.

[29]Foster Rhea Dulles, *America Learns to Play* (New York & London: Appleton-Century Company, 1940), pp. 85-86.

[30]Thomas Carlyle, *Past and Present* (New York & London: Dutton Everyman Edition, 1962), p. 193. Future references to this book will be included within parenthesis in the text.

[31]Walter E. Houghton, *The Victorian Frame of Mind* (New Haven & London: Yale University Press, 1957), pp. 251, 254, 256.

[32]Huizinga, *Homo Ludens,* pp. 191-192.

[33]This is included in the "Backgrounds, Sources and Contemporary Reactions" section of the Norton Critical Edition of *Hard Times*, edited by George Ford and Sylvere Monod (New York, 1966), p. 275. Future references to this edition of *Hard Times* will be included within parenthesis in the text.

[34]Nathaniel Hawthorne, "The Maypole of Merry Mount," *The Novels and Tales of Nathaniel Hawthorne* (New York: The Modern Library, 1937), p. 885. Future references will be included within parenthesis in the text.

[35]Henry David Thoreau, *Walden; or, Life in the Woods* (New York: Holt, Rinehart & Winston, 1964), pp. 2, 5. Future references will be included within parenthesis in the text.

[36]Ralph Waldo Emerson, *Selected Writings* (New York: Modern Library College Editions, 1950), p. 68.

[37]Houghton, *The Victorian Frame of Mind,* p. 202.

[38]Thomas Hughes, *School Days at Rugby* (Boston: Tichnor and Fields, 1858), p. 4. Future references will be included in parenthesis in the text.

[39]Edward C. Mack and W.H.G. Armytage, *Thomas Hughes* (London: Ernest Benn Limited, 1952), p. 19.

[40]See Albert F. McLean, Jr., *American Vaudeville as Ritual* (Lexing-

ton: University of Kentucky Press, 1965), p. 83ff. For the Turnerian interpretation of the rise of sport in the late nineteenth century, see Frederick Logan Paxon's essay, "The Rise of Sport," written in 1917 and included in his *The Great Demobilization and Other Essays* (Madison: University of Wisconsin Press, 1941).

[41]Mark Twain, *Life on the Mississippi* (New York: Bantam Books, 1945), p. 48. Future references will be included within parenthesis in the text.

[42]Thorstein Veblen, *The Theory of the Leisure Class: An Economic Study of Institutions* (New York: The New American Library, 1953), p. 169. Future references will be included within parenthesis in the text.

[43]Thorstein Veblen, "The Place of Science in Modern Civilization" in *The Place of Science in Modern Civilization and Other Essays* (New York: The Viking Press, 1932), p. 7. Future references will be included within parenthesis in the text.

[44]Thorstein Veblen, *The Instinct of Workmanship and the State of the Industrual Arts* (New York: W. W. Norton & Company, 1964), p. 18. Future references will be included within parenthesis in the text.

[45]"Two Tramps in Mud Time" originally appeared in Frost's 1936 collection, *A Further Range.* I quote from *The Poetry of Robert Frost,* edited by Edward Cornery Lathem (New York: Holt, Rinehart & Winston, 1969), pp. 275-277.

[46]Robert Lowell, "Endecott and the Red Cross," *The Old Glory* (New York: The Noonday Press, 1966), p. 14. Future references will be included within parenthesis in the text.

CHAPTER II

[1]Joseph Warren Beach, "How Do You Like It Now, Gentlemen?" in Carlos Baker, ed., *Hemingway and His Critics: An International Anthology* (New York: Hill & Wang, 1961), p. 233.

[2]Carlos Baker, "Introduction: Citizen of the World," *Hemingway and His Critics,* p. 13.

[3]Ernest Hemingway, "A Clean, Well-Lighted Place," in *The Short Stories of Ernest Hemingway* (New York: Charles Scribner's Sons, 1954), pp. 382-383. All references to Hemingway's short stories are to this volume and will be included within parenthesis in the text.

[4]Ernest Hemingway, *The Sun Also Rises* (New York: Charles Scribner's Sons, 1953), p. 148.

[5]Ernest Hemingway, *A Moveable Feast* (New York: Charles Scribner's Sons, 1964), p. 21. See also p. 50.

[6]Ivan Kashkeen, "Ernest Hemingway: A Tragedy of Craftsmanship" in John K. M. McCaffery, ed., *Ernest Hemingway: The Man and His Work* (Cleveland and New York: World Publishing Company, 1950), pp. 87-88. See also "Alive in the Midst of Death: Ernest Hemingway" in Baker, *Heming-*

way and His Critics, p. 165.

[7]*A Moveable Feast,* pp. 44, 43.

[8]George Plimpton, "An Interview With Ernest Hemingway" in Baker, *Hemingway and His Critics,* p. 24. See also the deleted portions of "Big Two-Hearted River," quoted by Carlos Baker, *Ernest Hemingway: A Life Story* (New York: Charles Scribner's Sons, 1969), p. 132.

[9]*A Moveable Feast,* p. 209.

[10]Ernest Hemingway, *The Wild Years,* ed. and introduced by Gene Z. Hanrahan (New York: Dell Publishing Co., 1963), p. 258.

[11]For various studies of ritual in "Big Two-Hearted River," see Malcolm Cowley, "Nightmare and Ritual in Hemingway" in Robert P. Weeks, ed., *Hemingway: A Collection of Critical Essays,* pp. 40-51, and William Bysshe Stein, "Ritual in Hemingway's 'Big Two-Hearted River,' " *Texas Studies in Literature and Language,* Winter, 1960, pp. 555-561.

[12]Charles A. Fenton, "No Money for the Kingbird: Hemingway's Prizefight Stories," *American Quarterly,* Winter, 1953, pp. 346, 347.

[13]*Ibid.,* p. 343.

[14]Ernest Hemingway, "Million Dollar Fright: A New York Letter," *Esquire*, November, 1935, p. 190B. Future references will be included within parenthesis in the text.

[15]Quoted in Carlos Baker, *Hemingway: The Writer as Artist,* 3rd edition (Princeton, New Jersey: Princeton University Press, 1963), p. 81. *Ernest Hemingway: A Life Story,* p. 359.

[16]Johan Huizinga, *Homo Ludens,* p. 3.

[17]Reuel Denney, *The Astonished Muse: Popular Culture in America* (New York: Grosset & Dunlop, 1964), pp. 122-123.

[18]Ernest Hemingway, *The Sun Also Rises* (New York: Charles Scribner's Sons, 1953), pp. 36-37.

[19]*Homo Ludens,* pp. 6, 10.

[20]Ernest Hemingway, *Death in the Afternoon* (New York: Charles Scribner's Sons, 1961), p. 16. Future references will be included within parenthesis in the text.

[21]Ernest Hemingway, *The Wild Years,* p. 224. William White, ed., *By-Line: Ernest Hemingway* (New York: Charles Scribner's Sons, 1967), p. 92.

[22]Ernest Hemingway, "The Dangerous Summer," *Life,* September 5, 1960, p. 85.

[23]*Ibid.,* p. 94.

[24]Ernest Hemingway, "The Pride of the Devil," *Life,* September 12, 1960, p. 78.

[25]*Ernest Hemingway: A Life Story*, p. 268.

[26]Ernest Hemingway, *Green Hills of Africa* (New York: Charles Scribner's Sons, 1962), p. 70. Future references will be included within parenthesis in the text.

[27]Lillian Ross, *Portrait of Hemingway* (New York: Avon Books, 1961), p. 68.

[28]Ernest Hemingway, *Across the River and Into the Trees* (New York: Charles Scribner's Sons, 1956), pp. 187-188.

[29]William White, ed., *By-Line: Ernest Hemingway,* pp. 239-240.

[30]*Ibid.,* p. 237.

[31]Ernest Hemingway, *The Old Man and the Sea* (New York: Charles Scribner's Sons, 1952), pp. 32-33.

[32]*Ernest Hemingway: A Life Story,* p. 499.

[33]Complete lyrics for this song, "Mrs. Robinson," are printed on the back cover of the record album *Bookends,* Columbia KCS 9529, performed by Simon and Garfunkel, words by Paul Simon.

[34]James A. Farley, "Introduction," *Lucky to be a Yankee* (New York: Rudolph Field, 1946), pp. 7, 8.

[35]Grantland Rice, "Forword," *Lucky to be a Yankee,* p. 9.

[36]Joe DiMaggio, *Lucky to be a Yankee,* p. 35. Future references will be included within parenthesis in the text.

[37]Joe DiMaggio, "It's Great to be Back," *Life*, August 1, 1949, p. 67.

[38]New York *World-Telegram,* March 4, 1949. See also Arthur Daley's "Sports of the Times," New York *Times*, March 16, 1949.

[39]New York *Times,* April 13, 1949.

[40]New York *World-Telegram,* March 25, 1949.

[41]New York *World-Telegram,* March 5, 1949.

[42]New York *Times,* March 16, 1949.

[43]New York *World-Telegram,* March 25, 1949.

[44]New York *World-Telegram,* April 1, 1949.

[45]New York *Times,* March 28, 1949.

[46]New York *Times,* April 14, 1949.

[47]*Life,* August 1, 1949.

[48]New York *Times,* July 29, 30, 1949.

[49]New York *Times,* August 26, 1949.

[50]New York *Times,* October 3, 1949.

[51]New York *World-Telegram,* June 30, 1949.

[52]New York *World-Telegram,* July 1, 1949.

[53]"Joe Comes Back," *Newsweek,* July 11, 1949, p. 62.

[54]New York *World-Telegram,* July 1, 1949.

[55]New York *World-Telegram,* July 2, 1949.

[56]New York *Times,* June 30, 1949.

[57]New York *World-Telegram & Sun,* April 11, 1950.

[58]New York *World-Telegram,* August 31, 1949.

[59]Ernest Hemingway, *The Old Man and the Sea,* p. 18. Future references will be included within parenthesis in the text.

[60]Mark Harris, *The Southpaw* (New York: Bobbs-Merrill, 1953), p. 32. Future references will be included within parenthesis in the text.

CHAPTER III

[1]Mark Harris, *The Southpaw,* p. 34.

[2]Gilbert Seldes, "Introduction," *The Portable Ring Lardner* (New

York: The Viking Press, 1945), p. 5.

[3]Clifton Fadiman, "Ring Lardner and the Triangle of Hate," *The Nation,* March 22, 1933, pp. 316-317.

[4]Virginia Woolf, "American Fiction," *The Moment and Other Essays* (New York: Harcourt, Brace and Company, 1948), pp. 126, 123.

[5]F. Scott Fitzgerald, *The Crack Up* (New York: New Directions, 1956), pp. 36-37. John Berryman most effectively opposes this position in "The Case of Ring Lardner," *Commentary,* November 1956, p. 421.

[6]Clifton Fadiman, "Pitiless Satire," *The Nation,* May 1, 1929, p. 537.

[7]John Berryman, "The Case of Ring Lardner," p. 418.

[8]Maxwell Geismar, "Introduction," *The Ring Lardner Reader* (New York: Charles Scribner's Sons, 1963), p. xxix.

[9]Gilbert Seldes, "Introduction," *The Portable Ring Lardner,* pp. 4, 5. Donald Elder has an excellent section on this same topic in his biography of Lardner which emphasizes that "for many of its old time fans" baseball "was never the same again" after the scandals. *Ring Lardner* (Garden City: Doubleday and Co., 1953), p. 161.

[10]See Howard W. Webb, Jr., "The Development of a Style: The Lardner Idiom," *American Quarterly,* Winter, 1960, pp. 486-487. See also John R. Betts, *Organized Sport in Industrial America* (Unpublished Doctoral Dissertation, Columbia University, 1951), p. 404n.

[11]Ring W. Lardner, "The Cost of Baseball," *Collier's*, March 2, 1912, p. 28.

[12]Ring W. Lardner, " 'Braves' is Right," *American* Magazine, March 1915, p. 19. All future references to this article will be included within parenthesis in the text.

[13]We should recall here the opposing point of view which suggests the commercial values implied in Lardner's, expressed in John Updike's comment that "insofar as the clutch hitter is not a sportswriter's myth, he is a vulgarity, like a writer who writes only for money." "Hub Fans Bid Kid Adieu," *Assorted Prose* (New York: Fawcett World Library, 1966), p. 107.

[14]Ring W. Lardner, "Some Team," *American* Magazine, April 1915, pp. 23-24. Future references to this article will be included within parenthesis in the text.

[15]Ring W. Lardner, "Tyrus: The Greatest of 'Em All," *American* Magazine, June 1915, and "Matty," *American* Magazine, August 1915. References to these articles included in parenthesis in the text.

[16]See Paul Gallico, *The Golden People* (Garden City: Doubleday & Company, 1965), pp. 199-217, for a considerably darker portrait of Cobb's character.

[17]Walton Patrick, *Ring Lardner* (New Haven: Twayne Publishers, 1963), p. 46.

[18]Ring W. Lardner, "Call For Mr. Keefe," *Saturday Evening Post,* March 9, 1918, p. 4.

[19]Ring W. Lardner, *The Real Dope* (Indianapolis: The Bobbs-Merrill Co., 1919), pp. 55-93.

[20]Ring W. Lardner, *You Know Me Al* (New York: Charles Scribner's

Sons, 1925), p. 43. Further references included within parenthesis in the text.

[21]Maxwell Geismar, "Introduction," *The Ring Lardner Reader,* p. xvii.

[22]See Howard W. Webb, Jr., "The Meaning of Ring Lardner's Fiction: A Re-evaluation," *American Literature,* January 1960, pp. 440-443. Walton R. Patrick also has an excellent analysis in *Ring Lardner,* pp. 92-95.

[23]Ring W. Lardner, "My Roomy," *How To Write Short Stories* (New York: Charles Scribner's Sons, 1925), p. 186. Further references included within parenthesis in the text.

[24]Grant Overton, "Ring Lardner's Bell Lettres," *The Bookman,* Sept. 1925, p. 46.

[25]Ring W. Lardner, "Champion," *How To Write Short Stories,* p. 158. Further references included within parenthesis in the text.

[26]Ring W. Lardner, "The Battle of the Century," *Saturday Evening Post,* October 29, 1921, p. 12. Further references included within parenthesis in the text.

[27]Ring W. Lardner, "The Venomous Viper of the Volga," *Cosmopolitan,* September 1927, p. 201.

[28]Ring W. Lardner, "Why We Have Left Hands," *Collier's,* July 6, 1929, p. 13.

[29]Ring W. Lardner, "Radio's All-American Team for 1932-33," *The New Yorker,* June 17, 1933, p. 39.

[30]Ring W. Lardner, "Sport and Play," in Harold B. Stearns, ed., *Civilization in the United States: An Inquiry by Thirty Americans* (New York: Harcourt, Brace & Co., 1922), p. 458. Future references included within parenthesis in the text.

[31]See Babe Ruth and Bob Considine, *The Babe Ruth Story* (New York: Scholastic Book Services, 1969), p. 51.

[32]Ring W. Lardner, "Along Came Ruth," *Saturday Evening Post,* July 26, 1919, p. 123. Further references included within parenthesis in the text.

[33]Ring W. Lardner, "The Courtship of T. Dorgan," *Saturday Evening Post,* September 6, 1919, p. 173.

[34]Ring W. Lardner, "Pluck and Luck: Or, The Rise of a Home Run King," *Collier's,* March 16, 1929, p. 65.

[35]John Lardner, "Introduction," *You Know Me Al* (New York: Charles Scribner's Sons, 1960), pp. 14-15.

[36]Quoted in Otto Friedrich, *Ring Lardner* (Minneapolis: University of Minnesota Press, 1965), p. 20.

[37]Ring W. Lardner, "Br'er Rabbit Ball," *The New Yorker,* September 13, 1930, p. 61. Future references included within parenthesis in the text.

[38]See also Lardner's autobiographical piece "Meet Mr. Cowley," in the *Saturday Evening Post,* November 14, 1931, p. 125, for a discussion of "left-handed fly-ball hitters."

[39]Quoted in Donald Elder, *Ring Lardner,* pp. 361-362.

CHAPTER IV

[1]"Play as a Church Function," *The Literary Digest* (66), September 11, 1920, p. 37.

[2]Gustav W. Axelson, "*Commy*": *The Life Story of Charles A. Comiskey* (Chicago: Reilly & Lee Company, 1919), p. 318.

[3]Morris R. Cohen, "Baseball," *The Dial* (67), July 26, 1919, p. 57. The essay was reprinted in condensed form in *Current Opinion*, December 1919, p. 318. It is also included in Cohen's 1946 selection of essays entitled *The Faith of a Liberal* (New York: Henry Holt and Company), under the title "Baseball as a National Religion," pp. 334-336.

[4]*Ibid.* [5]*Ibid.*

[6]*Ibid.*, p. 58.

[7]Even this fact is suspect. It is probable that one of the eight, George "Buck" Weaver, heard the offer and decided not to accept it. The story of this scandal is told briefly in many histories of professional baseball. Douglas Wallop's *Baseball: An Informal History* (New York: W. W. Norton & Co., 1969), pp. 168-179, is recent and representative. Two book length accounts are available. Eliot Asinof's *Eight Men Out: The Black Sox and the 1919 World Series* (New York: Holt, Rinehart and Winston, 1963), is the better, but Victor Luhrs' *The Great Baseball Mystery: The 1919 World Series* (New York: A. S. Barnes & Company, Inc., 1966), is good too. Luhrs' argument, that though the players agreed to lose the series, they may not finally have tried to do so, is always interesting, though sometimes implausible. Harold Seymour's *Baseball: The Golden Age* (New York: Oxford University Press, 1971), presents the scandal in the context of the history of professional baseball.

[8]The Chicago *Tribune*, October 1, 1919. The Kansas City *Star* and the New York *Times*, among other papers, carried the same or similar stories.

[9]New York *Times*, October 1, 1919. The next day the Chicago *Tribune* reported the same story circulating in Chicago.

[10]New York *Times*, October 6, 1919.

[11]New York *Times*, October 8, 1919.

[12]*The Sporting News*, October 9, 1919.

[13]New York *Times*, October 16, 1919.

[14]New York *Times*, October 2, 1919.

[15]New York *Times*, October 2, 1919.

[16]Chicago *Tribune*, October 8, 1919.

[17]It all depended on what paper you read. The Chicago *Tribune*, October 11, 1919, reported $10,000; the New York *Times* of the same date reported $20,000.

[18]Kansas City *Star*, October 11, 1919.

[19]New York *Times*, October 11, 1919.

[20]New York *Times*, October 16, 1919. See also John B. Sheridan's column in *The Sporting News*, October 16, 1919, for the same sort of argument. *The Sporting News*, October 7, 1920, printed a story told by Edd Roush very much like the one Mathewson tells here.

[21] *The Sporting News,* October 23, 1919.

[22] New York *Times,* January 11, 1920.

[23] *The Sporting News,* January 1, 1920.

[24] *The Sporting News,* January 1, 1920.

[25] *The Sporting News,* June 17, 1920.

[26] *The Sporting News,* October 23, 1919.

[27] "Editorial Comment," *Baseball* Magazine, February 1920, p. 530.

[28] Three or four minor scandals broke during the summer of 1920. Eliot Asinof, in *Eight Men Out*, p. 143, discusses only the most prominent, the Lee Magee case. Luhrs, in *The Great Baseball Mystery*, pp. 84-135, discusses the major league scandals both during and before the 1920 season. In addition, two minor league scandals, the Borton case and the Seaton-Smith case, were given considerable attention in the newspapers. For the Borton case see John J. Connolly, "The Gambling Evil on the Pacific Coast," *Baseball* Magazine, February 1921. For the Seaton-Smith case see *The Sporting News,* May 20, 1920, and June 3, 1920.

[29] *The Sporting News,* August 12, 1920.

[30] *The Sporting News,* September 2, 1920, quoted from the Shreveport *Journal.*

[31] The Chicago *Tribune,* September 21, 1920.

[32] New York *Times,* September 26, 1920.

[33] New York *Times,* September 27, 1920.

[34] Quoted in *The Sporting News,* September 2, 1920.

[35] *The Sporting News,* September 16, 1920.

[36] *The Sporting News,* September 30, 1920.

[37] Kansas City *Star,* September 19, 1920. This article provides a good summary of events up to that moment.

[38] Quoted in *The Sporting News,* September 16, 1920.

[39] *The Sporting News,* November 11, 1920.

[40] Chicago *Herald & Examiner,* September 28, 1920.

[41] New York *Times,* November 7, 1920.

[42] "Editorial Comment," *Baseball* Magazine, January 1921, p. 362.

[43] *Ibid.*

[44] James T. Farrell, *My Baseball Diary* (New York: A. S. Barnes & Co., 1957), pp. 104-105.

[45] Slightly varying accounts of this appear immediately after the event in the press. See, for instance, the Chicago *Herald & Examiner,* September 29, 1920, and the New York *Times,* September 30, 1920.

[46] *My Baseball Diary,* p. 106.

[47] Walter Camp, "The Truth About Baseball," *North American Review* (213), April 1921, p. 485.

[48] Chicago *Tribune,* October 1, 1920.

[49] "Baseball is Honest," *Collier's,* October 23, 1920, p. 13.

[50] Chicago *Herald & Examiner,* September 30, 1920.

[51] Kansas City *Star,* September 30, 1920.

[52] Kansas City *Star,* September 23, 1920.

[53] New York *Times,* September 24, 1920.

[54]New York *Times,* September 27, 1920.

[55]"The Baseball Scandal," *The Nation* (CXI), October 13, 1920, p. 395.

[56]"Editorial Comment," *Baseball* Magazine, December 1920, pp. 315, 314.

[57]Chicago *Herald & Examiner,* September 25, 1920. Many other assertions of professional baseball's "inherent" and "overwhelming" honesty appeared. For instance, see *The Literary Digest* (67), October 9, 1920, p. 12; *Collier's*, October 23, 1920, p. 13; Kansas City *Star*, December 4, 1920; New York *Times,* September 29, 1920, October 4, 1920, October 11, 1920, October 18, 1920, December 6, 1920; Chicago *Tribune,* September 29, 1920; *The Sporting News*, September 20, 1920, November 18, 1920.

[58]New York *Times,* September 30, 1920.

[59]*The Sporting News,* September 30, 1920.

[60]*The Sporting News,* October 7, 1920.

[61]Chicago *Tribune,* September 30, 1920.

[62]"The Flaw in the Diamond," *The Literary Digest* (67), October 9, 1920, p. 12.

[63]*The Sporting News,* November 4, 1920.

[64]Chicago *Herald & Examiner,* October 1, 1920.

[65]*The Sporting News,* October 7, 1920.

[66]*The Sporting News,* March 10, 1921.

[67]*The Sporting News,* November 4, 1920, Chicago *Tribune,* September 24, 1920, September 30, 1920.

[68]*The Sporting News,* October 7, 1920.

[69]Quoted in *The Sporting News,* March 3, 1921.

[70]"Editorial Comment," *Baseball* Magazine, June 1921, p. 290.

[71]*The Sporting News,* October 7, 1920.

[72]*The Sporting News,* October 7, 1920.

[73]New York *Times,* October 3, 1920.

[74]Chicago *Tribune,* September 30, 1920.

[75]Chicago *Tribune,* September 30, 1920.

[76]*The Sporting News,* October 21, 1920.

[77]*The Sporting News,* December 21, 1920. A poem called "The Burglar's Protest," printed in *The Sporting News,* October 28, 1920, makes the same sort of point.

[78]*The Sporting News,* March 24, 1921.

[79]*The Sporting News,* October 14, 1920.

[80]Chicago *Herald & Examiner,* October 2, 1920.

[81]*The Sporting News,* October 7, 1920. In the same issue an article indicative of the same point of view, by Bill Murphy of the St. Louis *Star*, is reprinted.

[82]Chicago *Tribune,* December 10, 1920.

[83]*The Sporting News,* December 30, 1920.

[84]*The Sporting News,* December 30, 1920.

[85]Chicago *Tribune,* February 15, 1921.

[86]*The Sporting News,* March 24, 1921.

[87] *The Sporting News,* October 28, 1920.

[88] *The Sporting News,* January 6, 1921.

[89] Kansas City *Star,* January 27, 1921.

[90] *The Sporting News,* February 3, 1921.

[91] *The Sporting News,* February 10, 1921.

[92] See Joe Vila's column in *The Sporting News,* June 16, 1921.

[93] *The Sporting News,* March 17, 1921.

[94] New York *Times,* March 18, 1921. For other versions of the same point of view, see Chicago *Tribune*, January 13, 1921, February 14, 1921; *The Sporting News,* January 6, 1921, March 24, 1921, June 16, 1921.

[95] *The Sporting News,* June 23, 1921.

[96] Washington *Post,* July 18, 1921. See also the New York *Times* of the same date.

[97] Chicago *Tribune,* August 1, 1921. For an account of the actual defense summary, see the *Tribune,* August 2, 1921.

[98] New York *Times,* July 30, 1921.

[99] New York *Times,* July 31, 1921.

[100] Washington *Post*, August 3, 1921.

[101] Chicago *Tribune,* August 4, 1921.

[102] *The Sporting News,* August 11, 1921.

[103] New York *Times,* August 4, 1921.

[104] Quoted in the Washington *Post,* August 4, 1921. For other uses of the multi-trial metaphor, see "Making the 'Black Sox' White Again," *The Literary Digest* (70), August 20, 1921, p. 13; "Acquittal, Yes; Vindication, No," *The Outlook* (128), August 1921, p. 594; *The Sporting News,* August 18, 1921; "Editorial Comment," *Baseball* Magazine, October 1921, p. 510.

[105] Quoted in *The Literary Digest* (70), August 20, 1921, p. 14.

[106] *The Sporting News,* September 8, 1921.

[107] *The Sporting News,* September 15, 1921.

[108] *The Sporting News,* August 11, 1921.

[109] *The Sporting News,* September 15, 1921.

[110] Gustav W. Axelson, "Commy," p. 126.

[111] See Victor Luhrs, *The Great Baseball Mystery,* p. 110.

[112] Chicago *Tribune,* September 6, 1919.

[113] *The Sporting News,* November 13, 1919.

[114] *The Sporting News,* November 27, 1919.

[115] *The Sporting News,* December 11, 1919.

[116] *The Sporting News,* October 23, 1919.

[117] *The Sporting News,* December 18, 1919.

[118] W. A. Phelon, "Striking Events of the Month in Baseball," *Baseball* Magazine, February 1920, p. 527.

[119] *Baseball* Magazine, March 1920, p. 582.

[120] *The Sporting News,* January 1, 1920.

[121] Charles Webb Murphy, "The World's Series from an Owner's View-point," *Baseball* Magazine, November 1919, pp. 419, 420.

[122] *Ibid.*, p. 420.

[123] Hugh S. Fullerton, "Baseball—The Business and the Sport," *Ameri-*

can *Review of Reviews* (LXIII), April 1921, p. 419.

[124]New York *Times,* December 13, 1919.

[125]*The Sporting News,* December 4, 1919.

[126]*The Sporting News,* August 26, 1920.

[127]*The Sporting News,* October 21, 1920.

[128]Chicago *Tribune,* January 10, 1920.

[129]*The Sporting News,* January 15, 1920.

[130]Chicago *Herald & Examiner,* September 28, 1920.

[131]*The Sporting News,* January 22, 1920.

[132]Chicago *Herald & Examiner,* September 8, 1920.

[133]*The Sporting News,* September 16, 1920.

[134]New York *Times,* October 2, 1920.

[135]Chicago *Herald & Examiner,* October 2, 1920.

[136]New York *Times,* October 6, 1920.

[137]"The Baseball Scandal," *The Nation* (CXI), October 13, 1920, p. 396.

[138]Chicago *Herald & Examiner,* October 18, 1920.

[139]Chicago *Herald & Examiner,* November 5, 1920.

[140]William Veeck, "The Lasker Plan," *Baseball* Magazine, December 1920, p. 324.

[141]Chicago *Herald & Examiner,* October 21, 1920.

[142]New York *Times,* October 19, 1920.

[143]See Chicago *Tribune* and New York *Times,* November 9, 1920. Both ran the story on page 1.

[144]New York *Times,* October 16, 1920.

[145]Ban Johnson, "What Baseball Needs Most," *Baseball* Magazine, December 1920, p. 326. Many others advanced this point of view. See Chicago *Herald & Examiner,* October 20, 1920, for a statement by Clark Griffith, owner of the Washington Senators. Frank Navin, owner of the Detriot Tigers, is quoted in the New York *Times* of the same date. See also the columns of James C. Isaminger (October 21, 1920), Paul W. Eaton (October 28, 1920), and John B. Sheridan (October 21, 1920), in *The Sporting News.*

[146]*The Sporting News,* October 21, 1920.

[147]*The Sporting News,* October 7, 1920. Connie Mack's statement, quoted in both the New York *Times* and the Chicago *Herald & Examiner* also suggests this. Elbert Sanders' column (October 7, 1920), and the editorial, "A Message for a Mr. Lasker" (October 14, 1920), in *The Sporting News* exemplify two kinds of frontal attack on the sponsors of the Lasker plan.

[148]*The Sporting News,* October 14, 1920. See also the response of Thomas A. Rice in his column (October 28, 1920), and of Otis Harris in the "Scribbled by Scribes" column (October 14, 1920).

[149]New York *Times,* November 10, 1920.

[150]Johnson, "What Baseball Needs Most," *Baseball* Magazine, December 1920, p. 326.

[151]*The Sporting News,* November 11, 1920.

[152]*The Sporting News,* November 4, 1920. See also New York *Times,*

October 30, 1920.

[153]See Bill Veeck, "Harry's Diary," in *The Hustler's Handbook* (New York: G. P. Putnam's Sons, 1965), pp. 277, 281. This essay, which analyzes the diary of Harry Grabiner, secretary of the Chicago White Sox, during the year 1920, is invaluable for understanding the various convolutions of the Johnson-Comiskey feud.

[154]New York *Times,* November 8, 1920.

[155]Victor Luhrs, *The Great Baseball Mystery,* p. 204.

[156]*The Sporting News,* December 30, 1920.

[157]"Editorial Comment," *Baseball* Magazine, December 1920, p. 315.

[158]*The Sporting News,* September 30, 1920.

[159]"The New Major League Agreement," *Baseball* Magazine, February 1921, p. 410. This article prints the full text of the agreement, which appeared in many other places. See, for instance, New York *Times,* December 13, 1920; *The Sporting News,* December 23, 1920.

[160]New York *Times,* November 13, 1920.

[161]New York *Times,* November 13, 1920. This article as a whole is a succinct summary of the various conflicts involved in the reorganization and of their resolution. The particular anecdote quoted here turned up almost everywhere. See, for instance, Chicago *Herald & Examiner,* November 13, 1920; *The Literary Digest* (67), December 4, 1920, p. 48.

[162]New York *Times,* November 21, 1920.

[163]Chicago *Tribune,* January 13, 1921. The ship of state metaphor appears also in *The Sporting News,* January 20, 1921. Landis is referred to as baseball's "pilot" in the New York *Times,* December 6, 1920.

[164]In *The Hustler's Handbook,* Bill Veeck's analysis of Harry Grabiner's diary concludes that Ban Johnson was behind this move to limit Landis' powers. See pp. 292, 294.

[165]*The Sporting News,* January 20, 1921.

[166]F. C. Lane, "Baseball's Dictator," *Baseball* Magazine, February 1921, p. 413.

[167]*Ibid.*

[168]Chicago *Tribune,* December 14, 1920, January 11, 1921.

[169]See Charles Webb Murphy, "How Judge Landis Will Help the Game," *Baseball* Magazine, April 1921, p. 536.

[170]Kansas City *Star,* December 10, 1920.

[171]*The Sporting News,* November 18, 1920.

[172]*The Sporting News,* November 25, 1920.

[173]*Ibid.,* pp. 36, 39.

[174]*The Sporting News,* December 18, 1919.

[175]*The Sporting News,* February 5, 1920.

[176]*The Sporting News,* January 27, 1921.

[177]F. C. Line, "Baseball's Dictator," *Baseball* Magazine, February 1921, p. 414.

[178]*Ibid.,* p. 448.

[179]"Judge Landis Under Fire," *The Literary Digest* (68), March 12, 1921, p. 42.

[180]William Fleming French, "Kenesaw Mountain Landis: The Most Interesting Man in America," *Illustrated World* (37), March 1922, pp. 34, 132.

[181]*Ibid.*, p. 36. [182]*Ibid.*

[183]"Judge Landis, America's Shame," *Non-Partisan Leader* (10-11), September 20, 1920, p. 15.

[184]"Judge Landis Slanders Lincoln," *Pearson's Magazine* (45), March 1920, p. 791.

[185]*The Sporting News*, February 12, 1920.

[186]New York *Times*, October 15, 1921.

[187]New York *Times*, October 16, 1921.

[188]Chicago *Tribune*, October 17, 1921.

[189]Chicago *Tribune*, October 19, 1921.

[190]Kansas City *Star*, October 17, 1921.

[191]Chicago *Tribune*, October 18, 1921.

[192]Kansas City *Star*, October 17, 1921.

[193]New York *Times*, October 17, 1921.

[194]Kansas City *Star*, October 17, 1921.

[195]New York *Times*, October 19, 1921. See J. G. Taylor Spink, *Judge Landis and 25 Years of Baseball* (New York: Thomas Y. Crowell Company, 1947), pp. 103-106, for an account of Landis' private dealings with Ruth during this time.

[196]Kansas City *Star*, October 22, 1921.

[197]New York *Times*, October 22, 1921. Ruth himself says that "Huston paid off the promoters and the players involved to get them to call off the trip." *The Babe Ruth Story* (New York: Scholastic Book Services, 1969), p. 97.

[198]New York *Times*, October 19, 1921.

[199]Chicago *Tribune*, October 25, 1921.

[200]Chicago *Tribune*, October 18, 1921.

[201]Chicago *Tribune*, November 3, 1921.

[202]*The Sporting News*, October 27, 1921.

[203]Chicago *Tribune*, October 31, 1921.

[204]Chicago *Tribune*, October 24, 1921.

[205]Chicago *Tribune*, November 3, 1921.

[206]New York *Times*, October 18, 1921.

[207]New York *Times*, October 18, 1921.

[208]*Baseball* Magazine, December 1921, p. 612.

[209]*The Sporting News*, November 3, 1921.

[210]Quoted in *The Sporting News*, October 27, 1921. For other references to pride as the cause of Ruth's actions, see the poem by George E. Phair, "Ox Landis and Froggy Ruth," in *The Sporting News*, November 10, 1921, Grantland Rice's column in *The Sporting News*, November 3, 1921. The Kansas City *Star*, November 17, 1921, November 18, 1921, also has comment in this vein.

[211]"Editorial Comment," *Baseball* Magazine, December 1921, pp. 578, 622.

[212]*Ibid.*, p. 622.

[213]*The Sporting News,* November 10, 1921. For other expressions of the need for discipline, see Damon Runyan's column in *The Sporting News,* October 27, 1921. An editorial in the same issue makes this point, as does James J. Long's column. See also New York *Times,* October 24, 1921, and Frank G. Menke's column in the November 3, 1921 *Sporting News.*

[214]Chicago *Tribune,* December 6, 1921. The New York *Times* of the same date also printed the whole statement.

[215]Chicago *Tribune,* December 11, 1921.

[216]*The Sporting News,* December 22, 1921. See also *The Sporting News,* December 15, 1921 and April 13, 1922, for other attitudes of the same sort. Harvey Woodruff, in "In the Wake of the News," made the same point Chicago *Tribune,* April 13, 1922 and May 23, 1922.

[217]Chicago *Tribune,* December 11, 1921.

[218]*The Sporting News,* December 15, 1921.

[219]Chicago *Tribune,* December 8, 1921. For other statements on discipline, see the *Tribune*, April 4, 1922, May 18, 1922; *The Sporting News,* December 15, 1921, January 19, 1922, April 16, 1922; *Baseball* Magazine, "Editorial Comment," February 1922, June 1922, July 1922; and Fred Lieb, "When Baseball Stars are Suspended" in the June 1922 issue.

[220]*The Sporting News,* December 22, 1921.

[221]Fred Lieb, "When Baseball Stars are Suspended," *Baseball* Magazine, June 1922, p. 291.

[222]*The Sporting News,* December 15, 1921.

[223]Chicago *Tribune,* December 15, 1921.

[224]*The Sporting News,* February 12, 1920.

[225]F. C. Lane, "The Home Run Epidemic," *Baseball* Magazine, July 1921, pp. 339-340. See also F. C. Lane, "Natural Slugging vs. Scientific Batting," in the August 1922 edition of *Baseball* Magazine.

[226]Quoted in Douglas Wallop, *Baseball: An Informal History* (New York: W. W. Norton & Company, 1969), pp. 50-51.

[227]Ty Cobb with Al Stump, *My Life in Baseball–The True Record* (Garden City: Doubleday & Company, Inc., 1961), p. 280.

[228]Kansas City *Star,* October 1, 1919.

[229]Chicago *Tribune,* September 20, 1919.

[230]*The Sporting News,* September 11, 1919.

[231]Kansas City *Star,* January 30, 1921.

[232]F. C. Lane, "Does Baseball Crookedness Pay?" *Baseball* Magazine, January 1921, p. 371.

[233]Chicago *Herald & Examiner*, October 9, 1920. There is a comparable remark in Phair's column of September 30, 1920, which is reprinted in *The Sporting News* of October 7, 1920.

[234]Ty Cobb with Al Stump, *My Life in Baseball–The True Record,* p. 145.

[235]*The Sporting News,* June 23, 1921.

[236]F. C. Lane, "Gladstone J. Graney, a Player Who Bats With His Brains," *Baseball* Magazine, July 1920, pp. 367-368.

[237]*The Sporting News,* April 6, 1922.

[238]F. C. Lane, "The Bunt as 'Scientific' Batting," *Baseball* Magazine, May 1921, p. 571. The Hornsby quotation is from his article on Batting in *Baseball* Magazine, July 1920, "Why Slugging is Natural Batting Style."

[239]*Ibid.*, pp. 572-573.

[240]*The Sporting News,* January 27, 1921.

[241]*The Sporting News,* March 16, 1922.

[242]F. C. Lane, "Is Base Stealing Doomed?" *Baseball* Magazine, June 1921, pp. 301, 297.

[243]F. C. Lane, "The Sensational Decline of the Stolen Base," *Baseball* Magazine, May 1922, p. 855.

[244]*The Sporting News,* April 6, 1922.

[245]F. C. Lane, "What's Wrong With the Three Base Hit?" *Baseball* Magazine, June 1922, p. 304.

[246]Hod Eller, "The Man Who Clinched the Title," *Baseball* Magazine, November 1919, p. 452.

[247]F. C. Lane, "What's Wrong With the Three Base Hit?" p. 303.

[248]*The Sporting News,* July 7, 1921.

[249]W. A. Phelon, "The First Lap of the Pennant Race," *Baseball* Magazine, July 1921, p. 353.

[250]This is the last stanza of a ten stanza poem printed in *Baseball* Magazine, June 1920. Other representative poems appear in *The Sporting News,* November 6, 1919, and November 27, 1919.

[251]*The Sporting News,* July 22, 1920.

[252]Grantland Rice, "The Swelled Head: Stories of Men Who Have Suffered From It," *American Magazine,* October 1919, p. 203.

[253]Ty Cobb with Al Stump, *My Life in Baseball—The True Record,* p. 173.

[254]*The Sporting News,* October 23, 1919.

[255]Paul Gallico, *The Golden People* (Garden City: Doubleday & Co., 1965), p. 36.

[256]*Ibid.*, pp. 36-37.

[257]New York *Times,* December 14, 1920.

[258]Chet Thomas, "Babe Ruth the Super Player," *Baseball* Magazine, November 1920, p. 586.

[259]Quoted in Joseph Durso, *The Days of Mr. McGraw* (Englewood Cliffs: Prentice-Hall, Inc., 1969), p. 206.

[260]Chicago *Herald & Examiner,* August 5, 1920. For other characterizations of Ruth as a "Freak" or "accident," see *The Sporting News,* May 26, 1921, and January 1, 1920.

[261]*The Sporting News,* April 15, 1920.

[262]*The Sporting News,* May 20, 1920.

[263]*The Sporting News,* January 19, 1922.

[264]*The Sporting News,* February 2, 1922.

[265]Sidney Reid, "Meet the American Idol!" *The Independent* (103), August 14, 1920, p. 170.

[266]*The Sporting News,* June 15, 1922.

[267]F. C. Lane, "Secret of My Heavy Hitting," *Baseball* Magazine,

August 1920, p. 420.

[268] F. C. Lane, "The Home Run Epidemic," *Baseball* Magazine, July 1921, p. 339. This article was condensed in *The Literary Digest* (39), June 25, 1921, pp. 51-52, 54 under the title, "The Babe Ruth Epidemic in Baseball."

[269] *Ibid.*, p. 40. [270] *Ibid.*, p. 373.

[271] *Ibid.*, pp. 340, 372.

[272] F. C. Lane, "The Decline in Run Scoring Efficiency," *Baseball* Magazine, July 1922, p. 374.

[273] *The Sporting News,* August 26, 1920.

[274] See, for example, New York *Times,* January 7, 1920, also Harry Frazee's article, "The Reasons Which Led Me To Sell 'Babe' Ruth," *Baseball* Magazine, April 1920. Frazee did not claim that Ruth's batting style itself was a detriment to the team.

[275] Chicago *Herald & Examiner*, September 11, 1920.

[276] New York *Times,* February 8, 1920.

[277] *The Sporting News,* May 26, 1921.

[278] Babe Ruth and Bob Considine, *The Babe Ruth Story* (New York: Scholastic Book Service, 1969), pp. 8-9.

[279] "A New Hero of the Great American Game at Close Range," *Current Opinion* (69), October 1920, p. 478.

[280] "Meet the American Idol!" p. 194.

[281] New York *Times,* September 25, 1920.

[282] *The Sporting News,* January 6, 1921.

[283] Hugh Fullerton, "The Ten Commandments of Sport, and of Everything Else," *American* Magazine, August 1921, p. 78.

[284] New York *Times,* June 22, 1922.

[285] *The Sporting News,* January 15, 1920.

[286] *The Sporting News,* April 1, 1920.

[287] *The Sporting News,* February 2, 1922.

CHAPTER V

[1] Marshall McLuhan, *Understanding Media: The Extensions of Man* (New York: McGraw-Hill Book Company, 1964), pp. 239-240. Used with permission of McGraw-Hill Book Company.

[2] For both the biographical information and the quotation, see "New Creative Writers," compiled by Anne Wood, *Library Journal,* February 1, 1955, p. 289.

[3] Eliot Asinof, *Man on Spikes* (New York: McGraw-Hill Book Company, 1955), p. 13. Future references will be included within parenthesis in the text.

[4] Eliot Asinof, *Seven Days to Sunday: Crisis Week with the New York Football Giants* (New York: Simon & Schuster, 1968), p. 9. Reprinted by permission of Simon & Schuster. Asinof also used material gathered during these years for setting and color in a mystery story, also published in

1968, by Simon & Schuster, called *The Name of the Game is Murder.* Future references to both these books will be included within parenthesis in the text.

[5]Eliot Asinof, "Big Shrimp of Pro Football," New York *Times Magazine* (December 12, 1965), p. 144.

[6]*Ibid.*, pp. 146-147. [7]*Ibid.*, p. 143.

[8]Eliot Asinof, "Crazy Fatso, the Putting Fool, May Now be the World's Best Golfer," New York *Times Magazine* (April 6, 1969), p. 38.

[9]Thomas Carlyle, *Past and Present,* p. 95. Future references will be included within parenthesis in the text.

[10]Herman Melville, *Moby Dick or, The Whale* (New York: Hendricks House, 1952), p. 106. Future references will be included within parenthesis in the text.

[11]Herbert Warren Wind, "The Sporting Scene: Packerland," *The New Yorker* (December 8, 1962), p. 226.

[12]William Phillips, "A Season in the Stands," *Commentary* (July 1969), p. 65.

[13]Richard Schickel, "On Pro Football," *Commentary* (January 1969), p. 65.

[14]*Ibid.* [15]*Ibid.*

[16]*Ibid.*, pp. 67-68. [17]*Ibid.*, p. 65.

[18]Quoted in Leonard Shecter, "The Toughest Man in Pro Football," *Esquire* (January 1968), p. 144.

[19]Jerry Kramer, *Instant Replay,* edited by Dick Schaap (New York and Cleveland: World Publishing Company, 1968), p. 166.

[20]Dave Meggysey, *Out of Their League* (Berkeley, Calif.: Ramparts Press, Inc., 1970), p. 14.

[21]Mike Holovak and Bill McSweeny, *Violence Every Sunday* (New York: Coward-McCann, 1967), p. 15.

[22]Phil Bengston with Todd Hunt, *Packer Dynasty* (Garden City: Doubleday & Company, Inc., 1969), pp. 206-207.

[23]Leonard Shecter, "The Toughest Man in Pro Football," p. 140.

[24]Vince Lombardi with W. D. Heinz, *Run to Daylight!* (New York: Grosset & Dunlap, 1967), p. 6. I would like to thank Prentice-Hall, Inc. for permission to quote from this book.

[25]Bengston and Hunt, *Packer Dynasty,* p. 167.

[26]Vince Lombardi with Tim Cohane, "Why the Pros Play Better Football," *Look* (October 24, 1961), p. 108.

[27]George Plimpton, *Paper Lion* (New York: Harper & Row, 1966), p. 180.

[28]Vince Lombardi with W. C. Heinz, *Run to Daylight!* p. 64.

[29]Jerry Kramer, *Instant Replay,* p. 3.

[30]Jack Olsen, *The Black Athlete: A Shameful Story* (New York: Time-Life Books, 1968), p. 188.

[31]*Packer Dynasty,* pp. 202-203.

[32]*Ibid.*, p. 112. [33]*Instant Replay,* pp. 1-2.

[34]"Vince Lombardi: The Packers Pay the Price," *Look* (October 24, 1961), pp. 102, 104.

[35]Lombardi and Heinz, *Run to Daylight!* p. 72. Another ceremony comparable to that of the Honors Assembly is the "hazing" of rookies. This is well described in George Plimpton's *Paper Lion*, pp. 24-30.

[36]Robert Daley, *Only A Game* (New York: Signet Books, 1967), p. 172.

[37]Jerry Karmer, *Farewell to Football*, edited by Dick Schaap (New York and Cleveland: The World Publishing Company, 1969), p. 7.

[38]F. Scott Fitzgerald, *The Great Gatsby* (New York: Charles Scribner's Sons, 1953), p. 6.

[39]*Farewell to Football*, p. 8; *Violence Every Sunday*, p. 46.

[40]Gary Cartwright, *The Hundred Yard War* (Garden City: Doubleday and Company, 1968), p. 55.

[41]*Instant Replay*, p. 261.

[42]*Ibid.*, p. 265.

[43]Robert Daley, *Only A Game*, p. 186.

[44]Quoted in *The Sporting News*, February 25, 1967.

[45]See Jack Olsen, *The Black Athlete*. Another, more radical book on the plight of black athletes is Harry Edwards' *The Revolt of the Black Athlete* (New York: The Free Press, 1969). Edwards, too, appears to feel Lombardi has solved these problems. See his discussion of the case of "Junior" Coffey, pp. 82-83. Dave Meggysey's *Out of Their League* also speaks of racism. See particularly pp. 123, 139, 146, 193.

[46]George Plimpton, *Paper Lion*, p. 187.

[47]*Instant Replay*, pp. 27, 28.

[48]*Ibid.*, p. 30.

[49]*Paper Lion*, p. 189.

[50]*Instant Replay*, p. 222.

[51]*Ibid.*, p. 250.

[52]*Run to Daylight!* p. 128.

[53]Lombardi and Cohane, "Why the Pros Play Better Football," pp. 108-109.

[54]Mike Holovak and Bill McSweeny, *Violence Every Sunday*, p. 12.

[55]*Ibid.*, p. 88.

[56]*Ibid.*, pp. 111-112.

[57]Dave Meggysey, *Out of Their League*, p. 154. See also p. 155.

[58]*Run to Daylight!* p. 7.

[59]*Ibid.*, p. 9.

[60]*Instant Replay*, p. 149.

[61]*The Hundred Yard War*, p. 129. See also Don Delillo's *End Zone* (Boston: Houghton-Mifflin Company, 1972).

[62]*Run to Daylight!* p. 108.

[63]*Ibid.*, p. 31.

[64]*Ibid.*, p. 100.

[65]*Instant Replay*, p. xiii.

[66]*Ibid.*, p. 202.

[67]*Ibid.*, p. 217.

[68]*Farewell to Football*, p. 8.

[69]*Instant Replay*, pp. 283-284.

[70]*Violence Every Sunday*, p. 102.

[71]*Ibid.*, p. 195.

[72]*Run to Daylight!* p. 51.

[73]*Ibid.*, p. 19.

[74]*Paper Lion*, p. 19.

[75]*Ibid.*, see pp. 63, 329, 285, 97.

[76]*Ibid.*, p. 97.

[77]*The Hundred Yard War*, p. 289. This image turns up again in Don Delillo's *End Zone*, p. 54.

[78]"Advice to Businessmen on How to Lead," *U. S. News and World Report* (February 20, 1967), p. 14.

[79]Harold B. Meyers, "That Profitable Nonprofit in Green Bay," *Fortune* (November 1968), p. 186.

[80]*Ibid.*, p. 186. [81]*Packer Dynasty*, p. 10.

[82]*Ibid.*, p. 30.

[83]"Capital Coach," *Newsweek*, February 17, 1969.

[84]William Johnson, "Arararararargh!" *Sports Illustrated* (March 3, 1969), p. 29.

[85]*Ibid.*, p. 33.

[86]Vince Lombardi and W. C. Heinz, "Secrets of Winning Football," *Look* (September 19, 1967), p. 70.

[87]Quoted in Terry Bledsoe, "Vince in Politics? Some Guess Yes," *The Sporting News*, August 24, 1968, p. 42.

[88]Quoted in Dave Brady, "Lombardi Runs to Daylight as 'Skin Skipper,' " *The Sporting News*, February 22, 1969, p. 19.

[89]Leonard Shecter, "The Toughest Man in Pro Football," p. 146.

[90]*The Hundred Yard War*, pp. 232-233.

[91]"Vince Lombardi's Philosophy," *The Sporting News*, February 25, 1967, p. 14.

[92]Quoted by Shecter, "The Toughest Man in Pro Football," p. 146.

[93]*Ibid.*, p. 146. [94]*Ibid.*, p. 68.

[95]"Vince Lombardi's Philosophy," *The Sporting News*, February 25, 1967, p. 14.

[96]Quoted in Terry Bledsoe, "Vince in Politics? Some Guess Yes," *The Sporting News*, August 24, 1968, p. 42.

[97]*The Hundred Yard War*, p. 233; "The Toughest Man in Pro Football," p. 146.

[98]Shecter, "The Toughest Man in Pro Football," p. 140.

[99]Lombardi and Heinz, *Run to Daylight!* p. 69.

[100]Jerry Kramer, *Instant Replay*, p. 78.

[101]*Ibid.*, p. 10. [102]*Ibid.*, p. 42.

[103]*Out of Their League*, pp. 11, 20, 182.

[104]Quoted in W. C. Heinz, "I Miss the Fire on Sunday," *Life* (September 27, 1968), p. 121.

[105]Quoted in William Johnson, "Arararararargh!" p. 33.

[106]Jerry Kramer, *Farewell to Football*, pp. 28-29.

[107]*Instant Replay*, p. 41. [108]*Ibid.*, pp. 141-142.

[109]*Farewell to Football*, pp. 146-147.

[110]*Run to Daylight!* p. 120.

[111]Lombardi and Heinz, "Secrets of Winning Football," *Look* (September 19, 1967), p. 70.

[112]"Arararararargh!" p. 30.

[113]See for instance, *Instant Replay*, pp. 40, 87, 146; "The Toughest Man in Pro Football," p. 146; "Green Bay's Salute to King Lombardi," *The Sporting News*, August 24, 1968, p. 42; *Packer Dynasty*, p. 221; "Capital Coach," *Newsweek*, February 17, 1969.

[114]*Run to Daylight!* p. 6.

[115]"Vince in Politics? Some Guess Yes," *The Sporting News*, August

24, 1968, p. 42.

[116]Herbert Warren Wind, "The Sporting Scene: Packerland," p. 226.
[117]"Arararararargh!" p. 30.
[118]*Instant Replay*, p. 42.
[119]*Packer Dynasty*, p. 224.

INDEX

D

E

F

T

U

V

W

Y